BREAKING GLASS CEILINGS
100 BLACK ACHIEVERS
WHO CHANGED THE WORLD

ELLISTON RAHMING, PhD
WITH BRIANA LOUISE CACUCI · FOREWORD BY MONTEL B. WILLIAMS

Distinction Publishing House
Dover, Denver, Colorado
United States of America
www.distinctionpublishinghouse.com

Copyright © 2021 by Elliston Rahming
All rights reserved.

Library of Congress Control Number 2021924358 (Print)
ISBN: 978-1-7374023-1-2 (Paperback)
ISBN: 978-1-7374023-2-9 (eBook)

No part of this publication may be reproduced, stored in a retrieval system, or transmitted, in any form or by any means, electronic, mechanical, photocopying, recording, or otherwise, without the written permission of the author.

Designed by Allison Denise Arnett

This book is printed on acid-free paper.

Printed in La Vergne, TN in the United States of America

CONTENTS

Dedication vii
Acknowledgements viii
Foreword ix
Preface xi
Methodology xv

SECTION A
"PEACE"

Chapter I Human and Civil Rights 2
Chapter II Politics and Government 37
Chapter III Religion 65

SECTION B
"PROGRESS"

Chapter IV Education 92
Chapter V Inventions 118
Chapter VI Science and Technology 143

SECTION C
"PROSPERITY"

Chapter VII Business and Entrepreneurship 177

SECTION D
"PLEASURE"

Chapter VIII Arts and Entertainment 204
Chapter IX Communications and Media 249
Chapter X Sports 289

Index of "Top 100" 315
Citations 320

DEDICATION

In memory of my father, Ishmael Rahming, who passed ten years ago at the age of ninety three, but whose candle of influence burns ever more brightly; to my mother Daisy Rahming who passed away in 2017, who was a tower of strength and pillar of support; to the memory of my life-long friend, Anthony "Tony" Roach, who left us too soon; to Dr. Robert Wintersmith, my mentor many years ago in Missouri at Washington University in St. Louis; to my son, Pelé, and daughter, Rashanda, who always have words of encouragement; and finally, to my anchor, Arthurlouise Rahming, whose devotion, insights, and support defy comprehension.

ACKNOWLEDGEMENTS

In an undertaking such as this, there are of necessity many whose thoughts, ideas, talents, and energy go into the mix to advance the project. Most notably, we thank our research assistant, Karin Adames, who helped to conceptualize the nature and scope of this endeavor. Her intellect, energy, and dedication proved invaluable.

We also thank the distinguished panel of judges that spent hours enduring an arduous selection process. The committee tried, whenever possible, to use objective criteria to determine who most merited inclusion. And to my proofreaders (Rolean Smith, Abbygail Gibson, Michele Stubbs, Rosetta Gibson, and Aleksandra Pyra) and to the memory of the late Della Thomson-Stevens who was my Secretary, I offer my gratitude. Finally, I thank television personality, Montel Williams, for his mentorship, friendship, and foreword.

– Elliston Rahming

FOREWORD

Carter Goodwin Woodson, African American author, editor, publisher, and historian was quoted as saying, "We should emphasize not Negro history, but the Negro in history. What we need is not a history of selected races or nations, but the history of the world void of national bias, race hate, and religious prejudice."

There have been other books written that compile for us the names of African Americans, who have made a significant impact on our lives and the course of history. Dr. Elliston Rahming has taken an approach that differs from most of these publications. His book, *Breaking Glass Ceilings: 100 Black Achievers Who Changed the World* takes the approach that we should not only look at the accomplishments of great African Americans, but also examine the achievements of blacks in other countries. All of these black individuals contributed to making our world more exciting, more aware, and more inventive, and therefore, they exacted huge impacts on our lives.

In his introduction, Dr. Rahming referred to an article in the *New York Daily News* that discusses "History's Black Hole," referring to the lack of memorializing the experiences and accomplishments of notable blacks in history. As I read this book, I realized that we needed to start a discussion that changes the reference from a "Black Hole" to a "Black Cup That Runneth Over," because you do not have to search far to find that the achievements of notable blacks throughout history are almost too numerous to chronicle in any one book.

We all know and recognize the names of impactful entertainers like Oprah Winfrey, but what about Mosunmola ("Mo") Abudu of Lagos, Nigeria, who has been recognized by *Forbes Magazine* as the first woman on the African continent to own a Pan-African TV channel and is very active in not only media, but also charitable work in her country. We all recognize the name of Reginald Lewis, but what about Patrice Motsepe, the South African billionaire, who established a charitable organization and donated half of his wealth to improve the lives of the poor, disabled, women, and youth in South Africa. We know about the black inventor, George Washington Carver, but what about Marie Van Brittan Brown, who, along with her husband, invented the closed-circuit TV system, used for home-security monitoring. Consider Patricia Bath, the first African American female to receive a medical patent for inventing the Laserphaco Probe used for cataract treatment. We have all cheered for Tiger Woods, who will go down in history as one of the all-time greatest golfers of all time, but let's also remember Charlie Sifford, who was the first African American to play in the PGA tournament and is considered the Jackie Robinson of golf.

The richness of the legacies created by the people in this book should awaken a curiosity in each of us, regardless of race or country, and push us to learn more about those who were not mentioned, but should never be forgotten. If these one hundred blacks were only some of the names that were vetted for this book, just imagine the hundreds of other blacks whose names were left on the table! I encourage everyone to read *Breaking Glass Ceilings: 100 Black Achievers Who Changed the World*. Then, continue to search for and read about the others upon whose backs our futures were launched.

– Montel B. Williams

PREFACE

Arthur Browne, writing in the January 10, 2016 global edition of *The New York Daily News,* opines an article entitled "History's Black Hole", "across every field of endeavor, from the ministry to medicine and from education to entrepreneurship, book merchants balk at memorializing black experience and accomplishments". Essentially, this book is a celebration of Black accomplishments over centuries and across continents and seeks to fill a portion of that "black hole".

Of the roughly 7 billion people who inhabit this planet, some 1.5 billion are classified as white and blacks account for 1.1 billion. The remaining 4 billion plus are somewhere in the middle. For the most part, black people live on three continents - Africa and North and South America. Yet, throughout the years there is a paucity of written material that records the positive influences and myriad contributions black citizens of the world have made towards global peace, progress, prosperity, and pleasure.

Having enjoyed slavery; having shaken off the cloak of colonialism; having triumphed over Jim Crow Laws in the United States, apartheid in South Africa and entrenched minority oligarchies throughout the diaspora, people of African descent, but for political power, are still in large measure considered separate and unequal, desegregated but not fully integrated; in the game but not the team owner; borrowers not lenders; employees, not employers.

The psychosocial underpinnings of this reality are incalculable. For many across the globe, at least psychologically, there is a benign embrace of second-class citizenship. It is only when the coin is flipped and one realizes that though unequal in power, prestige and influence, blacks have proven themselves equal to all others in ideas, intellect, and ingenuity.

Some of the greatest exploits in human endeavor were spawned from the hearts and minds of black folk, yet they are still underrepresented within mainstream compilations of achievers. For instance, the Nobel Prize has been awarded to some 800 persons since its inception in 1901, but only 14 of whom are black. Among the fourteen black recipients, eleven won for peace, two for literature, and one for economics-none for medicine, physics or chemistry.

It is that "black hole" that gave birth to this publication. It is an effort to showcase leading pioneers, movers and shakers within the global black community, past and present, whose contributions to peace, prosperity and pleasure helped to change the world for everyone, while inching us closer to an elaboration of those ancient and immutable ideals of "life, liberty and the pursuit of happiness".

It must be noted that conceptually, this book adds to the earlier work of others, such as Molefikete Asante's 2002 listing of "One hundred Greatest African Americans". We thought to expand our search to the global village.

This work, no doubt, will attract some criticism and perhaps even some controversy. No problem, because this suggests that a conversation has been ignited. In time, hopefully, criticism and controversy will give way to dialogue and debate until it becomes clear that, amidst the differences and distinctions, the push of history and the pull of the future impose upon mankind a shared patrimony that in the end will open eyes once blinded by divisions to a newer kinder humanity.

This book chronicles the accomplishments and contributions of mountain-movers who, arguably more than all others, were able to shape the course of human events and advance the refrain of ebony pride. Ultimately, this book is a clarion call for mankind everywhere to move beyond the superficiality of skin pigmentation and to rise towards Bobby Kennedy's ageless exhortation to "seek a newer world". Indeed, not just to seek it, but if need be, to build it.

METHODOLOGY

By its very nature, any undertaking of this magnitude must be collaborative and expansive. Therefore, in establishing a road map for this important endeavor, the first task was to determine the life-achievement categories.

This task was daunting; the possibilities approached infinity. In the final analysis, a decision was made to select ten broad categories in no particular order of precedence that cover the widest scope of human effort: Arts and Entertainment, Business and Entrepreneurship, Communications and Media, Education, Human and Civil Rights, Inventions, Politics and Governance, Religion, Science and Technology, and Sports.

After the categories were defined, the undertaking was to determine who would best qualify as a top-ten achiever throughout recorded history within each of the respective life achievement categories. We also considered regional and national proportionality. For instance, the United States has less than 5 percent of the world's population, yet it claimed 20 percent of the initial list of nominees.

After months, and in some cases, years, we agreed on a list of finalists. To assist in this exercise, a multidisciplinary panel of academics was assembled to delve into the backgrounds and achievements of thirty nominees within each category and narrow down the nominees to fifteen per achievement category. Thereafter, a second panel of multiethnic judges—drawn from a wider spectrum of society—was tasked with selecting ten finalists per category, based on one overarching criterion: The contribution of the nominee must have been so significant and so compelling that it helped to advance, change, influence, and impact the world (or a significant part thereof) for the better.

Hopefully, the depth of research that gave rise to this work vindicates the judges' decisions and helps to fill "history's black hole." It is also hoped that this work sparks a new wave of ebony pride, as embodied in the lives and work of these mountain movers — "Breaking Glass Ceilings: 100 Black Achievers Who Changed the World."

SECTION A
"PEACE"

CHAPTER I
Human & Civil Rights

INTRODUCTION
Human & Civil Rights

Generally, civil rights refer to those statutory rights that grant equal treatment in education, employment, and housing. They extend to freedom of speech, equality in public places, press freedom, voting rights, and the like. Human rights, on the other hand, are universal and inalienable; they apply to all persons equally. If we accept the United States' Declaration of Independence as a template, human rights center on "life, liberty and the pursuit of happiness."

Whether civil rights or human rights, a centuries-old struggle endures throughout most of the world in order to guarantee that these freedoms are amplified and expanded. At the same time, needless to say, persistent, entrenched, organized, and deliberate efforts to deny, delay, and derail both civil and human rights ensue.

In Africa (most notably South Africa), Brazil, Britain, the United States, the Caribbean, and elsewhere, a protracted tug of war persisted historically between the oppressors and the oppressed, between the haves and the have-nots, between tyranny and liberty, and between domination and self-actualization.

Injustices included colonialism throughout the world, slavery across North and South America, apartheid in South Africa, Jim Crow laws throughout the southern United States, fascism in Europe, and dictatorship across much of Asia. As it relates to black people, the denial of basic civil and human rights—while today not as stinging and obvious— still lurks in the shadows. There can be no denying that black people across the globe have been the recipients of significant gains as measured by enhanced civil and human rights. But this progress did not come easily.

The blood, sweat, tears, and sacrifice of many won these gains. In the arena of civil and human rights, the ten black persons who did most to change the world for the better are as follows:

Queen Ann Nzinga
(Ana de Sousa Nzinga Mbande)

Born: 1583
Died: December 17, 1663
Country: The Republic of Angola[1]

"Haughtiness and proudness is in my soul from the day I was born until my dying breath."

A historical warrior, Ana de Sousa Nzinga Mbande was born a princess in the late sixteenth century as part of the Ndongo Kingdom (modern-day Angola), and later became Queen Ann Nzinga. Great leadership of her empire marked her role during her lifetime during a time when it was under immense threat.

In 1624, Nzinga became ruler of Ndongo. During her reign, she faced great challenges to her kingdom, which she defended from attacks launched by multiple fronts. Her greatest enemies were the Portuguese, who were expanding their slave trade in competition with the British and French.[2] Nzinga is famously remembered for her participation at a peace conference in Luanda at which she represented her brother, King Ngola Mbandi. While at the peace conference, she negotiated with the Portuguese to put a stop to their invasion of her territories.[3] Both parties eventually signed off on an agreement to maintain peace; however, Portugal betrayed the agreement.

The discovery of the New World resulted in a greater demand for slave labor. As a consequence, business in the Old World shifted. With the formation of a new colony in Brazil, Portugal was in need of more slaves. Increasingly, territories—such as Nzinga's— became targets for Portuguese slave traders who captured slaves that could be sold and taken to work in the New World. In addition to slave trade, Portugal and other colonial powers made Nzinga's land their target. Clearly, the Portuguese were not honoring their end of the peace treaty agreement. Nzinga was forced to take action.

Forced by the Portuguese from their original territory, Nzinga and her kingdom were displaced and resettled farther west in Matamba.[4] The move meant that Nzinga could keep her kingdom intact. She began organizing her people and offering her land as a place of refuge for slaves who escaped and sought freedom. She also offered sanctuary for those who were trained as soldiers by the Portuguese. Nzinga's actions contributed to a stronger formation of her kingdom's military forces.[5] She led organized rebellion efforts in areas that were overtaken by the Portuguese. In addition, Nzinga reached out to the Dutch for their support, forming a militaristic alliance to combat the Portuguese.

The forces Nzinga assembled—including her new alliance with the Dutch—did not prove to be enough to drive out the Portuguese. However, after retreating a second time to Matamba, Nzinga focused on transforming Matamba into one of the central areas of commerce in the Old World, as it was strategically located near a port. Over the years, her efforts advanced her kingdom's position, developing it to an equal and competitive level with the Portuguese. She ensured her sovereignty was maintained throughout her kingdom.[6] Nzinga passed away in 1663, leaving behind a prosperous kingdom as a direct result of her successful strategic and militaristic negotiations.

Olaudah Equiano
(Gustavus Vassa)

Born: 1745
Died: March 31, 1797
Country: The Benin Empire (Modern day Southern Nigeria)

"I might say my sufferings were great; but when I compare my lot with that of most of my countrymen, I regard myself as a particular favorite of Heaven, and acknowledge the mercies of Providence in every occurrence of my life." [7]

Olaudah Equiano was born in the Kingdom of Benin, modern day Nigeria, in 1745. Equiano's childhood was severe. He grew up in the Ibo culture. Although his family-owned slaves, there was always a threat of becoming a slave as well. This threat became reality when he and his sister were kidnapped at an early age, separated, and sold into slavery.[8] For months following his capture, Equiano was traded as a slave from one master to another. Eventually he was brought to the African coastline; he was forced to board a ship— along with other slaves—that sailed to Barbados, where it was presumed he would be sold. However, there were no buyers for Equiano in Barbados, and he was shipped to Virginia, an English colony at the time. It was in Virginia that he was finally bought and forced once again to work as a slave. It was not long before Equaino was traded once more to a lieutenant of the Royal Navy, Michael Henry Pascal.[9] His new master, Pascal, gave Equiano the name he would be known widely for, Gustavus Vassa, following the name of the Swedish nobleman who helped his people gain independence from the Danish.[10]

Despite the unfortunate circumstances of Equiano's life, being a slave to a naval lieutenant opened opportunities to him that he would not have otherwise had as a worker on a plantation. Life as a slave to a man in the navy was not easy. However, it provided Equiano the chance to learn how to read and write, because Pascal sent him to school in London. In addition, Equaino had the opportunity to explore Europe.[11] During this time in the 1750s, Britain was fighting in the Seven Years' War, and as a result, Equiano's job aboard the ship was to carry gunpowder. He earned money as a slave, which he attempted to save in order to buy the freedom promised to him by Pascal following the war. Instead, Pascal betrayed him and reneged on his word. Equaino was sold to Captain James Doran who was unforgiving of Equiano's circumstances. After a time as a sea slave for Captain Doran, Equiano was brought back to the West Indies and resold, this time to a Philadelphian Quaker and merchant named Robert King, who treated Equiano humanely.[12] Equiano worked as a clerk for King and was given some liberty to conduct his own trade exchanges. As a result, Equiano finally saved enough money to purchase his freedom, which was granted to him in 1766. With his newfound freedom, Equiano returned to London to pursue further studies and eventually worked as an assistant to a scientist named Dr. Charles Irving. He later accompanied Irving on expeditions throughout the European and Asian continents.[13]

In 1789, he published his two-part autobiography entitled, *The Interesting Narrative of the Life of Olaudah Equiano.* This work goes beyond telling his life story; it also addresses the question of racism, refuting the views and sentiments of the time expressed toward blacks. His story forced people to see slavery through his perspective, and this gave impetus to the abolitionists in Britain. Equinao's book included a letter addressed to the queen of England, pleading his case regarding why slavery should be abolished. While slavery was not abolished until years later, Equinao's letter helped propel the antislavery movement at the time. Equiano passed away in March 1797.[14]

Samuel Sharpe

Born: 1801
Died: May 23, 1832
Country: Jamaica

"I would rather die upon yonder gallows than live in slavery." [15]

Samuel Sharpe was a Jamaican slave with strong human rights and religious beliefs. Born in Montego Bay, he is credited as being the chief architect and principal instigator of the 1831 slave rebellion.[16] This uprising turned out to be the catalyst that led to the abolition of slavery in Jamaica and throughout the British Empire.

In the 1830s, blacks in Jamaica could only congregate for religious reasons. Otherwise, they worked together in virtual silence in cane fields for ungodly hours and paltry pay. Sharpe was able to read and write, and thereby, he kept abreast of current affairs in England. He knew that there was talk of ending slavery, but in the interim, living and working conditions for slaves were inhumane. After religious services, Sharpe would discretely plant the seed of passive resistance into the minds of selected slaves.[17] They were then supposed to echo Sharpe's sentiments.

Sharpe instigated a plan for slaves to cease their labor starting on Christmas day, 1831.[18] He shared this plan with slaves whom he thought he could trust. Yet, he required them to kiss the Bible to affirm their loyalty and adhere to confidentiality. In a short while, Sharpe's plan spread throughout Montego Bay and other parishes. And as night follows day, word got out to slave masters and managers. Army troops descended, a battleship anchored near the shore, and Jamaica was on a virtual lock-down.[19]

Despite the forces arrayed against them, Sharpe and his followers had enough. Just after Christmas 1831, sugarcane fields and the Great House in Kensington Estate were set ablaze.[20] As signals that passive resistance was shelved, fires erupted randomly. Open rebellion began.

Two weeks passed before the rebellion was under control. In its wake, fourteen whites were killed and five hundred blacks lost their lives in the struggle or were executed. Sharpe was hanged publicly in May 1849. A bill to abolish slavery was passed in Britain in 1833, and slavery was thereby abolished, not just in Jamaica, but also throughout the British Empire.

In 1975, almost one hundred fifty years after his execution, Sharpe became a national hero in Jamaica. Thereby, the government conferred on him the title, "Right Excellent" as a prefix to his name. In addition, a college in Jamaica bears Sharpe's name (Sam Sharpe Teachers' College), and his likeness adorns the J$50 note.

Frederick Douglass
(Frederick Augustus Washington Bailey)

Born: (February 14), 1818
Died: February 20, 1895
Country: United States of America

"I prefer to be true to myself, even at the hazard of incurring the ridicule of others, rather than to be false, and to incur my own abhorrence." [21]

Considered one of the most important figures of the nineteenth century, Frederick Augustus Washington Bailey was born into slavery in 1818 in Talbot County, Maryland. His mother was a slave, and it is suspected that his father was the slave owner, Captain Aaron Anthony. There were restrictions for slaves who had children at the time, and therefore, Douglass' mother could not visit him often. As a result, his maternal grandmother raised him during most of his early childhood. When Douglass was approximately seven years old, his grandmother left him at the Wye House Plantation, which was under the ownership of the wealthy master, Colonel Lloyd. Douglass later reflected on his sense of feeling betrayed by his grandmother. Unfortunately, she did not have a choice. His responsibilities included lighter work, as he was too young to work in the field. Douglass lived mostly in the plantation home and was able to observe firsthand, the abuse and forced labor that slaves endured, particularly under the supervision of Aaron Anthony. Douglass did not have very much contact with his mother, who passed away when he was only ten years old.[22]

Aaron Anthony had a daughter, Lucretia Auld, who became a protector of Douglass. Through her husband, Thomas Auld, Douglass was sent away to Baltimore, Maryland to work for Lucretia's brother-in-law, Hugh Auld.[23] It was in the Auld household in Baltimore that Douglass learned the alphabet, which was taught to him illegally by Auld's wife, Sophia. Initially, Sophia did not see the harm in teaching Douglass, who was twelve years old at the time, the basics of reading and writing. She showed a different level of kindness and patience with him than what he had experienced prior to that point in his life. However, when Sophia's husband, Hugh, discovered the lectures, he forbade them from continuing.[24] Literate slaves were considered threats to slave owners, as their new knowledge gave them the impetus to mobilize against captivity and enslavement. While Sophia Auld abruptly ended the lessons following her husband's orders, her time instructing Douglass gave him enough knowledge to wish to continue learning on his own from white children in the neighborhood.[25] After Douglass saved enough money, he purchased a journal that he wrote in. He also discovered *The Columbian Orator*, which he would read when he was able to. Through *The Columbian Orator*, he gained information related to his situation and the plight of slaves, as well as information on human rights and freedom.[26]

Douglass moved back and forth between Auld family members until Lucretia Auld inherited him as property via a will. After she passed away, however, Douglass became the property of Thomas Auld, moving him from Baltimore to St. Michael's in 1833. That year, Douglass was sent away to a notorious slave breaker named Edward Covey.[27] As was his reputation, Covey treated all of his slaves harshly and abused Douglass daily. One day, however, Douglass decided to stand up for himself. This rebellion resulted in a fight between him and Covey that ended in a draw. To avoid word getting out that a slave defied and in essence won against one of the most notorious slave owners, Covey stopped punishing and abusing Douglass. He was then sent away in 1834 to live under the supervision of a kinder and more lenient slave owner, William Freeland. While living under Freeland, Douglass was able to form a Sunday school. There, he began to educate other slaves, teaching them how to read and write.

In 1835, Douglass and other slaves devised a plan to escape from Freeland. However, their plans were discovered, and they were captured and sent to jail. Following this incident, Douglass once again came under the care of Thomas Auld. The following year, Auld sent him to work for William Gardner and later, Walter Price. Douglass became one of the high earning slaves in the caulking trade in Price's shipyard. Finally, in 1838, Douglass found his way to freedom from slavery. He devised another plan: After disguising himself, he used fake documents—provided to him by a free black sailor—and fled by train. Douglass arrived first in Philadelphia and later, New York.

Shortly after gaining his freedom, Douglass married and relocated to New Bedford, Massachusetts, changing his last name to Douglass based on Sir Walter Scott's poem, "The Lady of the Lake." He subscribed to a weekly journal by William Lloyd Garrison, the *Liberator*.[28] In 1941, at a Massachusetts Anti-Slavery Society meeting, Douglass heard Garrison speak. Then, Douglass was asked to speak and share his story; Garrison and others became impressed with Douglass' oratorical skills. This affirmation helped further his career as an activist, leading him to speak out against slavery on tour.

In 1843, Douglass took part in the Hundred Conventions project, which consisted of a six-month anti-slavery tour. In particular among his peers, Douglass faced great challenges during his travels, as he was not accommodated despite being free. While in Indiana, he was beaten by a mob; however, this episode did not deter him from continuing to pursue what he viewed as his life's mission.[29] In 1845, he released his autobiography, *A Narrative on the Life of Frederick Douglass, an American Slave*, which became one of his most well-known published works.

Douglass' increasing recognition and fame drew a concern that his former owner, Hugh Auld, may attempt to lay claim on him as his property. He was encouraged to leave the US to tour Ireland and Britain. Douglass sailed to Liverpool in 1845, and he spent two years touring Ireland and Britain before returning to the US.[30] Eventually, Douglass settled in Rochester, New York, where he established *The North Star* newspaper. He was not only outspoken on abolitionist issues, but also with regard to equality for all, including women's rights. *The North Star* supported all of his aims with the motto, "Right is of no sex—Truth is of no Color—God is the Father of us all, and we are all Brethren."[31] Douglass' actions demonstrated his commitment for equal rights to all citizens, and in 1848, he participated in the First Women's Rights Convention held in Seneca Falls, New York. He continued to work toward supporting women's rights and also helped to shelter escaped slaves as part of the Underground Railroad network. In 1859, Douglass left for Canada and subsequently, Britain, to escape arrest, following the Harpers Ferry raid.

Douglass' tireless and audacious efforts in fighting for equality ultimately ushered in the abolishment of slavery in 1862. The following year, the Emancipation Proclamation took effect. In 1877, he was appointed US marshal in the District of Columbia and US minister resident and consul general to the Republic of Haiti in 1889. His legacy highlights the dangers of his time and the immense struggles he was forced to endure. Douglass will forever remain a symbol of someone who was well ahead of his time and never thought twice about making personal sacrifices toward improving the rights of others. Frederick Douglass passed away on February 20, 1895, in Washington, DC, following a heart attack or stroke.

Harriet Tubman
(Araminta Ross)

Born: 1822
Died: March 10, 1913
Country: United States of America

"Every great dream begins with a dreamer. Always remember, you have within you the strength, the patience, and the passion to reach for the stars to change the world." [32]

Born in 1822 in Dorchester, Maryland, Araminta Ross, better known as Harriet Tubman, was a slave who became one of America's most esteemed and revered abolitionists. Tubman's parents were also slaves, and her childhood consisted of working from an early age as a house servant; then when she grew older, being sent away to work in the fields.[33] In 1844, Tubman married her first husband, John Tubman, acquiring his last name; however, her marriage to John Tubman appeared to be constraining. Their goals did not align, because Tubman's ambition was to move north to freedom, which was not what her husband desired.

In 1849, tensions increased in Tubman's environment, as her master sought to sell her to another owner; she managed to escape slavery with her brothers by heading north. However, her husband still refused to flee. Tubman, undeterred by worry or reservations, reached Pennsylvania. Her brothers, out of fear, decided to turn back. Tubman was a courageous individual, and her efforts in expanding the Underground Railroad contributed to a more powerful, reliable, and fortified system of escape for slaves seeking freedom. The following year, Tubman made the audacious decision to return to the South after learning that her sister and nieces were going to be sold.[34] She saved them and brought them to freedom. Later, she also helped to save her brothers. Over the course of several years, Tubman returned nineteen times to the South to guide hundreds of slaves to freedom. She carried a pistol as a means of protection; her weapon also ensured that slave escapees with cold feet would not attempt to turn around, and consequently, place rescue missions in jeopardy. Tubman became one of the most legendary "conductors" of the Underground Railroad for her successful efforts in freeing slaves from the South and bringing them to freedom.

In 1858, Tubman was set to participate in the infamous raid on Harpers Ferry with the radical white American abolitionist, John Brown. Due to her sudden illness, Tubman was unable to partake in the raid. Missing the foray was to her benefit as the raid—with the goal of overtaking a US arsenal whereupon the weapons would be used to arm a slave revolt— failed. Brown was captured, and his two sons were shot dead along with several of his other men.[35]

A few years later, in 1861, the American Civil War broke out, and Tubman became actively involved. She worked for the Union government as a nurse and an informant. Tubman infiltrated territories perfectly, because of her appearance; she operated seamlessly and undetected. Following the war, Tubman continued to care for blacks and people in need. In Auburn, New York, she turned her residence into the Home for Indigent and Aged Negroes. Tubman passed away from pneumonia on March 10, 1913 and was buried with semi military honors. The US Department of the Treasury on April 20, 2016 announced that Tubman would appear on the twenty-dollar bill, replacing former US President Andrew Jackson.

Marcus Garvey
(Marcus Mosiah Garvey, Jr.)

Born: August 17, 1887
Died: June 10, 1940
Country: Jamaica

"A people without the knowledge of their past history, origin, and culture is like a tree without roots." [36]

Marcus Garvey was born in Jamaica on August 17, 1887. He rose to prominence through a movement that became known as Garveyism. He instilled an important ideology within black people to rise above the restrictions of discrimination and prejudice and form their own networks and economic plans. Garvey grew up in a large family, as the youngest of eleven children. Apart from one of his sisters, all of his siblings passed away when they were young. Garvey's father was a farmer, and his mother was a domestic worker.[37] When he was just fourteen years old, he traveled to Kingston, Jamaica, to become a printer's apprentice at P. A. Benjamins Manufacturing Company. Garvey used this opportunity to lead a printer's strike in 1907 in an effort to fight for higher wages. His participation in the strike encouraged further political activism. As a result, Garvey travelled outside of Jamaica to countries in Central America, first living with his uncle in Costa Rica. He arrived in Costa Rica in 1910, and while there, he worked on a banana plantation. In addition, he worked for *La Nacionale* as a writer and editor. The following year, Garvey moved to Panama—where he worked as an editor of another publication—before returning to Jamaica in 1912. That year, Garvey made the decision to move to London to attend school at Birkbeck College.

Garvey later founded the Universal Negro Improvement Association (UNIA) in Jamaica after being inspired by Booker T. Washington's autobiography, *Up from Slavery*. Unfortunately, the Universal Negro Improvement Association did not see success in Jamaica, but when Garvey relocated to New York, he discovered that the UNIA was well received there. The UNIA became a mass movement with offices opened across the nation as well as internationally. UNIA represented a source of inspiration, support, and motivation for black people. Through his success with the UNIA, Garvey formed other unions and organizations, including the Black Star Line and the Negro Factories Corporation in 1919. The Black Star Line was specifically established to support international trade for black businesses as well as provide transportation from Africa to the American continent. He also began a newspaper called *Negro World*.[38] Garvey's ambitions, however, ultimately fell short, as he was unable to see the full success of his initiatives. By 1922, many of the organizations he pioneered folded, and the following year, he came under scrutiny by the postal service; Garvey was subsequently indicted and convicted for mail fraud. He spent time in jail before being deported back to Jamaica in 1927. During his sunset years in Jamaica, he continued to be an active advocate for black people.

In 1935, Garvey moved back to London. In 1940, he suffered a cerebral hemorrhage, and later that year, he passed away from a second cerebral hemorrhage.

George Padmore
(Malcolm Ivan Meredith Nurse)

Born: June 28, 1903
Died: September 23, 1959
Country: The Republic of Trinidad and Tobago

"The oppression of Negroes assumes two distinct forms: on the one hand they are oppressed as a class, and on the other as a nation." [39]

Widely known as George Padmore, he was born Malcolm Ivan Meredith Nurse in Arouca, Trinidad, on June 28, 1903. Padmore's family line included survivors of slavery; yet they rose to great prominence. As a result, Padmore was raised in a middle-class black family. Immediately following his graduation from high school, he accepted a job with the Trinidad Publishing Company. Padmore later travelled to the United States for further studies, and in 1924, he moved to Tennessee to enroll at Fisk University. He did not remain at Fisk; he switched to New York University and later, Howard University.[40]

He never completed his studies at Howard University; instead, Padmore traveled to the USSR. In 1930, he organized the International Conference of Negro Workers. He also became the head of the Negro Bureau of the Red International of Labor Unions.[41] The opportunity to live abroad in countries around Europe opened more opportunities for Padmore. After he left Russia, he spent time living in Austria before moving to Germany, and subsequently, to England. By 1934, Padmore had come to know W. E. B. Du Bois who requested his help with efforts to unify blacks.[42] The changing political climate of Europe at the time and Hitler's rise to power, however, caused the scope of the communist party he served to change as a result. Padmore was in disagreement with communist colonial policies, which led him to decide to leave the party.[43]

Near the end of World War II, Padmore consolidated the services of the International African Service Bureau (IASB) by merging it with other organizations to create the Pan-African Federation. Padmore also came to know Kwame Nkrumah, who led Ghana to Independence in 1957. Prior to Ghana achieving its independence, Padmore became increasingly involved in studying Ghana's situation and its ability to overcome the repercussions of colonial rule and reestablish self-governance.[44] Through his association with Nkrumah, Padmore moved to Ghana and became Nkrumah's political advisor, focusing on African affairs.

Padmore focused his life's work on championing black causes and elevating their position internationally. His perspective demonstrated the parallels between black people suffering in America with black people who had overcome generations of colonial rule. The remainder of his career was spent working to support Ghanaians while promoting his own ideals. In 1959, while at a conference in

Libya, Padmore passed away, leaving behind a dedicated legacy of enlightenment regarding the image and future of blacks around the world.

Nelson Mandela
(Nelson Rolihlahla Mandela)

Born: July 18, 1918
Died: December 5, 2013
Country: The Republic of South Africa

"I learned that courage was not the absence of fear, but the triumph over it. The brave man is not he who does not feel afraid, but he who conquers that fear." [45]

Born Nelson Rolihlahla Mandela on July 18, 1918 in Mvezo, South Africa, he became one of the world's most-recognized and respected revolutionaries. His position since childhood was one of privilege, having been born into a royal Xhosa family. Mandela experienced the loss of his father at an early age; a Thembu regent, Jongintaba Dalindyebo, adopted him. Through these early opportunities in life, he became the first in his line to receive a formal education, ultimately producing a strong freethinker who was unafraid to speak the truth.[46]

Mandela attended the University College of Fort Hare for his Bachelor of Art's degree; however, he did not complete his studies, because he was expelled for participating in a student protest. Mandela's participation in the demonstration angered Dalindyebo, but he was determined to follow his own path. In 1941, he ran away from home to escape an arranged marriage and ended up in Johannesburg.[47] His first job in Johannesburg was working as a night watchman at a mine compound; then, he was employed as a law clerk, while he also completed his studies at the University of South Africa.

In 1943, Mandela entered law school at the University of the Witwatersrand. After six years, he left the university without completing his studies.[48] It was during this time that Mandela was introduced to South African anti-apartheid activist Walter Sisulu. In 1944, Mandela formed the ANC Youth League. South Africa experienced a reemergence of the National Party in government by 1948; the ANC Youth League helped the African National Congress (ANC) transform itself into a more militant organization. The National Party divided South Africa and enforced the rule of apartheid within the country, encouraging racism and white minority rule.

In June of 1952, the Defiance Campaign was launched as a way to unite people in the fight against the unjust rulings of apartheid.[49] Nelson Mandela, along with Walter Sisulu and others, were part of the first group of volunteer protestors supporting the campaign. Many dissidents, including Mandela, were imprisoned for a short period. The campaign's success bolstered protests across the country. The growing movement increased the government's concern that—if not controlled—more defiance could come in the future. Over eight thousand people were arrested for protesting; these arrests—and lack of humane treatment for the imprisoned—prompted the United Nations to recognize apartheid as a critical international issue. During this time, Mandela continued to take on leadership roles and was active in protests. He was considered an increasing threat, as a direct result of his defiance, and in 1960, he openly burned his passport as further evidence that he had dedicated his life to the cessation of apartheid.

In 1962, the armed wing of the Pan Africanist Congress (PAC)—known as Poquo—was notorious for leading violent uprisings that targeted whites. A series of brutal attacks by this faction were executed in an effort to destabilize the country.[50] During this time, Mandela traveled outside of the country—to places like Tanzania and Botswana—in order to gain and mobilize greater support outside of South Africa. He also made a trip to Ethiopia, where he met with Haile Selassie. Mandela continued his journeys, visiting Britain.

Eventually, Mandela returned to South Africa. It did not take long for his presence to become known, and he was arrested. Mandela was given a five-year sentence for traveling without a passport and inciting a strike. His imprisonment began in Pretoria, but soon, he was moved to Robben Island. In 1964, Mandela was brought to what became the historic Rivonia Trial. During this trial he continued his defiance by relentlessly accusing the court of being illegitimate in its approach to the law and determinations. In June of that year, Mandela was sentenced to life imprisonment at Robben Island on charges of sabotage.

The conditions at Robben Island were brutal. As a black prisoner, Mandela was subjected to harsher treatment, less rations of food, and more strenuous labor at a lime quarry than white inmates. He had a small cell that did not include plumbing or a bed. Despite his circumstances, Mandela managed to earn his law degree from the University of London. In addition, he educated fellow prisoners about their rights and encouraged them to demand more rights in the process.[51]

The 1980s brought a new spotlight to Mandela who, despite his imprisonment, had already become a beacon of hope for South Africa. A "Free Nelson Mandela" campaign gained strength, ultimately pressuring the government to release him from prison under a set of terms and conditions set by the National Party. Mandela refused to comply with the stipulated demands and remained in prison. F. W. de Klerk took office as South Africa's president in 1989, as part of the Nationalist Party. Bowing to international pressure and domestic tremors, he decided to free Mandela and end apartheid. Mandela and de Klerk each were awarded the Nobel Prize in 1993. The following year, Mandela ran for president and won the election, becoming South Africa's first black president; de Klerk remained in office as first deputy.

President Mandela formulated programs directed at supporting underprivileged blacks within his country. He also implemented the Truth and Reconciliation Commission, which focused on investigations that highlighted the violations committed during the apartheid era by opponents and supporters of apartheid alike. Mandela not only recognized the suffering that blacks endured over the apartheid years, but he also made a point to preach a gospel of reconciliation, not retaliation. He envisioned a new South Africa where blacks and whites coexisted as equals.

After leaving office, Mandela continued to inspire the world and founded many organizations that worked towards supporting human rights globally. He expanded his focus to not only support racial equality and acceptance among all races, but also address other international issues, including AIDS (to which he lost his son). Nelson Mandela dedicated his life to human causes in order to improve the quality of life for all. Mandela passed away from a recurring lung infection on December 5, 2013.

Dr. Martin Luther King Jr.
(Michael King Jr.)

Born: January 15, 1929
Died: April 4, 1968
Country: The United States of America

"If a man hasn't found something in life that he's willing to die for, then that man isn't fit to live." [52]

A humanitarian and civil rights activist, Martin Luther King Jr. was a champion of peace and equality. He was born on January 15, 1929, in Atlanta, Georgia. King was the middle child of a pastor and a schoolteacher. King's father influenced him from an early age by openly speaking out against racism and in particular, by using religion as a basis for his argument. When King was twelve years old, his grandmother died of a heart attack. The trauma of her sudden death was further compounded by the fact that he had left the house when he was not supposed to. Young King harbored a heavy sense of guilt at the time, leading him to consider suicide by jumping out of a two-story window. The world is better off, most would agree, because he did not jump.

King began studies at Morehouse College when he was fifteen years old, and he excelled in school. While at Morehouse, King elected to study sociology. However, the influence of one of his mentors drew him toward considering a career in religion like his father. King decided to move to Pennsylvania and attend the Crozer Theological Seminary after graduating from Morehouse in 1948. At Crozer, he obtained his Bachelor of Divinity degree in 1951. Following these studies, King pursued his PhD at Boston University in systematic theology, which he obtained in 1953.

While at Boston University, King met his future wife, Coretta Scott, and they were married in 1953. They moved to Montgomery, Alabama, and a year later, he became the pastor at a local church. At the time, Alabama (and Montgomery in particular) was a highly segregated city. In 1955, Rosa Parks—who refused to give up her seat to a white person on the bus in Montgomery—was arrested. This sparked outrage among the black community, and activists organized boycotts against the bus system that lasted for more than 380 days. King helped lead these protests, which were highly successful in the way they economically affected the transportation system.[53] Following his heavy involvement in the boycotts, King continued to gain the attention of the public. This scrutiny had its consequences, and in January 1956, King's house was targeted by white supremacists and bombed. King and his family survived, and that incident further fueled his ambition to speak out and take action against the racism of his time.[54] In 1957, he founded and became president of the Southern Christian Leadership Conference (SCLC); this organization dedicated itself—peacefully and without violent confrontations—to seek justice and equality for black Americans. Part of King's inspiration for fighting causes through nonviolent means came from the teachings of Mahatma Gandhi.

King left Montgomery, Alabama, with his family in 1960 and moved to his childhood city of Atlanta, where he took a job in the local church alongside his father. Despite the move, King remained active politically and continued to support protests and speak out against segregation. In 1963, he was involved in the Birmingham campaign where he participated in a series of boycotts and marches aimed at combating racism. His involvement in the protest campaign resulted in his arrest,[55] yet King continued to speak out against discrimination from his jail cell. In April of that year, he produced the prolific "Letter from Birmingham Jail" to formalize his position and establish the seriousness of the SCLC.

Following his release from jail, King began to organize what became one of the most historic and well-known events in the civil rights era, the March on Washington. He brought together civil rights and religious groups from all over the United States to participate in the march. The goal was for a peaceful demonstration that would highlight the plight that African Americans faced. The event took place on August 28, 1963, and was attended by over 300,000 peaceful protestors, marching for freedom and equality. During the March on Washington, King addressed the public with his powerful, "I Have a Dream" speech. The March on Washington contributed to the enactment of the Civil Rights Act of 1964, which legally ended discrimination based on race, color, religion, sex, or national origin. Nineteen sixty-four also marked the year that King was awarded the Nobel Peace Prize, making him the youngest to ever receive the honor.

King's tireless work and advocacy for equality benefitted the entire nation. When he returned to the United States after receiving his Nobel Peace Prize, he had new challenges to face. In 1965, a violent protest broke out in Selma, Alabama. King intervened and led a peaceful march that was supported by US President

Lyndon B. Johnson and troops he sent to help maintain peace. The efforts led to the Voting Rights Act of 1965, which broke the barriers that once prevented blacks from voting. The events that Selma spurred also changed the tone for King, as his vision no longer matched that of young protestors who resorted to violence in defiance of Dr. King's exaltations. As a result, King turned his attention to many different causes, including efforts to advocate for the poor, whose plight may have led to rioting in the first place.

King, however, would not be able to fulfill his vision for a poor people's campaign. He decided to travel to Memphis to support another strike that was taking place. It was in Memphis in 1968 that King was assassinated by a single gunshot. His slaying brought about enormous riots, demonstrations, and anger across the country.

Dr. Martin Luther King Jr. has remained a universal symbol for peace and nonviolence. He will forever be a beacon of hope in struggles that promote fairness, justice, and equality, irrespective of race, gender, nationality, or religion.

Kwame Nkrumah
(The Right Honourable)

Born: September 21, 1909
Died: April 27, 1972
Country: Ghana

"We must set an example to all Africa."

Kwame Nkrumah, the first Prime Minister and President of Ghana, has secured a place atop the highest perch of black achievement as a founding member of the Organization of African Unity and the leading figure to make Ghana the first British Colony to break from Britain in 1952 and declare its independence.

Educated both in Britain and the United States, Nkrumah was a pioneer in preaching a doctrine of Africa first. He embraced socialism – nationalizing the energy industry among others and advancing the idea that education and continent-wide relations with international partners were tickets to national progress.

While he rose to power on democratic principles, this was short lived. A constitutional amendment in 1964 transformed Ghana into a one-party state with Nkrumah not only as head of the sole political party, but President for life.

On the occasion of Ghana's Independence when he declared "We have a duty to prove to the world that Africans can conduct their own affairs with efficiency and tolerance and through the exercise of democracy" Nkrumah was hailed internationally as a great liberator and freedom fighter. Indeed, some called him "the redeemer".

All of this must have gone to Nkrumah's head. Not only did he disband all political parties but his own; not only did he declare himself President for life; he passed a draconian Prevention Detention Act that saw citizens locked up for up to five years devoid of charges, trials or convictions. He pretty much banned trade unions and tinkered with the powers of Parliament to advance his agenda.

For all his democratic failings and authoritarian excursions, Nkrumah is heralded for modernizing Ghana's economy by introducing factories, transforming Ghana's civil service; introducing near universal access to primary and secondary school education; ushering in a new era of overseas travel that helped to forge a new middle class; promoted gender equality and he significantly expanded Ghana's social safety network by creating a robust social services regime. Taken together, these initiatives and programmes served as a template for the rest of Africa. Moreover, his Ten-Year Development Plan was a first in an effort to codify long-term planning among African and Diaspora States.

Ironically, Nkrumah was essentially driven from power on February 24, 1966. He died in Bucharest Romania on April 27, 1972.

CHAPTER II

Politics & Governance

INTRODUCTION
Politics and Governance

Sociologists tell us that there are six basic institutions that regulate human development and interactions: family, school, church, economy, science and technology, and politics and governance. No matter where one lives, a form of governance and some measure of political process exist.

Whether formal or informal; democratic or autocratic; elected, appointed, or anointed; there is—on every corner of the globe—some form of governance. This chapter seeks to identify the black universal giants in governance and politics who best utilized the instruments of states craft to effect broad-based change at home and abroad.

Clearly, the intention is to highlight those associated with positive, productive, purposive change. In order to make the top-ten list in politics and governance, two overarching achievements were considered: the extent to which the candidate shaped the future of his/her country, and the extent of influence the candidate exerted in shaping world events for the better.

The size of a country or its economy proved irrelevant to this process. In the examination of Trinidad and Tobago's A. N. R. Robinson and the Bahamas' Sir Lynden Pindling, it is evident that Small Island Developing States (SIDS) can spur global action and direct ideas with universal appeal.

Having regard to the foregoing considerations, it is postulated that in the arena of politics and governance, the ten blacks who had the greatest impact are as follows:

Askia the Great
(Askia Mohammad I)

Born: 1443
Died: 1538
Country: Futa Tooro (Modern day northern Senegal and southern Mauritania)

The continent of Africa is comprised of 57 countries. Long before many of its territories became countries (Benin, Burkina-Faso, Guinea, Guinea-Bisson, Mali, Mauritania, Niger, Senegal, and Gambia), they were part of the Songhai Empire over which Askia the Great ruled as emperor. His reign extended from 1493 to 1528 when Askia Musa, his son, overthrew him.

Askia the Great came to power by default. He was a military commander and hardly in line to become emperor. In fact, Askia was not even in the bloodline of the royal family. As fate would have it, Sunni Ali, the emperor, died; the full expectation was that Sunni Baru, his son, would ascend the throne. In order to do so, Baru had to embrace the Muslim religion. Baru refused. Therefore, Askia the Great (known as General Ture) contested Baru's right to the throne, defeated him, and in 1493, became emperor.[56]

Askia the Great significantly increased trade to other continents and vastly expanded his empire's territory to the north and south. He was a strong proponent of education as an arm of social stability and economic development. Consequently, he built many universities and pre-tertiary institutions. A devout Muslim, Askia the Great imposed the teachings of Islam, as part of the empire's socio-religious fabric. Yet, he was careful to not allow Islamic structures to dictate public policy.

Askia introduced quasi-democratic principles for the first time, instituted a rational tax system, and modernized shipping regulations and methodologies. The Songhai Empire reigned for over two hundred years (1375-1591); for thirty-five of those years, Askia the Great—not withstanding multiple coup attempts—served as emperor.[57] His tomb has been declared a World Heritage Site.

Toussaint L'Ouverture

Born: May 20, 1743
Died: April 7, 1803
Country: The Republic of Haiti

"I was born a slave, but nature gave me the soul of a free man." [58]

L'Ouverture was a mostly unschooled, unimposing military genius who masterminded the liberation of slaves in Hispaniola (now Haiti and the Dominican Republic) and led the march towards Haiti's independence. Son of a slave, L'Ouverture was a strict adherent to Catholicism, an uncompromising vegetarian, and a man of simple tastes. In addition to these characteristics, he was extraordinary, visionary, and legendary.

In August 1791, L'Ouverture faced a major challenge. An unexpected slave revolt erupted in the north of Haiti and spread like wildfire. L'Ouverture was caught by surprise, so he remained neutral to the rebellion for a while. After approximately two weeks, however, he helped his former slave master escape; then, he joined hands with slave protestors who burned vegetable crops and killed hundreds of

Europeans and mixed-race inhabitants. L'Ouverture quickly concluded that the uprising suffered from poor leadership, so he formed his own army and trained them in guerilla tactics. Soon, L'Ouverture was recognized as a general. By 1793, when France and Spain went to war, L'Ouverture and a band of black soldiers from Hispaniola (Dominican Republic) led the fight in the north and significantly degraded the French fighting machine.[59]

After these confrontations in a classic case of duplicity, L'Ouverture—one year later— aligned himself with the French noting that France had decided to end slavery while Britain and Spain had not. This move catapulted him to the post of lieutenant governor. By this time, L'Ouverture's name and fame were secured. He began instituting progressive policies to move Haiti forward. L'Ouverture loathed laziness. He applied a militaristic approach to governance, abolished corporal punishment, and forced freed slaves to work with the incentive of sharing in the proceeds from plantation production. Perhaps his most enduring legacy is the goodwill he extended to former masters in a spirit of reconciliation. This benevolence helped to open the doors for aggressive trading between Haiti and Europe, as well as the United States. (Typically, Haiti exported plantation products and imported weapons and staple goods.)

After fighting for the abolition of slavery in Haiti, which claims one-third of Hispaniola, L'Ouverture defied Napoleon Bonaparte and marched into the other two-thirds of the island (now Dominican Republic). There, in 1801, he freed the slaves to the utter amazement of those of mixed race and the Europeans. Having accomplished this feat, L'Ouverture crafted a constitution that made him governor general of the entire island—for life. This lofty position was short-lived, however. In 1802, L'Ouverture was overthrown by a French invasion that utilized superior firepower and upgraded methodology. He was subsequently placed under house arrest where he died a year later at age sixty.[60]

Anwar Sadat
(Muhammad Anwar el-Sadat)

Born: December 25, 1918
Died: October 6, 1981
Country: The Arab Republic of Egypt

"Russians can give you arms, but only the United States can give you solutions." [61]

The role Anwar Sadat played in cementing a peace treaty between Egypt and Israel will live on as one of the great, shining, seminal moments that changed the course of history.

Muhammad Anwar el–Sadat, prior to assuming the presidency of Egypt, was a military man, who at age twenty completed military school and enlisted in the armed forces. His strategic and tactical acumen was in full bloom during World War II, when he masterminded an operation— in concert with Germany—to oust the British from Egypt. His plot was discovered, and the British arrested and imprisoned him, only to have him escape. Sadat was caught and again jailed; this time, he was accused of being involved in an assassination attempt of a high government official. He was found not guilty.

Military commander, Abdel Nasser, formed a revolutionary organization that attracted Sadat, and in 1952, they plotted to overthrow the Egyptian dynasty. They succeeded, and Nasser was elected president. Meanwhile, Sadat held several senior government posts before becoming vice president and then president upon Nasser's death in 1970.

Sadat set out to broaden Egypt's economy by expanding foreign trade while attracting major foreign direct investments. Although well intentioned, these initiatives erased a fledgling middle class and created a two-tier society—very wealthy and very poor. This sad state of affairs reached its zenith in 1977, when the country plunged into food riots.[62]

Where Sadat floundered on the domestic front, he flourished in foreign affairs, particularly as they related to relations with Egypt's epic adversary, Israel. He formed the view that the then Soviet Union's support of Egypt against Israel was at best lukewarm, so he chased scores of Soviet workers out of the country.

Sadat later initiated a surprise attack against Israel to reclaim a portion of disputed land. Israel responded adroitly, but Sadat's effort bore some fruit. This adventure significantly elevated the esteem with which he was held within the region, because up to that time, no other Arab leader was successful in reclaiming land from Israel.

Ironically, for a long time, Sadat wanted peace between Egypt and Israel. So, in 1977— against great opposition by many of his countrymen—he went to Israel, addressed its parliament, and laid out a path toward peace. In 1978, United States President Jimmy Carter mediated talks between Sadat and Israel's Prime Minister

Menachem Begin, and in 1978, the historic Camp David Accords were settled. Signed in 1979, it was the first peace treaty between Israel and any Arab country.

For their efforts to attain peace, which had previously been consistently elusive, Sadat and Begin shared the 1978 Nobel Peace Prize. In a twist of fate, Sadat was assassinated on Armed Forces Day, while watching a military display.

Kamala Harris
(49ᵗʰ Vice President of The United States)

Born: October 20, 1964
Country: United States of America

"If you are fortunate to have opportunity, it is your duty to make sure other people have those opportunities as well."

In 1872, Victoria Woodhall became the first woman to seek the Presidency of the United States. Over the years, a number of women of all stripes have sought the U.S. Presidency culminating in Hillary Clinton's historic attempt in 2008 and again in 2016.

Perhaps because Clinton came so close to shattering that elusive glass ceiling, no fewer than seven women entered the race for President of the United States in 2020, including Tulsi Gabbard, Elizabeth Warren, Marianne Williamson, Amy Klobuchar, Kirsten Gillibrand, Jo Jorgensen and Kamala Harris.

Although Harris' quest for the U.S. Presidency was short lived, Joe Biden chose her from amongst a galaxy of contenders as his running mate and on January

20, 2021, she was sworn in as the first woman to become Vice President of the United States.

Since 1884, some ten women have sought the U.S. Vice Presidency but until Harris' rise to political prominence, only two represented major parties, namely Geraldine Ferraro (Democrat) in 1984 and Sarah Palin (Republican) in 2008. Harris' selection by Joe Biden as his running mate and her election to a position just a heartbeat away from the Presidency of the richest, most powerful country on earth, did not come on a silver platter. Her stella achievements came the old-fashioned way – she earned it.

From her middle-class roots in Oakland, California, Harris has been a focused, purposeful aspirant who never allowed privilege to define her.

A graduate of Washington D.C.'s Howard University with a degree in Political Science, Harris earned her J.D. degree from the University of California's Hastings College of Law. She served as a District Attorney then Attorney General of California – the second largest Justice Department in the United States – before she joined Diane Feinstein as a Senator from California in 2017. As a U.S. Senator, she developed a reputation for withering questions posed to those who appeared before the Judiciary Committee. Her detractors say her story is one of being in the right place at the right time. To her supporters, Harris has carefully ordered her steps through preparation and perspiration.

When she took the Oath of Office on January 20th, 2021, Harris crashed a major glass ceiling, becoming not just the highest elected female in the history of the United States, but the first African American/Asian Vice President. From this lofty perch it is widely expected that in the fullness of time, she will launch a second Presidential bid.

Sir Lynden Pindling

Born: March 22, 1930
Died: August 26, 2000
Country: The Commonwealth of The Bahamas

"The Bahamian people have spoken and the voice of the people is the voice of God." [63]

Sir Lynden Pindling was an elected member of parliament in The Bahamas from 1956 to 1997 and the head of government from 1967 to 1992. He is the longest serving democratically elected head of government in the Western Hemisphere. Pindling helped to change the world in 1985; as host of the Eighth Commonwealth Heads of Government meeting, he was appointed chairman of the Commonwealth Eminent Persons Group. This organization was charged with pressuring South Africa—via diplomacy and onerous sanctions—to dismantle apartheid. Soon thereafter, Nelson Mandela was released from prison after twenty-seven years, and the liberation of South Africa became a reality. Not long after his assumption of the presidency of South Africa, Mandela visited The Bahamas to personally thank Sir Lynden.

Widely regarded as a master politician and in possession of a British law degree, Pindling was blessed with superlative oratorical skills, and yet, he embodied the "common touch." He purposefully built a political legacy by aligning himself with individuals he referred to as the "common man." Even before he became prime minister, Pindling was a key factor in bringing about the vote for women and eighteen-year-olds. He was also a key figure in dismantling the Property Vote, which was designed to sustain the political power base of the white oligarchy in The Bahamas.

In 1967, Pindling led a Quiet Revolution (without bloodshed), which placed political power in the hands of the black majority for the first time. He led the country to independence in 1973, and by 1992, he had built schools and clinics across the thirty inhabitant islands of The Bahamas. In addition, Pindling created myriad socio-economic institutions, including the College of The Bahamas, the Defence Force, Bahamasair, the National Insurance Security Scheme, the Central and Development Banks, one of the world's largest ship registries, the Bank of The Bahamas, and a Bahamianization policy that placed qualified Bahamian nationals at the front of the line to fill professional job vacancies. Perhaps his greatest achievements were enhancing year-round tourism, keeping the Bahamian dollar on par with the US dollar, and building a new middle class through an economy that is still the third strongest in the Western Hemisphere—behind only Canada and the United States.

In his later years, Sir Lynden was the subject of scandals and corruption charges fueled mostly by drug barons and political foes. Charges against him were not proven conclusively, and he was never indicted by anyone for any wrongdoing. Sir Lynden lost his battle with prostate cancer in August 2000.

The country's main airport bears his name, and the Lynden Pindling Foundation awards scholarships annually to deserving students. The Washington, D.C., Organization of American States in 2015 agreed to the placement of a bust of Sir Lynden Pindling within it Hall of Heroes, alongside national heroes from throughout the western hemisphere.

Colin Luther Powell

Born: April 5, 1937
Country: The United States of America

"There are no secrets to success. It is the result of preparation, hard work, and learning from failure." [64]

Had he answered the cacophony of calls, Colin Luther Powell might well have become the United States first black president. In 1992, there was a serious effort to have him sign on as George Bush's running mate instead of Dan Quayle. Powell declined. The chorus grew louder in 1996 when there was an all-out bid to have him compete for the presidency against Bill Clinton. Powell determined that he lacked the passion for hard-core politics. Instead, in 1997, he launched America's Promise, a nonprofit, multipronged, leadership development organization. This institution's goals were aimed at imbuing young people from across the country with positive values, high self-esteem, targeted goals, and certainty of purpose.

Yet, in 2000, his name reemerged prominently as a dream candidate to take the Republican Party's fight to the Democrats. He declined. The requests for Powell to rise higher did not come out of thin air. They came from sober-minded citizens on both political sides, who saw in Powell strength, intellect, integrity, and leadership—all of which he displayed during his stellar thirty-five years in the military. During his military career, he recorded a series of firsts: first black commander of the US Armed Forces, twelfth chairman and first black to serve as chairman of the Joint Chiefs of Staff, sixteenth and first black national security advisor, and sixty-fifth and first black US Secretary of State.[65]

Powell, who retired as a four-star general, saw action in Vietnam and Panama and planned the invasion of Haiti and Grenada. In addition, he masterminded the Persian Gulf War, at which time the Powell Doctrine came into force—namely, attack the enemy with such force that you achieve the maximum shock in the shortest period with minimal civilian casualties. Powell, who initially opposed the Iraq War, was later convinced, though wrongly, that Saddam Hussein possessed weapons of mass destruction. He became the principal spokesman for the war, and in the end, when his boss, President George W. Bush was proven wrong and Powell was proven right, he resigned. It is believed that their relationship never fully recovered.

Born in Harlem to Jamaican parents, Powell earned his MBA at George Washington University, and is decorated with two Presidential Medals of Freedom, the Woodrow Wilson Award for public service, the Academy of Achievement Golden Plate Award, the Ronald Reagan Freedom Award, and the Congressional Gold Medal among others.

Kofi Annan

Born: April 8, 1938
Died: August 18, 2018
Country: The Republic of Ghana

"We are not only responsible for each other's security, we are also responsible for each other's welfare." [66]

Some say that Kofi Annan was born with a head start that propelled him to the corridors of international civil service stardom. Not hardly. Although born to an aristocratic family in Kumasi, Ghana, Annan displayed a penchant for social justice since he was a teenager. This early orientation towards human rights, equalitarianism, and human inspiration pushed him up the ladder of international diplomacy, and in 1999, his efforts made him the first black secretary-general of the United Nations.

Annan is perhaps the most decorated secretary-general of the United Nations with whom he shares the 2001 Nobel Peace Prize for his role in promoting world peace. Eight countries have bestowed high honors upon him. Annan has received more than twenty international awards and some thirty honorary doctorate degrees for his work as a peacemaker.

Annan's diplomatic exploits are legendary. He supported the transition from military to civilian rule in Nigeria, promoted the efforts in East Timor to secure independence from Indonesia, certified Israel's withdrawal from Lebanon in 2000 and led talks between the two countries over the Bakassi peninsula, created a cabinet-style body to help him carry out his mandate at the UN, and sparked the formulation of the UN's Millennium Development Goals that aimed to reduce extreme poverty around the world. In reaching these lofty goals, Annan lifted the state of human affairs.[67]

Annan, who joined the United Nations in 1969, retired as secretary general on December 31, 2006. Since then, he established the Kofi Annan Foundation, which promotes improved global governance. In addition, Annan was appointed joint special envoy to Syria and honored as a Li Ka Shong Professor at the Lee Kuan Yew School of Public Policy of the National University of Singapore.

Ellen Johnson Sirleaf

Born: October 29, 1938
Country: The Republic of Liberia

"I work hard, I work late. I have nothing on my conscience. When I go to bed, I sleep." [68]

In 2006, she was ranked by *Forbes Magazine* as the fifty-first most powerful woman in the world. Although by 2014, she slipped to seventieth position in the magazine's ranking, Ellen Johnson Sirleaf is a political giant and world-class stateswoman. Currently, she is in her second term as president of Liberia.

First elected as president in 2006, Sirleaf holds the distinction of being the first elected female head of state in Africa. Her road to the top was paved with bumps, detours, and danger signs. A Harvard–trained economist, she once served as Liberia's assistant finance minister. However, this position was short-lived after she gave a withering address to Liberia's Chamber of Commerce, accusing the corporate community of essentially raping the national economy. Sirleaf later resigned her post after squabbling with the government over its spending habits. In 1979, Sirleaf was elevated to minister of Finance. She resigned in 1980 before

Samuel Doe seized power in a coup that resulted in the execution of all but four members of the old cabinet. Doe offered Sirleaf a cabinet post, which she accepted. Before assuming office, she lambasted the new government and secretly left the country.

While in self-imposed exile,[68(b)] Sirleaf gave of herself to the world. She held a remarkable list of positions: executive at the World Bank; a Citibank vice president in Kenya, assistant secretary general at the United Nations, professor at Ghana Institute of Management and Public Administration, and a member of the Eminent Persons Group (EPG). The EPG was appointed by the Organization of African Unity to delve into genocide in Rwanda.

In 1985, Sirleaf returned to Liberia with intentions of running for the vice presidency. Instead, she was placed under house arrest, charged with sedition, and sentenced to ten years of imprisonment. The government bowed to international pressure and soon released her but disqualified her from seeking the vice presidency.

Sirleaf then successfully contested a senate seat but refused to take her seat on the grounds that the overall election had been rigged. Having accused the new government of fraud, Sirleaf was again arrested and imprisoned. Upon her release, she fled to the United States.

Although banned from seeking public office for thirty years, Sirleaf returned to Liberia in 1997 to seek the presidency. She was not successful, and again, she left the country. (Some say she departed for her own safety.) In 2005, Sirleaf again offered for the presidency, and this time—after a run-off election—she emerged as Africa's first female president.

Liberia, Africa's oldest republic, was founded in 1822 by Caribbean slaves and freed Americans; it has a population of just over four million. Liberia has long been plagued by civil war, and one of Sirleaf's enduring legacies will be her commitment to democracy and the rule of law. Her achievements as president are impressive: she passed a Freedom of Information Bill, she placed some of her erstwhile political opponents in her cabinet as a means of promoting national unity, she significantly reduced the burdensome national debt, and she promotes anti-corruption as a cornerstone of her administration. Since Sirleaf took the reins of power, Liberia has existed in relative peace and in friendly relations with its neighbors.

For her life's work and contributions to the welfare and betterment of Liberia and peoples around the world, Sirleaf has been decorated with many awards, including the 2011 Nobel Peace Prize; the 2012 Indira Gandhi Prize for Peace, Disarmament, and Development; 1988 Franklin and Eleanor Roosevelt Institute Freedom of Speech Award; Ralph Bunche International Leadership Award; 2011 Africa Gender Award; and the 2006 Laureate for the Africa Prize for Leadership for Sustainable End to Hunger. In addition, she has earned honorary doctoral degrees from numerous world-renown universities, including Harvard, Dartmouth, Yale, Brown, Marquette, and Rutgers.

Ngozi Okonjo–Iweala

Born: June 13, 1954
Country: The Federal Republic of Nigeria

"No one can fight corruption for Nigerians except Nigerians. Everyone has to be committed from the top to the bottom to fight it." [69]

Dr. Ngozi Okonjo-Iweala was in February 2021 elected Director General of the World Trade Organization (WTO) becoming the first woman and the first African elected to head the world trade body. She once served as the managing director at the World Bank from 2017-2011.

The World Bank is a Washington DC–based international financial institution that provides loans to its 188 member states, primarily for infrastructural development in accordance with its motto "working for a world free of poverty." Ngozi Okonjo-Iweala, a Nigerian economist, knows the World Bank well. Apart from serving as the Managing Director, she also served as one of its vice presidents and as corporate secretary. In fact, Okonjo-Iweala, armed with an undergraduate degree from Massachusetts Institute of Technology (MIT) and a PhD in economics from Harvard, was once considered likely to become president of the World Bank. Indeed, she made a bid for the post in 2007, but was not successful.

Okonjo-Iweala had two stints as Nigeria's minister of finance and is credited with instituting policies that significantly reduced the country's national debt. At the time of this writing, she is using her expertise as a senior advisor at Lazard, a financial advisory and asset management conglomerate—headquartered in Bermuda—with offices in twenty-four cities across fifteen countries on four continents.[70]

In 2007, Okonjo-Iweala launched her not-for-profit think tank, Global Consulting, which teamed up with Gallop to introduce opinion polling to Nigerian politics. She is a fellow at the Brookings Institution and has served on the board of Oxford University's Blavatnik School of Government.

Okonjo-Iweala has a string of impressive honors including Nigeria's Minister of the Year (2004), Nigerian of the Year (2006), and *Euromoney magazine's* 2005 Finance Minister of the Year.[71]

Barack Obama
(Barack Hussein Obama II)

Born: August 4, 1961
Country: The United States of America

"Change will not come if we wait for some other person or for some other time. We are the ones we've been waiting for. We are the change that we seek." [72]

In 1968, a news reporter asked Senator Robert F. Kennedy—in the wake of the assassination of Dr. Martin Luther King Jr.—how long would it take before a black person became president of the United States. "Forty years," Kennedy replied. In November 2008, exactly forty years later, Barack Hussein Obama was elected the forty-fourth president of the United States.

In his own words, his rise to the presidency—and hence, leader of the free world is an improbable, almost imponderable story. Consider that in 2000, nine years before he took the oath of office, Obama traveled to Los Angeles, California, to attend the Democratic Party's National Convention. His credit card was turned down at the rental car company, and at the convention, he was told that there was no floor pass for him.

According to some analysts, Obama was twice elected president of the United States not only because white America had changed, but also because there was a new, dynamic demographic. By pulling together a coalition of blacks, Hispanics, Asians, LGBT voters, and other democrats—along with independent and first-time voters—Obama defied the odds and is regarded by many as a great president.

Among his outstanding accomplishments, his supporters point to the absence of any personal or official scandal, the protection of the homeland against external attacks, the rescue of the economy from the greatest recession since the great depression, the resuscitation of the auto industry, and the cutting of unemployment in half. In addition, his achievements include passing the Affordable Care Act, ridding the world of Osama Bin Laden, ending the war in Iraq, restoring relations with Cuba, pushing through congress a major trade pact, legitimizing same-sex marriage nationwide, reducing student-loan interest rates, creating alternative forms of energy that lowered gas prices, and passing equal pay for equal work legislation. In terms of his effectiveness as president, the jury is still out. Suffice it to say however that noted statistician, Nate Silvers, ranks Obama seventeenth among the forty-four US presidents.[73] In 2012, a Siena College poll placed Obama fifteenth among US presidents.[74] Some believe that history will treat him even more kindly.

CHAPTER III

Religion

INTRODUCTION
Religion

Whether Jewish, Christian, Muslim, Buddhist, Hindu, Bahia, Unitarian, or Rastafarian, just over seven billion (of the 7.4 billion people in the world) belong to a religion. Christianity and Islam claim more than half of the world's religious worshippers.

While there is wide disagreement over who God is, there is near universal belief in a Superior Being or a Higher Power, be that God, Buddha, Mohammed or whoever. Regardless of one's affiliation, there is little disagreement that religion, above and beyond all things, is a regulating, human management and behavior modification phenomenon that assists mightily in maintaining order and balance in the world. Needless to say, countless wars and acts of terror and crime found their genesis within religious underpinnings as well. But in the main, religion has been a stable force for good.

Conducting a search for the top-ten leaders in religion requires examination of individuals beyond their abilities to command the pulpit as preachers, teachers, or musicians. One's social outreach, universal appeal, participation in humanitarian causes, and overall leadership as a person of faith, vision, and sacrifice are all-important criteria.

It is difficult to imagine a world without the transformative influence of religion in all of its manifestations. Similarly, without the leading vessels—whose lives and words not only evangelize but also humanize religious teachings—the world would be a less harmonious place.

Given the foregoing, it is hereby postulated that the leading black religious leaders of all time are as follows:

Saint Augustine
(Augustine of Hippo)

Born: November 13, 354 AD
Died: August 28, 430 AD
Country: Thagaste (or Tagaste)

"Theology is a pilgrimage, and God is its end."

Saint Augustine, some say a successor to the Apostle Paul, was an ancient Bible scholar, well-schooled in logic, rhetoric, and philosophy. Through the ages, his writings helped to formulate a broader understanding of Christianity. St. Augustine is especially known for his ageless thoughts expressed in *City of God* and *Confessions*.

Born in Algeria, St. Augustine turned to Christianity at age thirty-three and is perhaps best known for the notion that individual freedom is predicated on God's grace. He is also widely regarded as a prophet—much like Jeremiah—whose narrative switches from a love of life to a life of love. This point is especially poignant when considering the environment during St. Augustine's time—one of social and moral decay of frightening dimensions. In fact, while a seventeen-year-old student at Carthage, St. Augustine forsook his Christian upbringing and became what is now called a party animal. His contemporaries would brag about their sexual conquests—straight and bisexual. Augustine, not to be outdone, embellished the extent of his prowess and uttered the immortal words "Grant me chastity and continence, but not yet."

Once he turned to Christianity, however, it was as if St. Augustine had his own Damascus Road experience. He engaged in profound, brilliant teachings that rebuked heresy. Indeed, as a father of the Catholic Church, St. Augustine's writings heavily and universally influenced that religion, even to this day. Some argue that his intonation, "Thou has made us for thyself, oh Lord, our hearts are restless until they rest in Thee" sits at the core of Catholicism. St. Augustine devoted his life to imparting divine revelations through his writings.

Saint Benedict the Moor, O. F. M.

Born: March 31, 1526
Died: April 4, 1589
Country: The Italian Republic

"Listen and attend with the ear of your heart." [75]

Benedict the Moor (a synonym for dark skinned) was denied being ordained a priest, because he was illiterate. However, as a member of the Catholic laity, he was beatified by Pope Benedict XIV and canonized by Pope Pius VII.

Benedict's parents were captured in Africa and taken to Italy as slaves in the sixteenth century. They were extremely poor, and this circumstance posed grave challenges to his education. Benedict worked as a shepherd during his teenage years and gave most of his earnings to those he considered more deprived than he was. When he became a member of a Franciscan–affiliated hermit society, he gave away all that he owned.[76]

Pope Pius IV disbanded the hermit society in 1564, and Benedict joined the Franciscan Friary of St. Mary and Jesus. Though not a priest, his teaching of the scriptures and healing of the sick attracted a following. By all accounts, Benedict lived a life of complete chastity and solemnity, serving God and mankind with humility and fervency.

Many wondered why Benedict deserved sainthood. Clearly, those who doubted his qualifications lacked an appreciation for the discrimination and persecution Benedict endured—as a black man in the fifteenth century—spreading Catholicism throughout Europe. In tribute to his service and sacrifice, some twelve Catholic churches and schools throughout the United States bear his name. In addition, a shrine was created in his memory in Palermo, Italy, by order of King Phillip III of Spain.

Richard Allen (Bishop)

Born: February 14, 1760
Died: March 26, 1831
Country: The United States of America

"If you love your children, if you love your country, if you love the God of love, clear your hands from slaves, burden not your children or country with them." [77]

Richard Allen was an iconic African American activist who founded the African Methodist Episcopal Church (AME) in 1794 in Philadelphia, Pennsylvania. Beyond the wide reaches of theology, Allen sought to birth a church with a decided social purpose—a place of solace, reflection, empowerment, and fellowship. At last, free blacks could come together and escape the stinging darts of discrimination and subjugation that had become their lot.

Allen also used the church as an educational venue to enhance literacy skills. He based his thinking on the notion that reading skills empower and enlighten, and therefore, Allen rendered his congregants as more fully functioning human beings. Allen was born a slave in Delaware. At a young age, his family's master ran into

72 | BREAKING GLASS CEILINGS

money problems, and as a result, he sold Allen's mother and several other family members. During this traumatic time, Allen taught himself to read and write. At the age of seventeen, he converted to Christianity and almost immediately began preaching. Being a slave preacher was not easy. Allen knew that slavery was wrong, but he also understood that disobedience was wrong as well.

In order for his master not to discourage their spirituality, Allen and his brother worked extra hard. Eventually, Allen's master became convinced that slavery was wrong and permitted Allen and his brother to purchase their freedom by working double time. Once he purchased his freedom, his name changed from Negro Richard to Richard Allen.[78]

Allen founded the AME Church in response to the naked discrimination he encountered by white church leaders, mostly in Baltimore, Maryland. At St. George's Methodist Episcopal Church, blacks and whites could not sit together, and he was confined to preaching primarily at 5:00 a.m. services, which were attended almost exclusively by blacks. Later in the day, while whites attended St. George's indoors, Allen held services outside in the commons.

Allen eventually broke away from St. George's. He converted a shoe shop into his first church; it was sanctioned by the larger Methodist body, but with the proviso that he would allow white clergymen to exercise general oversight. Allen endured this unwanted supervision for as long as he could. Then in 1816, he spearheaded a movement with black church representatives from Pennsylvania, Delaware, Maryland, and New Jersey to launch the AME Church with Allen as its founding bishop. Thus was born the oldest and largest formal institution in black America with a current membership in excess of 2.5 million.

In tribute to his enduring legacy and rich contributions to the advancement of mankind through the instrumentality of religion, the following carry his name: a university (Allen University in South Carolina), a charter school in Philadelphia (Richard Allen Preparatory School), a park (Bishop Richard Allen Park); a street in Massachusetts (Bishop Richard Allen Drive), as well as a major housing project in Philadelphia (Richard Allen Homes).

Haile Selassie

Born: July 23, 1892
Died: August 27, 1975
Country: The Federal Democratic Republic of Ethiopia

"We have finished the job. What shall we do with the tools?" [79]

He never claimed to be God, nor was he ever a Rastafarian. Yet, Haile Selassie, a Coptic Christian (belief in Jesus' divinity, but not his humanity) inspired the genesis of the Rastafarian religion, which today boasts more than one million followers around the world.

It all began with Jamaican civil rights icon, Marcus Garvey, who exhorted blacks to look to Africa, where a black king would be crowned and honored as the redeemer. As fate would have it, Selassie rose to power not long after Garvey's prediction; he toured the world, and infused blacks with pride in observing a black man ascend to such political heights. A widely held belief asserted that Selassie's roots could be traced to King Solomon and the Queen of Sheba. (His translated name means "power of the king.") That notion helps to explain why

Selassie was embraced—primarily by Jamaicans—as the "God of the black race", the "Lion of Judah", King of Kings", and "Elect of God."

Born Tafari Makonen in the Abyssinian Empire (now Ethiopia), Selassie was one of eleven children in a well-off political family. At age thirteen, his father made him commander of a local militia; Selassie enjoyed his own living quarters, servants, and security detail. By the age of fifteen, he was promoted to governor of a relatively small province. In 1916, at the age of twenty-four, Selassie was instrumental in the overthrow of the emperor, and he became heir to the throne. He served as emperor until 1928, when he was crowned king. Later, Selassie lost power, only to regain it in 1941; he continued to hold the reins until 1974.[80]

During his fifty-year rule, Selassie was on one hand, autocratic, demonstrating absolute control; yet on the other hand, he introduced democracy to his homeland. Indeed, he was a pioneering, progressive force that modernized Ethiopia. Selassie ushered in paid public servants, a court system that bestowed rights to the poor, a printing press, motor vehicles, prison reform, police accountability, import taxes, and generous scholarships for citizens of promise to study overseas. Perhaps, Selassie's crowning achievement was the introduction of Ethiopia's first constitution in 1931, which is known primarily for three provisions: the cementing of Selassie as the people's only king; the declaration that all Ethiopians are equal, and the creation of a two-tier parliament.[81]

Haile Selassie, one of the founders of the Organization of African Unity, is a source of black pride throughout the third world and the last of Ethiopia's three thousand years of dynastic rule. He was overthrown in a coup in 1974 and a year later, found dead in a tiny apartment that once was a part of his opulent, ornate palace.

Elijah Muhammad

Born: October 7, 1897
Died: February 25, 1975
Country: The United States of America

"Accept your place in the sun—the black man is the first and last, maker and owner of the universe." [82]

He had only a fourth-grade education, and he worked as a sharecropper at an early age. By sixteen, he was a factory worker. Yet, Elijah Muhammad rose to global prominence as leader of the Nation of Islam and a source of inspiration and enlightenment to the likes of Malcolm X, Louis Farrakhan, Muhammad Ali, and legions of other followers.

Born in Sandersville, Georgia, Elijah moved to Michigan in the early 1920s and aligned himself with Marcus Garvey's Universal Negro Improvement Association. Elijah, at one time, attended a speech on Islam by Wallace Fard. It changed his life. Fard taught that blacks could free themselves via self-reliance and feed off of their own culture. Elijah thereafter assumed a Muslim surname, "Karriem" and later, "Muhammad." This catapulted him to the leadership of the Nations Temple No. 2 in Chicago. (Elijah Muhammad changed the name, Allah Temple of Islam to Nation of Islam, and when Fard mysteriously disappeared off the face of the earth, Muhammad succeeded him.)

The Nation of Islam published its first newspaper, *Final Call to Islam*, in 1934 to expand its membership through education. In 1942, Muhammad was arrested, because he refused to register for the World War II draft. He later won bail and moved from Washington DC to Chicago, where he was arrested, because he advised his followers not to register for the draft or serve in the armed forces.[83] Muhammad was found guilty of sedition and spent four years in a Michigan prison. From prison he—like the Apostle Paul in the Bible—sent instructions to his followers. Muhammad's wife took care of the administrative aspects of the Nation of Islam. He also used his incarceration to convert many inmates to the Nation of Islam. Consequently, the movement expanded from four temples in 1946, fifteen in 1955, to fifty in 1959 in twenty-two states.

Muhammad's gospel of economic development spurred the growth of the Nation of Islam and attracted thousands of young, unemployed, and mostly uneducated black men, who found the traditional church unattractive. To Muhammad, blacks were the original human beings, and whites represented an offshoot of race that oppressed blacks for millions of years.

By the 1970s, the Nation of Islam owned bakeries, barbershops, grocery stores, restaurants, laundromats, schools, printing plants, a bank, and farms; its net worth was nearly $75 million. At the time of Mohammad's death in 1975, there were seventy-five Nation of Islam centers across the United States.

Today, under the leadership of Louis Farrakhan, the movement has an escalated following of 10,000-50,000 members.

E. E. Cleveland
(Pastor)

Born: March 11, 1921
Died: August 30, 2009
Country: The United States of America

"I have seen God for so long, do so much with so little, I now believe He can do anything with nothing—meaning me." [84]

Edward Earl Cleveland, known around the world as E. E. Cleveland, was an American civil rights activist, humanitarian, and pulpiteer of the highest renown, who preached as part of the Seventh-day Adventist church for sixty-seven years in some sixty-seven countries.

Born in Huntsville, Alabama, into a Seventh-day Adventist home, Cleveland started preaching at the age of six when a Saturday worshipping denomination was a mere dot on the global religious landscape. Today, twenty-million church adherents of this worldwide body operate 142 hospitals (seventy-three in the United States), as well as 852 schools— inclusive of elementary and high schools, colleges and universities.

E. E. Cleveland is an alumnus of Oakwood University in Huntsville, Alabama, and he worked his way through the church system to the position of associate secretary at the Seventh-day Adventist's world headquarters, becoming the first black man to serve the church at that level.

Cleveland determined that he was not suited for office work. He was an affable, magnetic person, who carved out his destiny as a pastor to the world—as an evangelist. During the course of his ministerial career, he held sixty crusades on six continents, preaching to hundreds of thousands, baptizing some sixteen thousand, and at the same time, training more than one thousand preachers.

In addition to his exploits behind the pulpit, Cleveland was a pioneer in the civil rights movement. When police surrounded one of his religious services—witnessing blacks and whites sitting together—they tried to enforce the law that forbade such racial comingling. Cleveland urged his listeners not to obey the police on the grounds that the officers sought to enforce an unjust law. In addition, Cleveland not only participated in Dr. Martin Luther King's March on Washington, he also organized the distribution of blankets and other essentials to participants. In 1968, he helped organize the Southern Christian Leadership Conference's Poor People's Campaign, and he has spearheaded Feed the Hungry initiatives across the United States. After Martin Luther King's assassination led to civil disturbances, Cleveland established food stations to relieve human suffering among protestors.

For his significant efforts to effect positive change through religion and social activism, Cleveland—author of twelve books—was well decorated with honors, including an induction into the Martin Luther King Jr. Collegium of Preachers and Scholars at Morehouse College. Furthermore, he is listed in England's *Men of Achievement*, profiled in *Who's Who in Black America*, and named in *Who's Who in Religion in America*. Cleveland consulted with President Ronald Reagan on international affairs and was cited in 1989 by former Alabama Governor Guy Hunt as Alabama's Most Distinguished Black Clergyman.

Francis Arinze
(Cardinal)

Born: November 1, 1932
Country: The Federal Republic of Nigeria

Born in 1932, Francis Arinze became a Christian at age nine. He was ordained a Catholic priest at the age of twenty. By the age of thirty-two, Arinze became the youngest person in the world to be elevated to the office of bishop within the Catholic faith. In an accomplishment almost unheard of—by the age of fifty-two—Arinze was made a cardinal. With all his accomplishments in the Catholic Church, there was little wonder at the possibility of Cardinal Arinze—under serious scrutiny—replacing Pope John Paul II. If Arinze had become the successor, he would have been the first black pope in history.

A member of Nigeria's Igbo tribe, Arinze serves as Bishop of Velletri Segni and is considered an interfaith ambassador. He is methodical and contemplative—erudite yet adorned with humility. Against the wishes of his father, fifteen-year-old Arinze entered seminary and pursued his first degree with a concentration in philosophy. After working as a professor for several years, he enrolled at Pontifical

University where he earned a doctoral degree in systematic theology.

In 1976, Arinze broke another glass ceiling, becoming (as archbishop) the first African to direct the affairs of his own diocese. As fate would have it, the infamous war between Nigeria and Biafra broke out not long after Arinze became archbishop. In fear for his life, he fled to Amichi and lived in exile for three years. Though he was a refugee, Arinze spent countless hours in horrific conditions looking after the needs of hundreds of fellow displaced people. During this time, it became readily apparent that Arinze was no ordinary man; he was the embodiment of Christian virtues and selfless values. Although he did not have much physical property, Arinze gave all he spiritually had—hope, faith, and courage—to endure in anticipation of a better day. When relief products (food, water, blankets, clothing, and medicine) arrived from fields afar, Arinze is credited with executing a most organized and fair distribution of goods.[85] This brought him widespread respect by the church, civil society, and international emergency relief agencies.

Cardinal Francis Arinze has touched the world by his devotion and contributions to his church. By his shining example, those who claim to follow Christ should strive to shine wherever they are—by turning difficulties into opportunities and setbacks into steppingstones.

Andraé Crouch
(Andraé Edward Crouch)

Born: July 1, 1942
Died: January 8, 2015
Country: The United States of America

"God just happens to use me; I'm not his first, second, not even his one-hundredth choice, but so be it. He chose me." [86]

According to Andraé Crouch, God literally taught him to play the piano when he was eleven years old. While speaking at a Billy Graham crusade, Crouch recalled that his father had been invited to preach at a local church and took him along. The pianist did not show up. So, when Crouch's father began to preach, he said to everyone's astonishment, "Andraé, come on up and play the piano." The dutiful son reluctantly complied, knowing he never played before. Crouch turned a miracle moment into a lifelong music career that touched millions around the world.

Crouch's place in history, as perhaps the greatest gospel music icon of all time, is secured. He has penned over three-hundred songs, among them, all-time favorite sing-alongs such as "Take Me Back," "Through It All," "It Won't Be Long,"

"The Blood Will Never Lose Its Power," "Let the Church Say Amen," "Soon and Very Soon," "My Tribute," "Jesus Is the Answer," "I Will Bless the Lord," and "I Don't Know Why Jesus Loves Me."

Born in San Francisco, California, Crouch's music crossed the great religious racial divide; his songs are loved and sung by worshippers of all races and virtually, all denominations. In fact, Crouch is arguably the most prolific gospel songwriter ever—irrespective of race in the modern era. Moreover, his music has crossover appeal for those with secular taste, thereby expanding its reach. This accomplishment eluded other black gospel music megastars, such as Mahalia Jackson, James Cleveland, Kirk Franklin, and others. Writing in the September 1982 edition of *Ebony Magazine*, Walter Rico Burrell opined that "Crouch has cleverly combined elements of disco, progressive jazz, rhythm and blues, pop, and even rock while walking a fine line between his traditional grassroots gospel background and outright Top 40 funk."[87] While this achievement was noteworthy, it engendered some criticism among church traditionalists. Crouch summarily rejected the criticism.

During his career, Crouch held concerts and performed at crusades worldwide. He won seven Grammy Awards, a Gospel Music Excellence Award, and two NAACP Image Awards. Additionally, he earned an Oscar nomination for his role as an expert in the gospel music that was featured in *The Color Purple*; Crouch wrote, directed, and sang some fifteen songs for the film.

Over the years, he assisted many up-and-coming gospel artists and secular performers. As a composer, arranger, keyboardist, and singer, Crouch's mark on the gospel music world is undeniable and indelible.

T. D. Jakes
(Thomas Dexter Jakes Sr.)

Born: June 9, 1957
Country: The United States of America

"Your latter days are supposed to be greater than your former days." [88]

Thomas Dexter Jakes has authored close to forty personal development and inspirational books. He is the mind and the force behind ten films. He is quite possibly the most highly sought-after preacher in the world with a two-year-advanced booking requirement. Moreover, his annual conferences attract up to one hundred thousand attendees around the world.

Thomas Dexter Jakes (T. D.) is bishop overseer of The Potter's House in Dallas, Texas, which boasts thirty thousand members. An anointed prophet and multi-gifted pulpiteer, Jakes' influence—through television and personal appearances—has few rivals. He has been a part of the church since childhood, first as a Baptist adherent, then Pentecostal, and now, nondenominational.

Born in South Charleston, West Virginia, Jakes dropped out of university, but never dropped his dream of becoming a preacher. He later earned degrees via distance-learning programs. In 1980, at the age of twenty-three, Jakes became pastor of a small church in West Virginia. Over the ensuing fourteen years, he pastored a number of churches, and in each case, membership flourished.

On a nonprofit basis, Jakes launched his own ministry in 1994 and focused on radio and television outreach programs that enjoyed national appeal. Two years later, in the ultimate display of faith, Jakes, his family, and fifty of his members packed up and relocated to Dallas, Texas, to form The Potter's House, which sits on thirty-four sprawling acres, and includes The Potter's School of Ministry, a leadership academy, a recording studio, and the five thousand seat edifice.

Time Magazine, in 2001, named Jakes "America's Best Preacher", but his influence and ministry extend beyond the United States. He has gone global and so have his various humanitarian outreach programs. Jakes and Serita (his wife of thirty-five years) created a mega movement that literally touches the world via preaching, teaching, media, music, movies, and charity for his life's work. Jakes has received a string of awards, including thirteen honorary doctoral degrees, as well as Grammy and Dove Awards.

Chris Oyakhilome
(Pastor)

Born: December 7, 1963
Country: The Federal Republic of Nigeria

"Success is causing the world around you to aspire to your inspiration." [89]

It is estimated that he has a net worth approaching $50 million from his vast business empire that consists of television stations, real estate, publications, and a recording studio. But Pastor Chris Oyakhilome is known mostly as minister of the largest church building in the world—which holds forty thousand members—the Believers' Loveworld Ministry in Lagos, Nigeria.

Oyakhilome is not a novice behind the pulpit. He has preached since he was a teenager. His ministry is decidedly youth focused, as evidenced by his million-plus, worldwide followers on Twitter. Primarily, the Twitter medium is used to construct a global prayer line, thereby extending Oyakhilome's reach and sphere of influence. Another estimated thirty million followers are linked to him on Facebook.

Hearing Oyakhilome's name has become commonplace around the world, mostly because of his healing ministry. In fact, he owns the record as the only preacher/healer to attract more than one million persons to a single event. So confident is Oyakhilome of his gift of healing, he now conducts healing seminars throughout the United States, Europe and Africa.

Oyakhilome is a graduate of Ambrose Alli University and holds several honorary doctoral degrees. In 2013, he launched the Future Africa Leaders Award, which honors enterprising, promising young Africans who demonstrate the potential to lead Africa into the next century. Pastor Oyakhilome, a firebrand preacher, writes a daily devotional that is translated into over six hundred languages and is available worldwide. Pastor Chris Oyakhilome, a spellbinding televangelist, has taken to heart a biblical mandate to "Go ye into all the world and preach my gospel."

SECTION B
"PROGRESS"

CHAPTER IV

Education

INTRODUCTION
Education

Education comes in many forms, and over time, formal methodologies for teaching and learning evolve. Throughout the transformations, one constant truth about education is that it can significantly and positively alter the course of a person's life. The gift of an education allows students to further develop their value systems, goal-setting orientations, and decision-making processes; it provides the tools to achieve and build off successes. Furthermore, education helps support ambitions and encourages new outlooks despite failures or setbacks. It also enhances and amplifies a person's natural talents and abilities. Throughout history, certain groups—who experienced oppression, discrimination, and enslavement—were denied prospects for education. Many of these maltreated people were disallowed opportunities to live enriched by what education offers—change and progress.

Through the ages, people of courage swam against prevailing tides to obtain an education, and in turn, they dedicated their lives to the betterment, upliftment, and empowerment of others through the transfer of knowledge. Ten such global leaders in education are as follows:

Daniel Payne
(Bishop)

Born: February 24, 1811
Died: November 2, 1893
Country: The United States of America

"That's my top goal, to go to college." [90]

Daniel Payne has the distinction of becoming the first black American to head a four-year tertiary institution within the United States. But his rise to the zenith of academia was as exhilarating as it was frustrating, as embodied with opportunities as it was fraught with difficulties.

Payne received his early education via private tutoring and excelled particularly in foreign languages. When he was eighteen (1829), he opened a school to teach black children to read and write. Five years later, the city council in his hometown, Charlestown, South Carolina, passed a law making it illegal to teach blacks to read and write. Payne reluctantly closed the school.

Buoyed by the closure of his school, he decided to become a preacher, and he matriculated at the Lutheran Seminary in Pennsylvania. After graduation, Payne left the Lutheran Church and united with the African American Methodist Episcopal Church (AME). After eleven years of ministry, he was elevated to the high office of bishop. Even today, Payne is widely regarded as a father of the church in consideration of his storied contributions.

Payne was AME's sixth bishop. An educator at heart, he was instrumental in the church's decision to purchase Wilberforce College in Ohio, which had closed in the aftermath of the civil war. Payne became the college president and led the institution for fourteen years. Payne's college presidency did not detract from his penchant for evangelism. In the post– civil war era, he relentlessly recruited church volunteers to minister to newly freed slaves. By this action, he quickly increased church membership by 250,000.[91]

Payne was a strong advocate of continuing education for AME's clergy. He therefore organized a wide range of classes for ministers to improve themselves. Payne saw his job as twofold: improve the ministry and improve the people.

Today, the downsized Wilberforce University has an enrollment of five hundred students and offers a full range of liberal-arts programs. The university also boasts an impressive list of notable alumni.

Alexander Crummell
(Minister)

Born: March 3, 1819
Died: September 10, 1898
Country: The United States of America

"Strive to make something of yourself; then strive to make the most of yourself."[92]

A native New Yorker, Alexander Crummell was a minister within the Episcopal Church and known for his scholarship that culminated in his establishment of the American Negro Academy in 1897—the first black think tank in the United States. The academy, which operated from 1897 to 1928, also functioned as a society of scholars who engaged in academic discussions and produced learned papers that contributed to the state of knowledge at the time.

Because of his race, Crummell, like many of his contemporaries, was denied admission to the college of his choice. He therefore travelled to England and enrolled at Cambridge University, graduating in 1853. Crummell crisscrossed England—lecturing about the twin evils of slavery and racism—in order to help defray the cost of his education. In 1853, he became the first black person to graduate from Cambridge.

Almost immediately, Crummell travelled to Liberia, where he remained for two decades in dual capacities as minister and university professor. He was instrumental in helping citizens of Liberia see the connection between education and economic empowerment.

It is noteworthy that Crummell launched the American Negro Academy when he was seventy-eight years old.[93] The stated goal of the ANA was "to lead and protect black people and to be a weapon to secure equality and destroy racism."

Patrick Francis Healy

Born: February 27, 1830
Died: January 10, 1910
Country: The United States of America

Patrick Francis Healy was born into slavery in Macon, Georgia. His white father was the owner of his unmarried, black mother. (During that time, a child assumed the status of the mother.) Young Patrick, therefore, was considered black. It is believed that his parents lived as a married couple, but then, mixed-race marriages were not allowed in Georgia.

Healy's parents preferred that Patrick develop an identity as a white person, so they sent him to New York. He later matriculated at a college in Massachusetts and embarked on a long-held goal of becoming a priest in the Catholic Church. Healy travelled extensively and learned several languages.

All of his accomplishments mattered little, as Healy was of mixed race and therefore, the subject of ridicule and exclusion. He decided that the psychosocial pressure within the United States was too much to bear. Healy consequently entered the Jesuit Order, travelled to Europe, and enrolled at the Catholic University in Belgium; he later graduated with a PhD —the first black to do so. He was ordained to the priesthood in 1864 and returned to the United States.

Shortly after his return to the US, Healy joined the faculty of Georgetown College—the first college in Washington DC—as a professor of philosophy. Not long thereafter, he became vice president of the college, and one year later, he assumed the presidency of what has become the largest Catholic university in the United States. Moreover, Healy has the distinction of being the first black president of a mostly white university.

As the twenty-ninth Georgetown University president, Healy led the institution from 1874 to 1882.[94] During his tenure, he transformed a relatively small college into a modern, world class academic community by expanding its medical and law schools, erecting multiple buildings, diversifying course offerings and elevating the criteria for both student and faculty recruitment.

Today, Georgetown University sits on 104 acres, houses fifty-four buildings, and hosts an overall enrollment approaching ten thousand students. *U.S. News and World Report* ranks Georgetown University twenty-one among national universities. Since its founding in 1789, Georgetown University has made significant contributions to the world via its thousands of diverse graduates in virtually every discipline. Healy is buried on the campus of Georgetown University and Healy Hall, dedicated to his memory, is a National Historic Site on campus.

Fanny Jackson Coppin

Born: October 15, 1837
Died: January 21, 1913
Country: The United States of America

"I am always sorry to hear that such and such a person is going to school to be educated. This is a great mistake. If the person is to get the benefit of what we call education, he must educate himself, under the direction of the teacher." [95]

Fanny Jackson Coppin was a pioneering, trailblazing educator with a vision and passion for education. She significantly and permanently changed the approach to education within the United States and beyond.

A former slave, Coppin's aunt bought her freedom. Coppin worked as a housekeeper while pursuing a high-school education at Rhode Island State Normal School. After high-school graduation, Coppin matriculated at Oberlin College, and upon completion of her degree in 1865, she became a teacher at the Institute for Colored Youth, a high school in Philadelphia. In addition to serving as head of the girls' high-school department, Coppin taught mathematics, Greek, and Latin.

Four years later, Coppin was named principal of the Institute for Colored Youth, becoming the first African American to be offered such a position.[96] Almost immediately, Coppin placed her stamp of innovation on the school's curriculum. She initiated an ambitious teacher training program that grew in popularity. Not only did Coppin introduce the art of teaching, but she also placed future teachers in classroom settings for practice purposes as a graduation prerequisite. Her program made it possible, for the first time, for scores of blacks to enter the teaching profession—fully trained.

Perhaps Coppin's greatest contribution to the development of education was the introduction of technical-vocational courses as an integral component of education. This curriculum offered a venture unheard of at the time. Armed with the belief that technical vocational education constituted a path to self-empowerment, just as profoundly as academic instruction, Coppin introduced ten such technical–vocational courses.

In 1902, after some thirty years at the institution, Coppin resigned, and the school moved to Delaware County, Pennsylvania. It is now known as Cheyney State University—the oldest, historically black institution of higher learning within the United States, offering BA and MA degrees in over thirty disciplines.

Coppin and her husband, Reverend Levi J. Coppin, sailed to Cape Town, South Africa, in 1904. For ten years, she taught black girls character development and self-discipline. Eventually, she founded the Bethel Institute, an academic program with a religious orientation.

After ten years in Cape Town, Coppin returned to Philadelphia and died shortly thereafter. Thirteen years after her passing, in 1926, Baltimore's High and Training School became the Fanny Jackson Normal School; today, it is known as Coppin State University, also an historically black institution of higher learning that boasts an enrollment in excess of four thousand students and sits on a sprawling fifty-two-acre campus in Baltimore, Maryland.

Booker T. Washington

Born: April 5, 1856
Died: November 14, 1915
Country: The United States of America

"Character, not circumstances, makes the man." [97]

Perhaps Reverend Jesse Jackson had Booker T. Washington in mind when he famously said, "I was born in the slum, but the slum was not born in me." Similarly, Washington must have said to himself, "I was born in a slave hut, but the hut was not born in me." From the bowels of poverty and discrimination in Franklin County, Virginia, Washington became a national figure in education, whose influence extended around the world.

A graduate of Hampton Normal and Agricultural Institute (now Hampton University) in Virginia, Washington was a tireless teacher in Washington DC—instructing children during the day and adults at night. He later served on the faculty at Hampton. After a time, Washington was asked to move to Tuskegee, Alabama, to perform a miracle. His mandate was to make something out of the fledgling Tuskegee Normal and Industrial Institute. During Washington's thirty-four-year presidency, the institution grew from two, small, ill-equipped buildings to more than one hundred buildings, fifteen hundred students, approximately two hundred faculty, and some $2 million in endowment.

Nestled in rural Alabama, Tuskegee University currently hosts more than three thousand students, sits on five thousand acres of land, and claims a considerable endowment. As the founder of Tuskegee University, Booker T. Washington touched lives and changed the world.

W. E. B. DuBois
(William Edward Burghardt DuBois)

Born: February 23, 1868
Died: August 27, 1963
Country: The United States of America

"The test of liberty is less than the price of repression." [98]

He was among the founders of the National Association for the Advancement of Colored People (NAACP) in 1909. Considered one of the great social thinkers of his day, W. E. B. DuBois effectively stirred protest movements to effect fundamental changes in the human condition.

Born in Great Barristan, Massachusetts, and blessed with a sharp intellect, DuBois graduated from Fisk University and completed his PhD in Sociology (first black American to do so) at Harvard University. At first, DuBois thought that education in general, and sociology in particular, was key to effecting social change. That view was short lived when he concluded that protests held the key to social change.

Just as Martin Luther King Jr. and Malcolm X were contemporaries who viewed social change through different lenses—King favored determined passivism and Malcolm leaned toward aggression or even violence—DuBois and Booker T. Washington held opposing approaches to social change. DuBois wanted protests; Washington wanted acceptance. DuBois wanted agitation; Washington favored accommodation. In short, DuBois saw blacks as victims, Washington saw them as instruments of reform. DuBois denounced Washington's approach to black empowerment as paternalistic and patronizing. As this characterization caught on within the black community, Washington's clout and esteem diminished.

DuBois, a long-term professor at Atlanta University, was relentless in encouraging blacks to reinforce their cultural identity by supporting the arts, black literature, and black theatre. He also preached economic gain and upward mobility through hard work and emboldened blacks to develop their own economy by supporting black-owned businesses. For twenty-four years, as editor of *The Crisis* magazine, DuBois wielded unmatched influence and access, as he promoted his social gospel of black unity and change.

Toward the end of his career, DuBois was embroiled in a string of controversies, which ultimately led to his complete disillusionment with the United States. He renounced his citizenship after relocating to Ghana, where he died in 1963.[99]

In recognition of the pivotal role he played in the struggle for equality for blacks in the United States and abroad, dormitories at the University of Pennsylvania, as well as Hampton University, bear his name. These universities particularly recognize DuBois's utilization of print media to educate and indoctrinate blacks. In addition, his childhood home is now a National Historic Landmark.

Furthermore, DuBois has the distinction of being among a few blacks to be honored with a Lenin Peace Prize by the USSR in 1955.

Mary McLeod Bethune (Mary Jane McLeod)

Born: July 10, 1875
Died: May 18, 1955
Country: The United States of America

"Invest in the human soul. Who knows, it might be a diamond in the rough." [100]

Sixty-two years after her death, Mary McLeod Bethune is still revered as one of the most accomplished women—black or white—of all time. Her life embodied the self-actualizing triumvirate of selflessness, service, and sacrifice.

In reality, Bethune had no peers. In her capacity as assistant to the secretary of war, she selected enlistees for the United States Army. She was a special envoy of the State Department during its 1945 meeting in San Francisco that led to the establishment of the United Nations. Her additional accomplishments include the following: director of the Division of Youth Affairs at the federal level, special United States envoy at the inauguration of Liberia's new president in 1952, advisor to President Franklin D. Roosevelt, founder of the National Council of Negro Women, president of the Florida Federation of Colored Women, and founder and president of Bethune-Cookman College (now University) in Daytona Beach, Florida.

Born in Mayesville, South Carolina, her parents were former slaves. Bethune was one of seventeen children. Though poor, each member of her family exuded a sense of self-respect and intrinsic dignity. Bethune graduated from Barber-Scotia College in North Carolina; then, she pursued further studies at Chicago's Moody Bible Institute. After teaching at various schools throughout the United States, Bethune moved to Daytona Beach, Florida, and in 1904, she launched her own school: Daytona Normal and Industrial Institute for Negro Girls.

Bethune had very little money and had to skillfully appeal to mostly white benefactors for assistance in making the institution viable. Given the realities of discrimination at the time, Bethune's success was based upon her thoughtful diplomacy; she fed donors honey, not vinegar and compromise, not contention. After twenty years, Bethune's institution merged with Jacksonville–based Cookman Institute for Men and morphed into Bethune-Cookman College (now University) with the help of the United Methodist Church. When Bethune retired as President in 1947, Bethune-Cookman College had one thousand students. Today, the university has an enrollment of more than four thousand, and the campus has expanded to eighty acres. In a tradition set by Dr. Bethune, the nationally renowned university upholds high academic standards, as well as a worthy Wildcats football team and marching band.

It should also be noted that because blacks were not admitted to the Daytona General Hospital in Bethune's day, she established a mini hospital adjacent to the college campus.

Mary McLeod Bethune—a woman of vision—fought racism without bitterness. Her work helped to change the world and continues to positively impact lives today.

Benjamin Elijah Mays

Born: August 1, 1894
Died: March 28, 1984
Country: The United States of America

"It is difficult to know who is damaged more—the segregated or segregator." [101]

While Dr. Martin Luther King Jr. was a student at the all-male Morehouse College in Atlanta, Dr. Benjamin Mays served not only as college president, but also as Martin Luther King's personal mentor. They forged a friendship that climaxed when Dr. Mays eulogized thirty-nine-year-old Dr. King in April 1968 with the words, "It isn't how long one lives, but how well."

Born in Epworth, South Carolina to freed slave parents, Mays was the youngest of eight children. He ascended to high-school valedictorian; yet, because of his race, he was denied admission by multiple colleges and universities. (This raw, unrelenting racism was common in the southern United States.) Mays ended up at Bates College in Maine. Again, Mays excelled academically; however, after graduation from Bates, he was denied admission to the seminary of his choice, because of his race. This roadblock did not deter him. Eventually, Mays was admitted to the University of Chicago, but even there, he encountered overt racism. Blacks and whites did not share the same dormitories, and Mays battled against this discrimination. Nearby restaurants refused to serve Mays due to his race, and he fought against this injustice as well.

Mays exemplified dogged determination in the struggle against racism. After earning his MA degree, he taught at several colleges, worked for the National Urban League, and served in the national office of the Young Men's Christian Association in Atlanta. The latter position allowed him to target young men in southern states, encouraging them to stay in school, stay out of trouble, and maintain their dignity. Mays also promoted racial pride, not as a means to scorn other races, but instead, as a way to develop positive self-esteem regarding one's race.

Eventually, he returned to the University of Chicago. In 1935—at age forty—he fulfilled a lifelong dream: to earn a PhD from a mostly white institution, as a means of demonstrating that there is no ceiling atop black intellect. Armed with his PhD, Mays joined the faculty at Howard University. After six years at Howard, he accepted an offer to relocate to Atlanta and assume the presidency of a floundering, failing institution: Morehouse College.

Mays was president of Morehouse College from 1940 to 1969. Over that period, he rebranded the institution by strengthening and broadening its academic offerings, stabilizing its finances, constructing some twenty buildings, and more than doubling its enrollment. Today, Morehouse takes pride—as one of only two historically black colleges—in producing a Rhodes Scholar. In addition to Dr. Martin Luther King, noted graduates include Spike Lee, Samuel Jackson, Jeh

Johnson, Herman Cain, Edwin Moses, and others. Morehouse is ranked tenth among thirty colleges and universities in Georgia.

In recognition of his life's work, Mays has been decorated with fifty honorary doctoral degrees, and his portrait adorns the South Carolina State House.

Dr. David Olaniyi Oyedepo (Bishop)

Born: September 27, 1954
Country: The Federal Republic of Nigeria

"Dedication is the mystery behind the distinction. How dedicated you are determines how distinguished you will ever become in the kingdom." [102]

A native of Osogbo, Nigeria, Dr. David Oyedepo is a multifaceted leader, who wears many professional hats. Not only is he the senior minister of one of the largest churches in the world—Faith Tabernacle in Nigeria with a fifty-thousand seat capacity—but Oyedepo is also an architect, author, and educator.

Armed with a doctorate in human development from Honolulu University in Hawaii, Bishop Oyedepo sits as chancellor of the prestigious Covenant University as well as Landmark University. Both fully recognized, tertiary institutions, Covenant boasts an enrollment of some eight thousand students and is described by Webometrics as Nigeria's premier university. He has established several additional universities across Nigeria and elsewhere, patterning them after Covenant. Oyedepo sets as the goal of these institutions the preparation of tomorrow's leaders to positively impact the world.

In addition to the two universities—Covenant and Landmark—Oyedepo presides over Canaan land—a five-thousand-acre mini city—in Otah, Ogun, Nigeria. The land houses a progressive, Christ-based primary school and Faith Academy, a high school with an enrollment approaching two thousand. Oyedepo's church, commonly referred to as Winners Chapel, has branches in over three hundred Nigerian cities. In addition to a presence in virtually all of Africa's fifty-plus nations, Winners Chapels can be found in the United States, United Kingdom, and the Middle East.

Oyedepo's inspiration reportedly came from an eighteen-hour encounter in the early 1980s, whereupon God instructed him to liberate the world. In pursuit of his divine mandate, Oyedepo founded Dominion Publishing House, which has some five million prints. Furthermore, Oyedepo is the publishing firm's leading author with more than seventy books and magazines that bear his name.[103]

Dr. Oyedepo—who reportedly has a net worth in excess of $100 million—is widely regarded as a visionary with global impact in ministry, education, and leadership.

Melinda F. Emerson

Country: The United States of America

"You never lose in business, either you win, or you learn." 104

Although still relatively young, Melinda Emerson has found a way to impact the world. Known globally as Small Biz Lady, she has carved out a reputation as a premier small business coach within the United States.

Emerson conveys advice to some three million entrepreneurs weekly via the internet. She is also a pioneer in social-media marketing, boasting the longest-running, live chat on Twitter for operators of small businesses.

As CEO of Quintessence Multimedia, Emerson created an electronic medium for her Fortune 500 clients to reach owners of small businesses. Her substantial clients include Johnson & Johnson, Verizon, Enterprise Rent-A-Car, Citizen's Bank and Comcast.

Forbes Magazine opines that Emerson is the leading woman for entrepreneurs to follow on Twitter. Apart from teaching entrepreneurship through her bestselling book, *Become Your Own Boss in Twelve Months: A Month-by-Month Guide to a Business That Works*, Emerson is regularly seen sharing her expertise on MSNBC, Fox News, and NBC. She also pens articles for *Black Enterprise*, the *Washington Post*, and the *New York Times*, among others.

In 2012, Emerson, an alumnus of Virginia Tech University, launched the Melinda F. Emerson Foundation for Small Business Success.[105] It serves as a platform for Emerson to teach how to "end small business failures among minority- and women-owned businesses through entrepreneurship education and technical assistance." The foundation offers free information, educational materials, and executive educational opportunities to women and minorities. Due to her insightful, fresh approach, Emerson is highly sought after as a small business start-up and development coach.

CHAPTER V

Inventions

INTRODUCTION
Inventions

No one positively knows man's first invention. It is widely speculated that it may have been a sharp-edged tool, a shelter-related item, or a curative substance. Without doubt, each generation creates new inventions that make living easier and simpler. Sometimes these discoveries add to man's longevity, improve safety, enhance security, and advance efficiency, productivity, and durability.

Almost everyone is familiar with the pioneering inventions—from airplanes to light bulbs, radio to television, hotplates to microwaves, air conditioning to airbags, rotary to cellular telephones, automobiles to jet skis, and paper maps to GPS—the list is endless. These many inventions play important roles in improving the quality of our lives.

It is important to acknowledge the personalities behind the ingenuity. This recognition is particularly essential as it relates to black inventors, since historically, they have not been associated with compelling intellect or stellar scientific and technological acumen. Black creators are rarely viewed as equals in the vanguard of human progress beyond sports and entertainment. The undeniable reality is that many inventions—now taken for granted— found their origins in the minds of black geniuses. Consequently, blacks are responsible for thousands of patents.

Who are the leading innovators, and how have their contributions improved the universal quality of life? In the arena of inventions, the ten black persons who did the most to change the world for the better are as follows:

Thomas L. Jennings

Born: 1791
Died: 1856
Country: The United States of America

On March 3, 1821, Thomas L. Jennings became the first African American to be awarded a patent for his invention of the dry-scouring cleaning process. Jennings was born in 1791 in New York. Not much is known about his childhood except that he was born a free man who later became a successful businessman. Not only was he the first black man to obtain a patent for dry scouring—a dry-cleaning process that is still widely used—but he also became a leader within the abolitionist movement.

As a young man, Jennings worked as a clothier in New York. By conversing with customers, he realized the struggles they faced when cleaning their delicate pieces of clothing. Traditional washing and scrubbing methods proved to be too harsh and often damaging to fragile fabrics. This problem inspired Jennings to find a way to clean clothes, using little or no water. He ran experiments on different cleaning methods and tested various stain removal solutions. Since Jennings was a free man, he applied for a patent in his name, and thereby, he made history when he was awarded a patent for the process he called dry scouring in 1821.

After receiving the patent, Jennings became wealthy for there was a demand for his dry scouring services. His accomplishments—during a time when blacks lived under segregation and enslavement with limited rights—proved to be remarkable. He earned the exclusive rights to his product, and this ownership paved the way for black inventors in America. Reportedly, Jennings used the first bit of income he earned to buy his family members their freedom.[106]

While Jennings' forward-thinking invention led to the dry-cleaning process we use today, Jennings also maintained a progressive outlook for the future of blacks in America. This vision was most evident by his support of the abolitionist movement.

Jennings is credited with establishing the Legal Rights Association (1855), a civil rights organization that was formed in response to a serious incident involving his own daughter, Elizabeth Jennings. As the story goes, Elizabeth was on her way to work via public transportation when she was literally thrown out of what was labeled a "whites only" streetcar. With the strong support of her father, Elizabeth went to court for this injustice and won her case after the jury deemed the actions taken against her were unlawful.[107] Because of battles like Elizabeth's, the Legal Rights Association was created to strengthen the fight against racism and discrimination, particularly through the courts. Jennings passed away in New York in 1856.

Lewis Howard Latimer

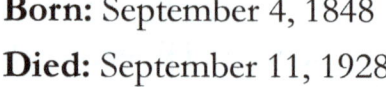

Born: September 4, 1848
Died: September 11, 1928
Country: The United States of America

"The two fortresses which are the last to yield in the human heart are hope and pride." [108]

Born to runaway slaves on September 4, 1848, in Chelsea, Massachusetts, Latimer started his career as an office boy with Crosby & Gould, a patent law firm; he earned $3 per week. Latimer taught himself drafting and eventually became head draftsman, earning $20 weekly.

In 1874, Latimer and W. C. Brown co-invented an improved water closet for trains. Two years later, in 1876, he drafted the drawing used by Alexander Graham Bell in his patent application for the telephone.

Latimer next worked as the assistant manager and draftsman for the United States Electric Lighting Company after moving to Bridgeport, Connecticut. The owner, Hirman Maxim, was the rival of Thomas Edison. Edison created a light bulb that lasted only a few days. Maxim desired to extend its lifetime. Latimer encased the filament in the bulb in cardboard, which prevented the carbon from breaking. This improved the longevity and efficiency of the light bulb, making it less expensive to utilize. The cost efficiency allowed the new and improved bulb to be used in streetlights and homes.

For his ingenuity, Latimer was in great demand. He was called upon to be the lead planner in the first electric plants in Philadelphia, New York, and Montreal, Canada. Directors of installation projects for railroad stations, government buildings, and major thoroughfares in Canada, London, and New England sought Latimer for his expertise as an overseer.[109]

In 1890, Latimer worked for Thomas Edison in the legal department of Edison Light Company as a patent expert, inspector, expert witness on the board of patents, and chief draftsman. *Incandescent Electric Lighting: A Practical Description of the Edison System* was written by Latimer in 1890 with C. J. Field and John White Howell. The research in this book became the industry standard in electrical lighting.

Latimer was an original and only black member of the Edison Pioneers, the thirty-seven person engineering group of the Edison Light Company, which later became General Electric.

An inductee into the National Inventors Hall of Fame, Latimer held eight patents that changed our lives, including the electric lamp, water closets for railway cars, the process for manufacturing carbons, and an apparatus for cooling and disinfecting.

George Washington Carver

Born: Exact date unknown (1861-1864)
Died: January 5, 1943
Country: The United States of America

"When you do the common things in life, in an uncommon way, you will command the attention of the world." [110]

George Washington Carver was born into slavery in Diamond, Missouri. His family was dirt poor, but he was determined to obtain a first-class education. He graduated from Iowa State University and went on to become a prized botanist, inventor, and legendary professor of agriculture at Tuskegee Institute (now University) in Alabama.

In 1865, after the civil war ended slavery, owners, Moses and Susan Carver, decided to keep George and his brother, James.[111] Because blacks were not allowed at the local schools, George and his brother were taught to read and write by Susan. Carver later became the first black to attend Iowa State University, where he graduated with both Bachelor of Science and Master's degrees. Carver was fascinated by the properties of peanuts as well as potatoes, thus began his groundbreaking experiments.

Believing that his inventions should be shared freely, Carver never patented his inventions of more than one hundred uses for the sweet potato, over three hundred uses for the peanut, and the many benefits of different plants. Other opportunists exploited his research on plants and subsequently earned millions on cosmetics, glycerin, nitroglycerin, soaps, shampoos, paints, stains, dyes, synthetic rubber, fuel, alcohol, road-paving materials, axle grease, linoleum, plastics, insecticides, soybean milk, soybean oil, and biodiesel fuel among others.

Carver elevated the lowly peanut from passed-over obscurity to an in-demand cash crop, establishing the US peanut industry and ranking the peanut as one of the top five national crops. His invention did not end with peanuts. Carver established the first weather station in Macon County, Alabama. He also discovered that by removing the acid from the southern pine tree, the pulp could be used to manufacture paper. Thus, the pulp wood paper industry was born.

Carver was the first black in the United States to have a national monument erected in his image; the bust and a statue of Carver as a young boy are located in a national park located in Diamond, Missouri. Carver has also been honored with three museums that bear his name: they are located in Tuskegee and Dothan, Alabama, and Austin, Texas.

While teaching at Tuskegee Institute, Carver taught his students eight virtues during indoctrination:
- Be clean both inside and out.

- Neither look up to the rich nor down on the poor.
- Lose, if need be, without squealing.
- Win without bragging.
- Always be considerate of women, children, and older people.
- Be too brave to lie.
- Be too generous to cheat.
- Take your share of the world and let others take theirs.

Garrett Morgan
(Garrett Augustus Morgan Sr.)

Born: March 4, 1877
Died: July 27, 1963
Country: The United States of America

"If you can be the best, then why not try to be the best?" [112]

Garrett Morgan was born the son of former slaves in Claysville, Kentucky. His grandfather was a Confederate colonel, and his mother was part Native American. His unique physical appearance presented many obstacles for him; he had to endure and overcome racism and discrimination. Morgan's level of education did not extend beyond middle school; however, he had a natural inclination toward engineering.

In 1895, Morgan moved to Cleveland, Ohio, where he worked in mechanics at a textile factory that also served as a sewing-machine repair shop. This experience taught him important mechanical and technical skills that he soon put to use in his own business. After obtaining a sewing-machine patent, he opened his first company in 1907, which served as a sewing machine and shoe-repair shop.

Morgan produced all of the equipment used in his shop, and despite his struggles with racism, his business thrived.

Morgan was challenged by the reoccurring damage to wool threads caused by the friction from the machine needle; he set out to fix this problem. Instead, he accidentally invented a hair-straightening cream. The cream was so successful that Morgan soon opened another business, which he called the G. A. Morgan Hair Refining Company.

Morgan continued to generate new ideas and introduce his inventions to the public. One such invention was a respiratory safety helmet; its design influenced the modern-day gas mask. His idea for the device was inspired by firefighters, many of whom died in the course of firefighting due to smoke inhalation.[113] His safety helmet was designed to filter smoke and incorporate a cooling mechanism simultaneously. The US military invested in his safety helmets, and on one occasion, they saved the lives of several men trapped in a tunnel underneath Lake Eerie.

In addition to the safety helmet, Morgan is credited with the creation of the traffic signal. His signal improved the safety of both pedestrians and motorists. General Electric bought this technology from him after he was awarded the patent in 1923.

Although his products were highly acclaimed, Morgan struggled to sell them in certain areas of the US, such as the South, due to the entrenched racism that pervaded his era.

Morgan is believed to have been the first black person to own a car in Cleveland, Ohio. However, he did not use his wealth purely for personal ease and comfort. He was a regular contributor to the NAACP, and in the 1920s, he launched the *Cleveland Call*, a newspaper that served as a voice for blacks in Ohio.

Morgan passed away on July 27, 1963.

Frederick McKinley Jones

Born: May 17, 1893
Died: February 21, 1961
Country: The United States of America

Frederick McKinley Jones is remembered and recognized for inventing and patenting the first automatic refrigeration system in trucks, keeping foods fresh during transport. In the course of his life, Jones was awarded over sixty patents with forty of those granted to him in the area of refrigeration.[114]

Jones was born in Cincinnati, Ohio. His mom passed away when he was nine years old. Shortly thereafter, Jones moved to a rectory in Covington, Kentucky, where he was raised by a priest. During his teens, he returned to Ohio, where he was employed at the R. C. Crothers Garage as an assistant to an automobile mechanic. The time Jones spent working on cars helped him develop the mechanical and engineering skills that later contributed to his successful inventions. In addition to repairing automobiles, the R. C. Crothers Garage also built race cars, which Jones helped to design and build. (It has been said that one of Jones' racecars beat an airplane in a race.)

When World War I broke out, Jones advanced his skills by serving as a sergeant in the US Army in France, where he specialized in electrical rewiring. After military service, Jones returned to the US in 1919, moving to Minnesota and further utilizing his engineering and electrical skills. During this time, he invented the radio-station transmitter as well as the portable X-ray machine.

In 1927, while employed at Ultraphone Sound Systems, Jones converted silent movie projectors into audible devices. This design revolutionized cinema and the movie-going experience. Additionally, Jones invented one of the first machines to automatically dispense movie tickets and change. In 1935, Jones built his breakthrough invention—an automatic refrigeration system for trucks. He pioneered the concept, following a conversation with a truck driver who explained the challenges of carrying produce and meats across the country.

Of equal significance, when World War II broke out, demand for a safe method of storing blood for transfusions became a great focus for the military. With his refrigeration expertise, Jones delved deeper into his research, leading him to develop new refrigeration systems for military field hospitals. His discoveries also worked well in kitchens.[115] His outstanding accomplishments in refrigeration and engineering earned him the honor of first African American to be inducted into the American Society of Refrigeration Engineers in 1944. Jones passed away on February 21, 1961.

Marie Van Brittan Brown

Born: October 30, 1922
Died: February 2, 1999
Country: The United States of America

Marie Van Brittan Brown is recognized, along with her husband, for inventing the first home security device using a motorized camera. Her vision, imagination, and insight are also credited with contributing to the creation of the modern-day home surveillance system.

Brown, born on October 30, 1922, in Jamaica, New York, was a nurse and sometimes worked odd shifts. Consequently, she and her husband, Albert L. Brown, were seldom home at the same time. In fact, Brown was often home alone. She felt uneasy about her situation, given the rate of crime in her area. Brown and her husband sought to change their status quo by devising a solution to alleviate their fears and insecurity.

In 1969, they developed a security device and obtained a patent—the first of its kind. The device consisted of a camera attached to the door. This camera allowed the homeowners to view someone at the door without opening it. The camera adjusted for four different peepholes, making irrelevant the height of the person. The system was connected wirelessly—via a radio-controlled connection to a television monitor— and recorded everything that the camera saw. Additionally, a voice mechanism worked both ways, allowing homeowners to directly speak with anyone on the other side of the door. If there was cause for concern, with the push of a button, the security system sounded an alarm. Then, the alarm transmitted a signal to a contact of choice. If there was no issue with the visitor at the door, he or she could be let in automatically when the owner pressed a button.[116]

Brown's invention significantly improved the standard of home security, providing greater safety and peace of mind. It also led to the modern-day surveillance systems. Brown passed away on February 22, 1999.

George Edward Alcorn Jr.

Born: March 22, 1940
Country: The United States of America

George Edward Alcorn Jr. is the inventor of the imaging X-ray spectrometer, which contributes to research on atoms and sheds light on the solar system. In addition to the imaging X-ray spectrometer, Alcorn has over twenty-five patents under his name. His progressive inventions and significant advances in science and space have been rewarded by his elevation to assistant director of the NASA's Goddard Space Flight Center.

Alcorn was born in Indianapolis, Indiana, to middle-income parents who worked hard to support him and his brother's educational aspirations. His outstanding academic achievements in high school earned him a scholarship to attend Occidental College, where he majored in physics and graduated with honors in 1962. Alcorn completed his master's degree in nuclear physics at Howard University the following year. He cut his "professional teeth" while a student at the university, working in the space division of North American

Rockwell as a research engineer. During this time at Rockwell, he worked on research related to NASA's Apollo space missions.

In 1964, Alcorn applied for a research grant through the National Aeronautics and Space Administration (NASA). With the grant from NASA, he began research related to negative ion formation and simultaneously pursued a PhD at Howard University. He completed his PhD in atomic and molecular physics in 1967; then, Alcorn held positions at Philco-Ford, where he worked in the company's aerospace sector before joining International Business Machines (IBM).

Alcorn joined NASA in 1978, and by 1984, he received a patent for his invention of the imaging X-ray spectrometer. He later became project manager; in this role, he oversaw and managed new technologies and inventions that benefitted the International Space Station.

By 1992, Alcorn was promoted to lead the Goddard Space Flight Center (GSFC) Office of Commercial Programs. Over the years, Alcorn spent considerable time encouraging minorities in the fields of science and engineering. In addition to teaching courses—electrical engineering at the tertiary level—he devotes time on the weekends to educating science honor students in inner-city schools.

The Government Technology Leadership Award, a prestigious honor from *Government Executive* magazine, was presented to Alcorn in 1999 for the Airborne Lidar Topographic Mappin Applied Engineering and Technology Directorate.[117] Alcorn has held many leading positions in the science, technology, and engineering industries. He is also the recipient of many prestigious honors, awards, fellowships, and scholarships.

Patricia Era Bath

Born: November 4, 1942
Died: May 30, 2019
Country: The United States of America

"Believe in the power of truth.... Do not allow your mind to be imprisoned by majority thinking. Remember that the limits of science are not the limits of imagination." [118]

Dr. Patricia Era Bath made significant contributions to the medical world, specifically within ophthalmology. Bath is the first African American woman to have a medical patent. Her innovations in medicine led her to the development of the Laserphaco Probe in 1986, which is used in the treatment of cataracts. Bath is also noted for being the first African American female to complete her residency in ophthalmology. In 1983, she became the first female chair in ophthalmology in the United States at UCLA.

Bath was born in Harlem, New York, on November 4, 1942. While life growing up was not always easy, her parents provided her with unending support; they encouraged her to be open-minded and appreciative of other cultures, as well as to work hard academically. Bath did well in her studies and proved her potential early. While in high school, she applied for a scholarship through the National Science Foundation, which she was granted in 1959. This opportunity allowed Bath to attend a program at Yeshiva University's Summer Institute, studying biomedical science in New York.

While at the institute, Bath was given the opportunity to conduct research. She studied the relationships among cancer, nutrition, and stress. In 1964, Bath completed her courses in science, obtaining a BS in chemistry. She continued her academic pursuits and obtained her MD in 1968 from Howard University Medical School. Additionally, Bath was the recipient of the Outstanding Student in Ophthalmology—an Edwin J. Watson Prize. She then attended New York University's School of Medicine. In 1973, Bath began working in New York as an assistant surgeon.[119]

Bath's successes were a direct result not only of her dedication and work ethic, but also her ability to perform despite the racism and sexism that she experienced in professional and academic arenas. After working as an assistant surgeon, Bath pursued her research in Europe, where she experienced greater support and freedom. Leaving the constraints she felt in the US, Bath researched abroad in France, West Germany, and England.

Upon returning to the United States, Bath became the cofounder of the American Institute for the Prevention of Blindness (AIPB) in 1977, which maintains that human eyesight is a priority and a basic human right. She is known for developing the Laserphaco Probe, which restored eyesight to many patients—some had been blind for up to thirty years and longer. Bath continues to mentor others, employing her lifetime experience as a world leader in the prevention and treatment of blindness.

Shirley Ann Jackson

Born: August 5, 1946
Country: The United States of America

"We need to go back to the discovery, to posing a question, to having a hypothesis and having kids know that they can discover the answers and can peel away a layer." [120]

Shirley Ann Jackson was born on August 5, 1946. She grew up in Washington DC, where she was encouraged and supported by her parents to do well in school. By high school, Jackson developed a special interest in science and mathematics, so much so that she took advanced courses in these subjects. Her academic successes led her to Massachusetts Institute of Technology (MIT), making her one of the first African Americans to attend the landmark institution. In 1968, Jackson earned her BA in theoretical physics and went on to pursue her doctoral work also at MIT.[121] She earned her PhD in theoretical elementary particle physics in 1973, the first woman to earn this degree from MIT.[121] Her life as a student was not only filled with classroom challenges, but also was marked by great difficulty, as a result of discrimination from her peers.

After graduation, Jackson was offered a research job at the Fermi National Accelerator Laboratory (Fermilab). In her new position, she worked on research related to subatomic particles. She later moved to Switzerland, where she worked for the European Organization for Nuclear Research. Jackson was also employed by the Stanford Linear Accelerator Center, Aspen Center for Physics, and Bell Telephone Laboratories. Her time at Bell Telephone Laboratories proved to be very successful. Through advances in physics and scientific research, Jackson realized major breakthroughs. Her findings led to the inventions of devices, such as fiber optic cable, portable fax machine, touchtone telephone, and other technological advancements.[122]

In 1976, Jackson accepted a position as professor of physics at Rutgers University. She retired from Rutgers in 1995, and accepted an appointment by United States President Bill Clinton to chair the US Nuclear Regulatory Commission (NRC).

Since 1999, Jackson—a recipient of the National Medal of Science—has served as president of Rensselaer Polytechnic Institute (RPI). RPI is a private university, located in Troy, New York. Founded in 1824, RPI is the oldest technological research university in the United States.

Mark Dean

Born: March 2, 1957

Country: The United States of America

"Most industry leaders, including corporate boards, aren't willing to do what it takes to make a difference and create a diverse workforce." [123]

Mark Dean was born in Jefferson City, Tennessee, on March 2, 1957. From a young age, he demonstrated a strong aptitude and uncommon ability to solve problems by thinking "out of the box." Dean graduated from the University of Tennessee in 1979 with an honors BS degree in electrical engineering. He also earned his master's degree at Florida Atlantic University (1982), in electrical engineering. In 1992, Dean obtained his PhD in engineering from Stanford University.[124]

Dean began his professional career as a computer scientist at IBM. He quickly proved his value to the company and rapidly climbed the corporate ladder. Before long, Dean was the team lead and developer of the Industry Standard Architecture (ISA) bus specification that is used widely in PCs.[125] In addition to this co-invention, Dean is credited with conceiving the colored PC monitor. In 1999, Dean developed the gigahertz micro-processing chip—the first of its kind.[126]

Dean's position with IBM permitted him to expand his ideas. He is widely regarded as one of the most successful African American inventors of all time. Dean holds over twenty patents. He continues to support and inspire young blacks around the world.

CHAPTER VI
Science & Technology

INTRODUCTION
Science and Technology

Research suggests that within the last two hundred years more scientific advancements have been made than in all of history prior to the 1800s. Though today taken for granted, the automobile, MRI scanning device, television, computer, airplane, GPS, and the Internet are all less than two hundred years old. In every field of endeavor, we commonly rely on science and technology to provide answers and solve problems more quickly and with more precision than ever before.

Scientific discoveries are seldom derived from inspiration. More often than not, innovations are generated as results of painstaking trial and error research in the laboratory or field. Once perfected, the outcomes of these discoveries assist in making people's lives simpler in thousands of ways.

As in other important areas, black scientists have not been given their due by the mainstream media or historians. Scores of black scientists have contributed significantly to the general understanding of the physical world. This chapter profiles ten researchers whose life work has benefitted mankind without regard to race, creed, gender, or nationality.

Dozens of scientists qualify for this honor, but on the basis of the universal impact criterion employed herein, the ten blacks who have made the most significant contributions in the arena of science and technology are as follows:

Daniel Hale Williams

Born: January 18, 1856
Died: August 4, 1931
Country: The United States of America

"A people who don't make provision for their own sick and suffering are not worthy of civilization." [127]

A progressive far beyond his time, Daniel Hale Williams was an American doctor who was recognized for successfully performing the second known pericardium surgery. This medical success also made him the first African American doctor to succeed in performing the surgery. Williams was born on January 18, 1856, in Hollidaysburg, Pennsylvania and grew up with his parents and six siblings. However, the tragic event of losing his father to tuberculosis when he was nine years old pulled his family apart. His mother could no longer support the family on her own and was forced to make the difficult decision of sending some of her children away, including Williams, to live with relatives.

As a result of this unavoidable move, Williams became apprentice to a Baltimore, Maryland, shoemaker. However, he eventually returned to his mother, because he disliked the work. He then followed in his father's footsteps and was employed as a barber for a short period. Yet, he decided that this profession was not in his future, either. After spending time in Wisconsin, Williams apprenticed to Dr. Henry Palmer—a well-known surgeon in the area. At the age of twenty, Williams had found his calling and decided to further train at the Chicago Medical College (better known today as Northwestern University Medical School).[128] Upon graduating in 1883, he moved into private practice in a diverse south side Chicago neighborhood.[129] In addition to managing his medical practice, Williams taught courses at Chicago Medical College and was appointed the City Railway Company's surgeon, making him the first African American to hold the position.

Despite his significant achievements, Williams endured the discrimination that African Americans faced during that time. He was an activist in his own right and did not fear speaking out against the injustices that society imposed upon him. Williams struggled with the idea that because of skin color, African Americans were prohibited from receiving medical attention at hospitals. Additionally, black doctors were not allowed to have staff positions within hospitals. After the governor of Illinois appointed Williams to the state's Board of Health, he focused on eliminating the medical hardships that African Americans still faced at that time. His vision was for a desegregated hospital—one where both black and white doctors studied, and black nurses had access to training.[130] On May 4, 1891, Williams accomplished his goal and opened the Provident Hospital and Training School for Nurses.

Only a few years after Provident Hospital's inauguration, Williams made another significant mark in history, as the first African American doctor to successfully perform a pericardium surgery for repairing a wound. In 1893, a Chicagoan named James Cornish was rushed to Provident Hospital following a severe stab wound to his chest. Williams acted quickly to operate on Cornish whose bleeding was profuse. Williams performed the surgery on Cornish without blood transfusions or proper anesthesia, while four white and two black doctors observed him. As a result of that operation, Williams became one of the first to successfully perform the pericardium. Without his skilled surgery, Cornish could have died from his potentially lethal wound.

A year later in 1894, Williams was appointed to the prestigious post of chief surgeon at Freedmen's Hospital in Washington DC. His medical talents contributed to reducing the mortality rate within the hospital by increasing ambulance services and implementing improvements to surgical procedures.

In a response to the American Medical Association's barring of black medical professionals for years, Williams cofounded the National Medical Association for black professionals in 1895. This organization provided black medical students and professionals with greater opportunities. Following his successes and the significant medical changes Williams inspired in Washington DC, he returned home to Chicago. In 1913, Williams was the first black doctor to be inducted into the American College of Surgeons.

William's contributions not only to medicine, but also to the politics of his time established immediate and lasting changes during a time of considerable difficulty for black medical professionals and patients. His legacy continues to inspire generations to serve all citizens equally and with respect.

Percy Lavon Julian

Born: April 11, 1899
Died: April 19, 1975
Country: The United States of America

"I don't think you can possibly embrace the kind of joy which one has who has worked with plants and plant structures, such as I have, over a period of forty years. How wonderful the plant laboratory seems." [131]

Percy Lavon Julian was the oldest of five siblings and was born in Montgomery, Alabama, on April 11, 1899. Ambition and the value of education were deeply ingrained in Julian's family lineage.[132] Julian's grandfather was a freed former slave who had two of his fingers cut off—as punishment—for learning to write. He was raised by parents who would eventually become university educated during the era of Jim Crow laws. His father had given up the opportunity to attend DePauw University—until years later—in order to support his family. All the while, Julian's parents defied the times and pushed for their own children to pursue higher education, doing whatever they could to support them.[133]

Julian attended school through the eighth grade—a typical occurrence given that blacks were severely limited from having opportunities to attend high school and other institutions for higher education. Julian was fortunate that a mentor of his father's, Stuart (who had encouraged Julian's dad to attend DePauw), was still a schoolteacher at the same school that his father and mother had attended. Stuart helped Julian secure admission to DePauw University in Greencastle, Indiana, making him one of the few African Americans to be accepted into the college that year.[134]

Greencastle and DePauw were not easy for Julian. Segregation meant that he could not live in student housing, and it took him a few days to find a location to eat, where he would not be denied services. These challenges, however, were not the only ones Julian faced during his transition. Because he was prevented from pursuing a proper high-school education in Alabama, Julian faced setbacks and challenges. He struggled with work that other students were well prepared for. During his first year, he enrolled in evening high-school classes to help him catch up, while also working in a fraternity house to pay additional expenses. Despite having to overcome these obstacles, Julian proved his academic worth, particularly excelling in chemistry. He graduated in 1920 as valedictorian and was initiated into Phi Beta Kappa honor society.

After Julian graduated from DePauw, he initially aspired to continue on his education route and obtain his doctorate in chemistry. Segregation prevented him from embracing this goal, and in lieu of further study, Julian became a chemistry instructor at Fisk University. Eventually, Julian was awarded an Austin Fellowship in chemistry in 1923, which allowed him to attend Harvard University, where he pursued a master's degree and doctorate. Harvard University, however, rescinded its offer for Julian to pursue a PhD after white students protested being taught by him as a doctoral candidate. This barrier did not discourage Julian.

In 1929, he left his instructor position at Howard University to devote his time to the Rockefeller Foundation fellowship that had been awarded to him.[135] The fellowship presented a chance for him to attend the University of Vienna and study alongside Ernst Späth, a distinguished European chemist. His time and training in Europe proved to be important to his career, because Julian finally earned his doctorate. In Vienna, he also enjoyed greater acceptance among his peers in contrast to the racism that plagued him in the United States.

After obtaining his doctorate in 1931, Julian returned to Howard University, and later, in 1933, to DePauw as a Minshall Laboratory Research Fellow. By 1935, Julian had created a treatment for glaucoma, earning him international acclaim. Even with his success and worldwide recognition, the university did not appoint Julian as a full-time professor, because of his race.[136] This unjust oversight frustrated Julian; consequently, he left academia to pursue industrial opportunities. Julian also overcame challenges in the business world, as many companies did not want him working for them, because he was black. Julian was not discouraged. He persisted and became the lab director at Glidden Company. Here he made breakthroughs and invented new solutions—many of which were based on soybeans. One such invention, Aero-Foam, was used during World War II, because of its ability to extinguish oil and gas fires. Aero-Foam saved the lives of many US soldiers when aircraft carriers and ships caught fire. Julian also synthesized hormones and cortisone, developing a treatment for rheumatoid arthritis that was affordable for everyone.

Based on his natural talent for chemistry, Julian gained worldwide fame and personal wealth over the years. Toward the end of his career, he founded Julian Laboratories, which he eventually sold for millions in 1961. Julian also opened the Julian Research Institute, a nonprofit organization that he managed until his death from liver cancer in 1975.

Charles Richard Drew

Born: June 3, 1904
Died: April 1, 1950
Country: The United States of America

"I feel that the recent ruling of the United States Army and Navy, regarding the refusal of colored blood donors, is an indefensible one from any point of view. As you know, there is no scientific basis for the separation of the bloods of different races except on the basis of the individual blood types or groups." [137]

He is considered one of America's foremost medical pioneers of the twentieth century for his contributions to science and medicine. Charles Richard Drew was born in Washington DC, on June 3, 1904 and was raised in a middle-class African American family. His childhood years were marked by average grades. However, Drew enjoyed great athletic success, as he was constantly awarded medals for his achievements in sports, particularly in swimming. His strong athleticism carried him through high school, eventually securing him an athletic scholarship to Amherst College in Massachusetts in 1922, where he ran track and played football. Segregation made Drew's academic and athletic pursuits difficult. He was the best athlete on his college football team; yet, his teammates refused to make Drew captain during his senior year. Academically, he became interested in studying science and medicine after receiving encouragement from a biology professor.[138] After earning his bachelor's degree in 1926, Drew wished to enter medical school, but he did not have the money to do so. Instead, he was forced to teach biology and coach at Morgan College. Two years later, he still had ambitions to pursue a medical degree, and therefore, he enrolled at McGill University in Canada. Drew excelled at McGill, proving that he had a passion and talent for medicine. He was presented with numerous prizes and was welcomed into the medical honor society as well. By the time he graduated in 1933, Drew had a strong academic record, earning both Doctor of Medicine and Master of Surgery degrees.[139] Following his graduation, Drew entered a residency program at Montreal Hospital in Canada and studied transfusion therapy.

When he returned to the United States in 1935, Drew accepted a job at Howard University, where he worked as an instructor at the medical school. Three years later, he began studies at Columbia University on a Rockefeller Fellowship. At Columbia he continued to study blood science and developed a method for storing blood plasma.[140] His thesis was titled *Banked Blood: A Study in Blood Preservation* and was claimed to be a remarkable body of work.

Drew's significant work in blood banks and key findings for processing and storing blood led to his appointment as head of the Blood for Britain project. This organization sought to safely transport blood and plasma to Britain—a country enduring attacks by the Germans at that time. The Blood for Britain project was deemed an enormous success, collecting over 14,500 blood donations and 5,000 liters of plasma saline—all shipped to England in a time of desperate need.

The Blood for Britain project ended in 1941. As a result of his pioneering work with the project, Drew was sought by the American Red Cross. The Blood for Britain blood banks—developed by Drew—shipped their blood and plasma to military personnel. Drew became upset and discouraged after learning that the American Red Cross categorized blood types based on the race of the donor. Displaying offensive racism at the time, the American Red Cross standards would not even allow Drew—a black man—to participate in the program that he created. This objectionable rule resulted in Drew resigning his position with the Red Cross, as he deemed this practice to be unscientific and racist. Later that same year, he returned to Howard University, serving as the head of the Department of Surgery and chief of surgery at Freedmen's Hospital. In his efforts at the hospital, Drew was relentless in ensuring that young black doctors received crucial support and proper training in order to become successful in the medical profession.

Charles Drew passed away in 1950 at an early age, following a car accident while driving to a medical conference.

Meredith Charles "Flash" Gourdine

Born: September 26, 1929
Died: November 20, 1998
Country: The United States of America

"My father told me, 'if you don't want to be a laborer all your life, stay in school.'" [141]

Born in Newark, New Jersey, to a working-class family, Meredith Charles Gourdine's father instilled in him a very strong work ethic. Gourdine was sent to Brooklyn Technical High School and would often help his father after school with different painting projects. Performing laborious tasks with his father affirmed his goal to achieve higher responsibilities throughout his life. Consequently, Gourdine excelled in school in order to pave a way for better opportunities.

His success in academics and athletics opened the doors to universities he sought to attend. Gourdine chose Cornell University in upstate New York. Over the course of the first two years, Gourdine paid his own way through college; however, his athletic talents landed him a track and field scholarship, which supported him for the remainder of his college career. Gourdine performed exceptionally well in track and field, winning American championship titles. He was eventually chosen to represent the United States at the 1952 Summer Olympics in Helsinki, Finland. Gourdine excelled at track and field and was ultimately awarded a silver medal in the long jump.[142]

In 1953, Gourdine graduated from Cornell with a bachelor's degree in engineering and physics; then, he decided to enter the US Navy. After his time in the navy, Gourdine received the Guggenheim Fellowship with which he pursued his PhD in engineering science at the California Institute of Technology (Caltech), graduating in 1960. While a PhD candidate, Gourdine worked in a series of labs. He graduated from Caltech with experience as a technician at Ramo-Wooldridge Corporation and Caltech Jet Propulsion Laboratory. Subsequently, Gourdine was employed by Plasmodyne Corporation; then, he became chief scientist at the Curtiss-Wright Corporation in 1962.

After a couple years with the Curtiss-Wright Corporation, he established Gourdine Laboratories with $200,000 he largely borrowed from his close family and friends. Located in New Jersey, Gourdine Laboratories grew to encompass over a hundred employees. He also established Energy Innovation, Inc. in Houston, Texas, for which he was CEO.

Gourdine's inventions allowed him to efficiently convert coal into energy. He also invented the Incineraid System, which dispersed smoke and fog in order to produce clean surrounding air. All told, Gourdine collected over thirty patents for his various inventions. In 1994, he was inducted into the Engineering and Science Hall of Fame. In his later years, Gourdine suffered severely from diabetes, and after enduring complications from multiple strokes, he passed away in November 1998.

Wangari Maathai

Born: April 1, 1940
Died: September 25, 2011
Country: The Republic of Kenya

"For me, one of the major reasons to move beyond just the planting of trees was that I have tendency to look at the causes of a problem. We often preoccupy ourselves with the symptoms, whereas if we went to the root cause of the problems, we would be able to overcome the problems once and for all." [143]

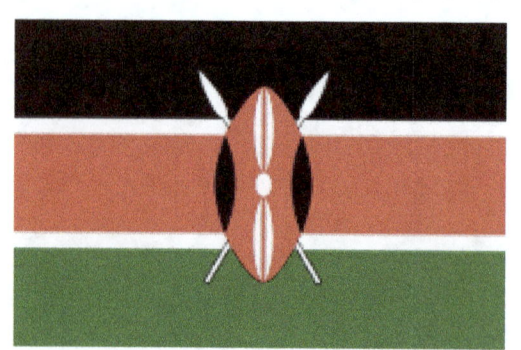

Wangari Maathai was born into a Kikuyu family on April 1, 1940, in Ihithe, British Kenya, in the Nyeri District. At the age of three, she moved with her parents to Rift Valley, where her father worked on a white-owned farm to support the family. However, the lack of educational opportunities in the rural area prompted Maathai to return to Ihithe to attend school. In 1951, at the age of eleven, her parents enrolled her in St. Cecilia's Intermediate Primary Boarding School in Nyeri. There Maathai received her educational and spiritual foundations, studying English and Catholicism, eventually converting to that religion. The following year marked the beginning of the Mau Mau Uprising in Kenya, which involved a majority of

Kikuyu groups, as well as the British military and white settlers within the country. Despite the turmoil and increasingly dangerous circumstances, Maathai remained untouched by the politics and fighting within her homeland and focused on her studies. She accomplished outstanding academic achievements and placed at the top of her graduating class in 1956. Her scholastic success opened the door for her to attend a challenging high school, where she also excelled.

The end of Maathai's high-school career coincided with the end of the Mau Mau Uprising in 1960. During that period, Kenyan students—who demonstrated great potential—were increasingly awarded funds to study abroad. Through the Joseph P. Kennedy Jr. Foundation, Maathai—among more than three hundred Kenyans—was presented a chance to complete her undergraduate studies in the United States. Maathai attended College of St. Scholastica in Kansas; she majored in biology and minored in chemistry. Maathai also studied at the University of Pittsburgh, graduating in 1966 with a master's degree in biological sciences.[144] Furthering her scholarly quest, Maathai obtained her PhD in anatomy from the University of Nairobi in 1971, making her the first woman from her region in Africa to earn this degree.

After completing the PhD program, Maathai took on various roles within local organizations, including director of the Kenyan Red Cross Society in 1973. The following year, she was invited to join the Environment Liaison Center; her experience with the organization opened her eyes to the importance of environmental preservation. Maathai became an associate professor and then the chair of the Department of Veterinary Anatomy at the University of Nairobi. Just prior to these posts in 1976, Maathai joined the National Council of Women of Kenya (NCWK), where she first proposed her tree-planting concept to citizens. Shortly thereafter, Maathai established her grassroots, environmental organization, called the Green Belt Movement in 1977. Its mission and efforts were ignited by her work in rural Kenya; in these communities, women in particular gathered firewood used for fires and fences. Maathai observed that these women travelled far to collect these resources due to environmental degradation from evaporating streams. The area suffered from food insecurity as a result.

Aimed specifically at communities throughout Kenya, the Green Belt Movement addressed the critical livelihood concerns within these communities by empowering women and providing them with resources to conserve their environment. The Green Belt Movement promoted the planting of seedlings and trees to prevent erosion and the storing of rainwater; the women were given earnings for their efforts.

Maathai eventually became the chairman of the NCWK in 1981 and served for six consecutive years, during which time, she expanded the Green Belt Movement and other projects for the purpose of conserving the environment.[145] Through her leadership, Maathai contributed to the planting of over thirty million trees and new skills for over 30,000 inhabitants. Consequently, she initiated an improvement in the immediate and long-term quality of life for residents. In 1986, the Green Belt Movement expanded, reaching other countries in Africa—known as the Pan African Green Belt Movement.

Maathai's community-based tree planting initiatives proved that she was an activist whose efforts extended far beyond environmental conservation. Maathai also sought to highlight the political and social issues that plagued her homeland. Her drive to reduce poverty and protect the environment led to international recognition. Maathai addressed the United Nations General Assembly on many occasions and served on various commissions.[146]

From 2002 to 2007, Maathai was the representative for the Tetu constituency in Kenya, and from 2003 to 2007, she served as Kenya's assistant minister for Environment and Natural Resources. In 2004, she was awarded the Nobel Peace Prize. Maathai was appointed Goodwill Ambassador to the Congo Basin Forest Ecosystem the following year, eventually becoming the Congo Basin's Co-Chair. In a 2009 speech, the UN Secretary General named Maathai the UN Messenger of Peace. She also supported the UN Millennium Development Goals, as part of the advocacy group of experts. In 2010, Maathai became the trustee of the Karura Forest Environmental Education Trust and established her own foundation, the Wangari Maathai Institute for Peace and Environmental Studies.

On September 25, 2011, Wangari Maatthai passed away at the age 71, following her battle with ovarian cancer. Her life's journey led to many personal achievements, including over a dozen honorary degrees from prestigious academic institutions and over fifty additional awards worldwide. Maathai's legacy, however, will be the green footprint she left on the world and her lifelong dedication to making it a safe, supportive, and protected environment.

Charles Frank Bolden

Born: August 19, 1946
Country: The United States of America

"Always do your best in whatever you do, set goals and seek challenges, become a role model for those behind you, and always have God in your heart." [147]

The United States National Aeronautics and Space Administration (NASA) is an arm of the federal government founded in 1958 and tasked with managing US space-exploration programs. NASA employs a staff of close to twenty thousand and manages an annual budget of approximately $20 billion. Sitting at the helm of NASA is former astronaut and retired US Marine Corps Major General Charles Frank Bolden Jr.—the first black person to head NASA on a full-time basis. A native of Columbia, South Carolina, Bolden matriculated at his hometown C. A. Johnson High-school and graduated in 1964. He received his undergraduate degree in electrical science from the US Naval Academy in 1968, and in 1977, Bolden earned his MS degree in systems management at the University of Southern California. After college, Bolden boasted a 34-year career in the military as a US Marine Corps fighter pilot in such places as Thailand and

North and South Vietnam. Later, in 1980, he was selected to join an elite group of NASA astronaut trainees.[148]

For fourteen years, Bolden distinguished himself as one of the premier space scientists in the United States, irrespective of race. He traveled to orbit on four space flights, piloted Space Shuttle Discovery in 1990, and spent close to seven hundred hours in space, inclusive of piloting Columbia in 1986 and Atlantis in 1992. Bolden holds the distinction of pioneering the Launch Complex 39 slidewire baskets, which allow for speedy exit from a space shuttle on the Launchpad in emergencies.

Despite a sharp reduction in NASA's budget, Bolden presses on as a top-rated space scientist to prove, once and for all, that NASA is vital to the modernization of our way of life, and its programs offer the best guides to information beyond our planet. As NASA administrator, Bolden takes pride in asserting that one of his objectives is to place astronauts on Mars. (Incidentally, he is the first person to hear his voice broadcast from the surface of Mars).[149]

For his many contributions to space science, Bolden received some ten honorary doctoral degrees. In addition, he holds a NASA Outstanding Leadership Award, Defense Distinguished Service Medal, Vietnam Gallantry Cross, NASA Exceptional Service Medal, among others.[150]

Wanda M. Austin

Born: 1954

Country: The United States of America

"If you have something to contribute, have courage and stick to your convictions so that your voice can be heard." [151]

Dr. Wanda M. Austin was born in 1954 and raised in a low-income neighborhood in Bronx, New York. Her father worked as a barber, and her mother was employed as a nurse. Austin's mother in particular encouraged her to become involved in extracurricular activities. Austin excelled in mathematics, claiming that she liked math, because the answers were matter of fact and undisputed—unlike in English class.[152] Austin attended Bronx High School of Science and graduated with strong results, which led to being awarded a scholarship to Franklin & Marshall College.

While at Franklin & Marshall College, Austin pursued a bachelor's degree in mathematics with the ambition of becoming a teacher. She advanced her education at the University of Pittsburgh where she originally planned on obtaining her master's degree in mathematics. However, after tutoring engineering students in math, the idea of becoming an engineer appealed to her as well. Consequently, Austin obtained master's degrees in mathematics and systems engineering.[153]

After graduating from the University of Pittsburg, Austin joined Rockwell International in Anaheim, where she worked on radar modeling systems as part of the technical staff. She eventually decided to leave Rockwell. In 1982, she accepted an entry-level position at The Aerospace Corporation, becoming one of the few women to work as an engineer for the company. This position opened opportunities for her. At Aerospace, she soon labored on massive US programs and projects at Aerospace for the pentagon and Air Force Communications satellites and the Global Positioning System (GPS) constellation of satellites. Austin earned her PhD in systems engineering at the University of Southern California in 1988, as she continued her career with The Aerospace Corporation. Austin's hard work and determination prompted her steady rise within The Aerospace Corporation and the Science Technology Engineering and Mathematics (STEM) community. She became internationally recognized for her efforts as one of the major architects for the US National Security Space (NSS) programs.[154]

Prior to being named The Aerospace Corporation's president and CEO in 2008, Austin held many supporting-role positions. She provided support to the National Reconnaissance Office as well as various space missions over the years. In 2009, she served on the NASA Advisory Council (NAC) and US Human Space Flight Plans Committee. The following year, Austin was awarded the American Institute of Aeronautics and Astronautics (AIAA) von Braun

Award for Excellence in Space Program Management. That same year, she was appointed to the Defense Science Board (DSB). Additionally, Austin serves on the California Council on Science and Technology, the National Academy of Engineering, and the American Academy of Arts and Sciences. In 2012, Austin was named the recipient of the Horatio Alger Award and the National Defense Industrial Association (NDIA) Peter B. Teets Industry Award. Three years later, in 2015, US President Barack Obama selected Austin to serve on the President's Council of Advisors on Science and Technology (PCAST).[155]

As a woman, Austin's significant achievements and accomplishments allowed her to not only build an unparalleled career in an industry that has not always welcomed women, but also pave the way for young girls and women to follow in the mathematics, science, and engineering fields. She has been the proponent of many initiatives including MathCounts, US FIRST Robotics, and Change the Equation. Austin also serves on the Board of Directors for the Space Foundation and on the Board of Trustees for the University of Southern California and the National Geographic Society.

Philip Emeagwali

Born: August 23, 1954
Country: The Federal Republic of Nigeria

"My focus is not on solving nature's deeper mysteries. It is on using nature's deeper mysteries to solve important societal problems." [156]

Often referred to as the Bill Gates of Africa, Dr. Philip Emeagwali—Nigerian inventor and scientist—is credited as being the inventor of the world's fastest computer.[157] Born in Akure, Nigeria, August 23, 1954, and raised in the Eastern Nigerian town of Onitsha, Emeagwali enjoyed school as a child.[158] He excelled particularly in mathematics. His classmates referred to him as "Calculus."[159] By the time he turned fourteen, Emeagwali already mastered math and outshined not only his classmates, but also his instructors.[160]

The outbreak of the 1967 Nigerian Civil War and family financial struggles forced Emeagwali to temporarily change his academic journey and leave school for a period. Despite these obstacles, he managed to receive a general education certificate from the University of London through its distance-learning study program. In 1971, Emeagwali was awarded a full scholarship to study mathematics in the United States at Oregon State University.[161] He graduated with a bachelor's degree in mathematics in 1977. Following graduation, he enrolled at George Washington University where he obtained a dual master's degree in civil engineering and marine engineering. He also attended the University of Maryland, where he obtained his master's degree in mathematics. Emeagwali then earned his PhD from the University of Michigan in scientific computing.

His impressive academic achievements reflect his perseverance and ambition and also reveal his natural talent for understanding mathematical intricacies. Emeawgwali is credited most for contributing to the effectiveness and speed of the Connection Machine. According to Emeagwali, he received inspiration for constructing the machine from nature, more specifically, from bee colonies.[162]

After observing ways in which computers could be developed to emulate and mimic the efficiency and strength of honeycombs, Emeagwali created a computing system that would work just as quickly and powerfully for humans.[163]

Emeagwali's mathematical expertise and computing abilities contributed to the improvement of oil-extraction processes. During his time at the University of Michigan, he wrote a thesis on employing microprocessors to expedite computer calculations in an effort to make oil drilling more efficient.[164] His methods helped to formulate a novel approach to oil extraction, resulting in oil fields becoming more productive. Thereby, Emeagwali's research saved the oil industry millions of dollars per year.[165]

In 1989, Emeagwali developed his computing code, which contributed to the invention of the world's fastest computer with 65,000 processors that performed at a speed of 3.1 billion calculations per second.[166] This step forward led to new knowledge of how computers communicate simultaneously and interactively. Emeagwali is also heralded as one of the fathers of the modern-day Internet. In 1989, Emeagwali was awarded the Gordon Bell Prize for his computing ingenuity, the equivalent of the Nobel Prize.[167] His computer-performance breakthrough made a significant contribution to advance science, mathematics, and technology.

Neil deGrasse Tyson

Born: October 5, 1958
Country: The United States of America

"I wanted to become something that was outside of the paradigms of expectation of the people in power. So, fortunately, my depth of interest was so deep, and so fuel-enriched, that every one of these curveballs that I was thrown and fences that were built in front of me and hills that I had to climb, I'd just reach for more fuel and I kept going." [168]

Neil deGrasse Tyson was born in Manhattan, New York, on October 5, 1958 and grew up in the Bronx. When he was nine years old, he toured the American Museum of Natural History's Hayden Planetarium; this visit left a deep and lasting impression, igniting his interest in astronomy.[169] Two years after stargazing at the Hayden Planetarium, Tyson's parents purchased his first telescope, which further supported and encouraged his growing interests in the universe.[170]

Tyson's name was already synonymous with astronomy when he attended Bronx High School of Science. At the age of fifteen, he gave astronomy lectures in his community and served as editor in chief of the high-school Physical Science journal. Prior to graduating, Tyson received a handwritten letter from astronomer and Cornell University professor, Carl Sagan. The letter encouraged him to attend Cornell for his undergraduate studies. However, after completion of high school in 1976, Tyson decided to pursue undergraduate studies at Harvard University.

Tyson obtained his bachelor's degree in physics from Harvard in 1980. He then earned his master's in astronomy from the University of Texas at Austin in 1983.[171] Tyson began teaching astronomy in 1986 at the University of Maryland, but eventually, he returned to New York to earn his MPhil in astrophysics in 1989 and his PhD in astrophysics from Columbia University in 1991.[172] The PhD research he conducted on galactic bulge supported related discoveries in the field of astrophysics. Over the course of his career, Tyson has held positions at Princeton University and the University of Maryland. In 1994, as a research affiliate with Princeton University, Tyson joined the Hayden Planetarium as a staff scientist. Two years later in 1996, he became director of the planetarium.

In 2001, President George W. Bush appointed Tyson to serve on the Commission on the Future of the United States Aerospace Industry in order to aid research and development in the aerospace industry with national-security interests.[173] The commission was comprised of twelve members, including some of the top names in aerospace defense and astrophysics (among them, former astronaut Buzz Aldrin, John Douglass, former assistant secretary of the Navy, and Heidi Wood, managing director at Morgan Stanley). President Bush appointed Tyson for a second time in January 2004, as part of the President's Commission on Implementation of United States Space Exploration Policy, which consisted of nine members, including politicians and scientific experts. The commission earned the nickname "Moon, Mars and Beyond" because it focused on developing America's civil space program and space exploration as it relates to human, as well as robotic missions to the Moon, Mars and other areas of the universe.

Tyson's appointment to the Moon, Mars and Beyond program impelled his selection as part of NASA's Advisory Council. Throughout the late 1990s to 2005, Tyson contributed monthly essays to Natural History Magazine. His success within the field of astrophysics and his strong communicating talents led him to host the PBS Nova series Origins in 2004 and collaborate with astronomy writer, Donald Goldsmith, on the book inspired by the series.[174] Goldsmith and Tyson also worked on the 400 Years of the Telescope documentary in 2009.

Over the years, Tyson's media presence has grown significantly, and he has appeared on television shows on various networks. He hosted Nova science NOW on PBS from 2006 to 2011. In addition, he was invited on numerous occasions to participate in The Universe, a series on the History channel. In 2009, he co-hosted the radio show, StarTalk.

Through his public presence as an acclaimed scientist, Tyson addresses the disparities of gender and race in Science Technology Engineering and Mathematics (STEM); he often shares his life story of overcoming stereotypes and expectations in order to influence dreamers to break long-established societal boundaries.

Juliana Rotich

Born: 1977

Country: The Republic of Kenya

"I think there is a role for us as women to contribute to the future of technology." [175]

An old gospel chorus begins with the phrase, "It only takes a spark to get a fire going." To countless women in Kenya and increasingly around the world, the spark is the application of technology to modern-day challenges, and the fire is the wealth of initiatives and innovations designed to improve the quality of life. At the forefront of this exciting march forward is Juliana Rotich. Born in Kenya, Rotich graduated from the information technology program at the University of Missouri. This driven technology entrepreneur set as her life's work a triumvirate of achievements by utilizing technology to "build things, fix things and by so doing, help others." Noting that much of Africa is beset by constant power outages, Rotich developed BRCK—a backup generator for the internet; the generator has the potential to offer reliable connectivity throughout the developing world. To date, Rotich's mobile Wi-Fi device brings the web to schools throughout Africa and beyond.

Not yet forty years old, Rotich is a key advisor to Microsoft 4Afrika, a trustee of the iHub in Kenya, as well as the Spain-based Bankinter Foundation for Entrepreneurship and Innovation. She's on the Kenya Vision 2030 Delivery Board and sits on the World Economic Forum Global Agenda Council with a focus on data-driven development.

Perhaps Rotich's greatest contribution to date is her development of Ushahidi Inc., which develops free software for modernizing information flow globally. Ushahidi (Swahili for "testimony") utilizes crowd-sourced geolocation—via mobile phone and web-reporting data—to generate crisis reporting. This groundbreaking technology was first employed during the 2007-08 presidential elections in Kenya and has since been used to transmit crowd portrayal of critical events in Haiti, Pakistan, Tanzania, Japan, New Zealand, and Chile. Rotich is a partner in a bid to raise $50 million to invest in science-based small businesses throughout Africa. In addition, she is a highly sought technology-conference presenter and strategic thinker. She has presented academic papers at myriad forums, including Smart City Expo in Barcelona (2015); Global Digital Leaders in Berlin (2015); MIT Media Lab (2015); Net Explorateur Forum with UNESCO in Paris (2014); World Economic Forum on Africa in Abuja (2014); and London School of Economics Africa Summit (1914).

As a result of Ushahidi, it is now more difficult for information to be confined to the viewpoints of those in authority during crisis situations. Ushahidi is a tool to democratize information, increase transparency, and allow ordinary folk en masse to describe events as they unfold. Rotich has been described by Fortune magazine as "one of the world's fifty great leaders." At her present pace, it may not be long before she takes her place amongst the world's top twenty-five.

SECTION C
"PROSPERITY"

CHAPTER VII

Business and Entrepreneurship

INTRODUCTION
Business & Entrepreneurship

Often, the question is asked, "Why do people go into business?" The trigger response is that people go into business to make profits. In order to make the cut for inclusion in this historic chronicle, one must view business and entrepreneurship not only as profit-making machines, but also as tools for effecting change.

From the standpoint of entrepreneurship, the goal was to seek out those who—against the greatest odds or despite the direst circumstances—began from virtually nothing and transformed their dreams into awesome forces to be reckoned with. In the area of business, the objective was to identify black corporate giants who ascended to the helm of a global conglomerate and added value to it for the common good.

In the United States within the white community, Donald Trump, Sam Walton, Henry Ford, Nelson Rockefeller, Warren Buffet, Bill Gates, and others are household names. Similarly, who has not read about Nicky Oppenheimer and Christoffel Wiese in South Africa, Blair Perry-Okeden in Australia, Nassef Sawiris in Egypt, Nathan Kirsh in Swaziland, Carlos Slim Helu in Mexico, Issad Rebrab in Algeria, Gordon "Butch" Stewart in Jamaica, or Jack Ma in China? These are all white global business leaders. But who are their black counterparts? Who are the top blacks—men and women—who achieved the greatest measure of business and entrepreneurial success, and at the same time, utilized their fortune, fame, and influence to effect social change?

It is one thing to amass wealth. It is quite another story to use that wealth, at least in part, as a vehicle to challenge the status quo, to open new doors for others to explore opportunities hitherto unknown. On this basis, it is felt that in the arena of business and entrepreneurship, the ten black persons who climbed the highest and accomplished the most to change the world for the better are as follows:

Madam C. J. Walker

Born: December 23, 1867
Died: May 25, 1919
Country: The United States of America

"Don't sit down and wait for the opportunities to come. Get up and make them." [176]

Sarah Breedlove, who later became Madam C. J. Walker, was a political activist, freedom fighter, and pioneering entrepreneur. She blended her acumen, creativity, and business savvy into becoming the first female self-made millionaire—black or white—within the United States.

As a political activist and freedom fighter, Walker started her campaign against discrimination and injustice at an early age. She especially protested lynching. At one point, as a member of the executive committee of the New York NAACP, Walker helped to organize a ten-thousand-person march to appeal to United States President Woodrow Wilson to use his authority to stop lynchings.[177]

Born in a small town near Delta, Louisiana, Walker was orphaned at the age of seven. As a young woman, she suffered hair loss from a prolonged scalp ailment. In an attempt to cure this malady, in 1905, Walker developed a line of hair-care products, targeting African Americans. While living in Denver, Colorado, working for a black hair-care manufacturer, her husband, Charles, encouraged her to change her name to Madam C. J. Walker, stating that the name had marketing appeal.[178]

The moniker stuck. She developed the "Walker Method" and is credited with inventing the hot comb and dozens of pomade formulas. Her creations led to the formation of Madam C. J. Walker Laboratories. The company formulated not just hair-care products, but also cosmetics. She traveled throughout the United States, demonstrating and promoting her products. In addition, she trained an army of young black beauticians in sales and hair-care techniques. Walker was adamant about empowering others. She preached self-reliance and especially wanted women to become economically independent.

In 1908, Walker moved to Pittsburg and opened a factory and school of beauty. Two years later, she relocated the business to Indianapolis, where her venture took flight.[179] Her agents promoted her products nationwide and promoted Walker's social gospel of "cleanliness and loveliness"—a clarion call to black pride, self-development, and economic empowerment. Walker pioneered vocational conventions that brought her sales agents together for motivation and education, and she often offered scholarships and other performance prizes.

Walker was a visionary. She traveled outside of the United States on several occasions, promoting her products and methods of hair care, while recruiting local agents. (One could say that she was an original Mary Kay or Avon.) Eventually, Walker moved to Harlem. Her business remained in Indianapolis, where she donated handsomely to the creation of a YMCA in Indianapolis. In Harlem, she awarded scholarships, contributed heavily to the National Conference on Lynching, the NAACP, and many other organizations.[180]

After her death, Walker's Irvington, New York, home—"Villa Lewaro"—was dedicated as a National Landmark. The US Postal Service, in 1998, issued a Madam C. J. Walker postage stamp to mark Black History Month.[181]

Reginald F. Lewis

Born: December 7, 1942
Died: January 19, 1993

"Keep going, no matter what." [182]

A native of Baltimore, Maryland, with a middle-class upbringing, Reginald F. Lewis was the consummate businessman. In fact, during the 1980s, through intellect, ingenuity, blood, sweat, and tears, he rose to become the richest black man in the United States.

To those who knew him well, they saw his success coming since he was a youngster. He was captain of his high school's football, baseball, and basketball teams. He was the first and only person to be admitted to Harvard Law School before he applied.

After Harvard, Lewis worked for fifteen years with a top New York law firm. Then, in 1983, he formed TLC Group L.P. to engage in venture capital work. He purchased the McCall Pattern Company—a sewing-patterns conglomerate—for $22.5 million as his first major adventure. At the time, the company's profits were in decline; Lewis reversed this trend within one year. Lewis later sold the company for $90 million, yielding a 90-to-1 return with 81.7 percent belonging to him.

In 1987, Lewis purchased Beatrice International Foods for $985 million; he rebranded the company as TLC Beatrice International, specializing in beverages, groceries, and snack foods. At the time, TLC Beatrice International was the largest black-owned and managed business in the United States.[183] That same year, the company posted revenue of $1.8 billion, cementing it as the first black-owned company to record more than $1 billion in annual sales. By 1992, sales climbed to $2.2 billion, and TLC Beatrice was listed 512 among Fortune magazine's list of one thousand largest companies.

Under the foundation that bears his name, Lewis awarded $1 million to Howard University for scholarships, and in 1992, he donated $3 million to Harvard Law School—at that time, the school's largest grant.[184] Today at Harvard, one finds the Reginald F. Lewis International Law Centre. In Maryland, an 82,000-square-foot building houses the Reginald F. Lewis Museum of African American History and Culture.

Lewis died in 1993 at the age of fifty after battling brain cancer. In the words of Frank Sander, one of Lewis' professors at Harvard Law, "Those of us on the faculty who saw in him then, the promise of greatness, had no idea of the extraordinary achievements he was to attain."

Mohammed Hussein Al Amoudi

Born: July 21, 1946
Country: The Federal Democratic Republic of Ethiopia

"There is a natural link between the effective running of my businesses and the effective direction of philanthropic funds. I apply business principles to my philanthropic work so that maximum value is given to the causes I support." [185]

He was born and raised in Ethiopia to mixed-race parents—his mother, an Ethiopian, and his father, Saudi Arabian. Mohammed Hussein Al Amoudi migrated to Saudi Arabia at a relatively young age, and although he assumed Saudi citizenship, Al Amoudi solidified his Ethiopian roots. Today, he is widely regarded as a corporate citizen of the world.

Al Amoudi's not only Ethiopia's richest man, but also is the second richest citizen of Saudi Arabia with a net worth of $11 billion. Al Amoudi's business success is attributable to the basic principle of not placing all his eggs in one basket.

His business interests run the spectrum: cement production, hotel ownership, agriculture, healthcare, tire manufacturing, and construction. Al Amoudi owns the largest construction firm in Ethiopia, and all combined, he commands a workforce of seventy thousand employees. One of Al Amoudi's highest accomplishments to date was the construction of the $30 billion underground oil storage complex in Saudi Arabia in 1988.[186]

Al Amoudi has major business interests not just in Ethiopia and Saudi Arabia, but also in Sweden, Morocco, the Middle East, and Europe. He was listed by Forbes Magazine (2015) as the second wealthiest black billionaire (after Aliko Dangote) with a net worth just shy of $19 billion.

Al Amoudi's philanthropy is as diverse as his investments. To date, he has funded a breast cancer research center in Saudi Arabia and the King Abdullah Institute for Nanotechnology at King Sand University. In addition, Al Amoudi pledged $88 million to support construction of the Renaissance Dam in Ethiopia to significantly increase hydroelectric power.

Al Amoudi has been honored by the Arab Economic Forum for his unstinting commitment to sustainable development.

Folorunsho Alakija

Born: 1951

Country: The Federal Republic of Nigeria

"Do not accept 'NO' for an answer." [187]

Folorunsho Alakija's story is both inspirational and aspirational. Though born with a head start—the daughter of a rich Nigerian father with eight wives and fifty-two children—Alakija, in her own right, distinguished herself as a world-class business leader and twenty-third century entrepreneur. Whether Forbes Magazine's estimation of her worth ($3.3 billion) or the Daily Mail's estimate ($7.3 billion) is considered, it is beyond dispute that Alakija is the world's richest black woman, replacing Oprah Winfrey.

Alakija left Nigeria at a relatively young age and completed her formative years of education in England. She then returned to Nigeria in the early 1970's and acquired a secretarial job at the Merchant Bank of Nigeria. By all accounts, the job was going well when Alakija had a light bulb moment. Management considered her a model employee; yet, the bank hired new, younger employees at higher wages and in higher positions, because they possessed college degrees. In her mind, this practice was unfair.

Alakija resigned from the bank and headed back to England; this time, she studied fashion design, something she always wanted to do. After graduation, she returned to Nigeria. With three months of prospecting and planning under her belt, she launched her own design line under the "Supreme Stitches" label. Alakija made a small fortune in the clothing industry and won the Best Designer in Nigeria Award one year. But she was unfulfilled; she wanted a bigger challenge.[188]

In 1993, Alakija founded Famfa Oil Ltd. and received a license to explore for oil. She literally struck gold. Famfa Oil has controlling interest in a 617,000-acre oil field; the Nigerian government controls the remaining interest as OML 127. Ironically, in 2000, the government high handedly and unilaterally repossessed 90 percent of its exploration grant. Alekija took the government to court and won. Today Famfa owns 60 percent of Nigeria's oil, producing two hundred thousand barrels of oil each day. According to Texaco, hired initially by Alekija for their oil drilling expertise, she sits on one billion barrels of oil. Consequently, Alekija can extract two hundred thousand barrels of oil per day for the next thirteen years from present reserves without breaking a sweat.

While Alekija enjoys the finer things in life—such as her $50 million private jet and over $100 million in real estate—she is also a noted philanthropist. Through her Rose of Sharon Foundation, Alekija assists widows and orphans worldwide by way of scholarships and microbusiness grants.

Kenneth Chenault

Born: June 2, 1951

Country: The United States of America

"Execution—performance—is the bottom line measure for everything we attempt to do. To be successful, our EQ or execution quotient must equal our IQ." [189]

American Express (Amex) is a household name around the world and synonymous with corporate success. Founded in 1850, this multinational, financial-services entity is ranked eighty-eighth among Fortune 500 rankings. Fortune magazine notes Amex as eleventh on its "Top 50 World's Most Admired Companies" list (2014). Boasting assets of $161 billion, 118 million active credit cards, annual sales of $33 billion, and net income of $5.1 billion, Amex enjoys staggering success.[190] It would have been imponderable twenty years ago that a black man would one day captain this mega financial-services ship. In 2001, Kenneth Chenault quieted all the naysayers.

A product of Mineola, New York, and an alumnus of Harvard Law School, Chenault piloted American Express—a global giant—as one of the first African Americans to lead a Fortune 500 conglomerate. Chenault joined Amex in 1981 after a brief stint practicing law. Almost instantly, his fertile business acumen distinguished him from the pack of both black-and-white peers. Chenault introduced bold, innovative ideas and products that helped Amex compete more robustly with its competitors. One of Amex's signature contributions has been access to credit by small businesses globally. By 1997, sixteen years after he first walked through the front door, Chenault sat in an office with "President and Chief Operating Officer" embossed on his business card. Four years later, he was elevated to CEO.

As fate would have it, Chenault's appointment coincided with the tragedy of September 11, 2001; in addition to damages to its Manhattan headquarters, Amex lost eleven employees. This incident caused many people to forego traveling for a period, and as a result, a sizeable portion of Amex's business was adversely affected. Chenault led the way out of this temporary setback by launching new services, not all of which were generic to Amex's traditional brands.

Chenault was again challenged by the near global collapse of 2008. American Express was issued a license to become a holding bank, and thereby, it qualified for assistance under Troubled Assets Relief Program (TARP) and weathered the storm until the days of economic recovery.

Ebony magazine, in 1995, noted Chenault among its fifty "Living Pioneers" in the African American community. In addition, he is a much sought-after commencement speaker. Junior Achievement inducted him into the US Business

Hall of Fame in 2002. Chenault, reported to have a net worth of $90 million, supports numerous nonprofits.[191]

Kenneth Frazier

Born: December 17, 1954
Country: The United States of America

"I think the entire pharmaceutical industry has a lot of work to do to restore public trust." ¹⁹²

One might say that Kenneth Frazier was born with business in his DNA, considering that by age sixteen, he was raising tadpoles and marketing them in the neighborhood to help pay his way through college at Penn State University. Frazier is a product of Philadelphia, Pennsylvania. Armed with a Harvard law degree and significant legal and corporate experience, he sits as chairman and CEO of Merck and Co., Inc., one of the leading pharmaceutical conglomerates in the world. With a workforce of 68,000 and revenues of $40 billion (2015), Merck specializes in manufacturing and distributing medicines, animal health products, and vaccines.¹⁹³

After completing law school, Frazier joined a firm in Philadelphia and was headed for stardom as a trial lawyer. He came to legal prominence when he successfully secured a retrial—and eventual acquittal—for Willie "Bo" Cochran, who had spent nineteen years on death row. At the same time, Merck was a client of Drinker Biddle, Frazier's law firm. In 1999, fourteen years after Harvard and mastering the art of advocacy, Frazier signed on at Merck as general counsel in its public affairs division. Many may recall the litany of lawsuits directed at Merck at that time—amounting potentially to $50 billion—over its Vioxx drug. Few know that it was Frazier who led Merck's legal defense against these lawsuits. He successfully fought in court in some cases and settled in others for under $5 billion.

In 2006, Frazier was promoted to executive vice president and retained the job of general counsel for Merck. In 2010, he assumed the position of president of Merck, and a year later, Frazier joined the board of directors as CEO, thus becoming the first African American to command a pharmaceutical conglomerate with universal reach.204 In 2014, Frazier was compensated to the tune of $22 million.[194]

Frazier has an insatiable desire to help people in developing countries. He also has a particular focus on Alzheimer's, the disease that killed his father.

Next time you visit your neighborhood pharmacy, note if your medication was manufactured by Merck. Then, remember the name, Kenneth Frazier, because he had a hand in making your convenient remedy possible.

Arnold W. Donald

Born: 1955

Country: The United States of America

"Travel is one of the great equalizers in bringing the world closer together." [195]

Only in the United States of America, some would say, could a black boy rise from "dirt poor" formative circumstances—with four biological and twenty-seven foster siblings—to the zenith of the international cruise industry. As president and CEO of Carnival Corporation, Arnold W. Donald operates some one hundred cruise ships with 120,000 employees, spanning sixty countries.

Most persons are familiar with Carnival Cruise Lines' twenty-four ships that service mostly the North American market. What is less known, perhaps, is that Carnival Cruise Lines' corporate umbrella encompasses Princess Cruises' eighteen ships; Holland America Lines' fifteen midsize ships that ply the seas of 100 countries; Seabourn's all-suite, upscale fleet; Cunard Cruises; P & O Cruises; and AIDA Cruises.

Founded in 1972 and headquartered in Doral, Florida, the entire carnival fleet has a passenger capacity of over two hundred thousand, and in 2015, the company realized a gross income of $15 billion. Sitting as captain of the Carnival Corporation—the number one cruise company in the world—is Arnold W. Donald. Some say Donald was wired at conception to become a business tycoon; the first sign of this phenomena came when—barely out of diapers—he started his first business, selling candies to family members.

Born into a working-class family in New Orleans, Louisiana, Donald attended the all-black, all-male St. Augustine's College with its mantra, "Gentlemen, prepare yourselves. You're going to run the world." Donald took that to heart; he internalized it; he embraced that adage as a summons to rise above life's circumstances and soar to heights unknown.

It was not, therefore, a big surprise when—as a high school junior—he decided that one day he would lead a Fortune 500 company. So said, so done. After earning a BA degree from Carleton College, a BS degree in mechanical engineering from Washington University in St. Louis, and an MBA from the University of Chicago, Donald discovered that for him, the sky was not the limit.[196]

Donald served as a senior vice president of global giant Monsanto Corporation and president of the company's $4 billion agricultural division. His stellar achievements and innovations—leading the agriculture sector—earned him the Agri-Marketer of the Year Award in 1996.

While at Monsanto, this sales and marketing guru convinced his bosses to allow him to purchase their Equal (sugar-substitute) division. They agreed, and Donald founded Merisant—now a $400 million company and pacesetter in the sugar-alternative industry.

As for Carnival, Donald had already retired when he received the call, inviting him to become the new captain of the Carnival Corporate ship. Having served on Carnival's Board of Directors for a decade, the industry's challenges were not new to him. Donald describes his job as a "blast," and at times, he has to pinch himself to believe he has achieved this position. However, in light of Donald's preparation, perspiration, purposefulness, and perspective, it is no wonder that he presides at the helm.

At Carnival, Donald is creating a culture around three focal points: give passengers golden moments of service and pleasure; cut costs; and enhance revenue. By all accounts, the Carnival ship is in good hands with Arnold W. Donald wearing the captain's hat.

Aliko Dangote

Born: April 10, 1957

Country: The Federal Republic of Nigeria

"Nothing is going to help Nigeria like Nigerians bringing back their money. Give me $5 billion today, I will invest everything here in Nigeria." [197]

In a real sense, Aliko Dangote has been in business since primary school—selling candy in his neighborhood in Nigeria. In his mind, he was born to be a businessman.[198] It is not surprising that after he completed his business studies at the Al-Azhar University in Egypt, Dangote returned to Nigeria, borrowed 500,000 Nigerian dollars from a relative, and launched Dangote Group—a small trading entity; Dangote was just twenty-one years old.

Since then, the Dangote Group has become not just multinational, but also multifaceted. The conglomerate enjoys major dominance in telecommunications, oil and gas, flour and sugar refining, cement manufacturing, food processing, banking, freight forwarding, and the production of salt, ginger, cotton, cocoa and nuts. In addition, Dangote controls the largest sugar refinery in all of Africa, the third largest in the world. Outside of Nigeria, Dangote has substantial business interests in Benin, Zambia, South Africa, Ghana, Cameroon, and Togo. Combined, he commands a workforce of over ten thousand.

Forbes Magazine ranked Dangote as the richest black person in the world with an estimated net worth of $19 billion (USD). In 2014, *Forbes Magazine* named Dangote, the "African Person of the Year." He is a recipient of Nigeria's second-highest honor, Grand Commander of the Order of the Niger (2011), and he is Nigeria's foremost employer in the construction trades.[199]

According to the Nigerian government, Dangote, in 2014, donated $1 million to assist in the fight against Ebola. He also pledged $1.2 billion to the Dangote Foundation to promote scholarships, healthy lifestyles, and youth entrepreneurship across Nigeria. This charity is in keeping with his prized reputation as Africa's most generous son.

Ursula Burns

Born: September 20, 1958
Country: The United States of America

"I realized I was more convincing to myself and to the people who were listening when I actually said what I thought, versus what I thought people wanted to hear me say." [200]

Forbes Magazine, in 2014, rated Ursula Burns as the twenty-second most powerful woman in the world. Not bad for a child of immigrant parents, who was raised by a single mother at the Baruch housing projects in New York City.

Burns joined Xerox as an intern in 1980, armed with a BS degree in mechanical engineering from New York University Polytechnic School of Engineering. The next year, she earned her MS degree in mechanical engineering from Columbia University and signed on full time at Xerox. In 2009, after a series of rapid promotions, Burns was installed as CEO of Xerox, becoming the first African American woman to head a Fortune 500 company with a compensation package that averaged $13 million annually.[201]

In 2015, *Forbes Magazine* listed Burns as twenty-ninth among the world's one hundred most influential women. Xerox, after all, has close to 150,000 employees, and its 2014 earnings approached $20 billion. Founded in 1906, Xerox is a world leader in document technology with some 19,000 active patents and a presence in over 180 countries.

Burns has served on various corporate boards, including American Express; Datto, Inc.; MIT; and Exxon Mobil. She pioneered the launch of Change the Equation, aimed at enhancing mathematics, science, and technology education throughout the United States. President Barack Obama, in 2010, placed Burns on his Export Council as its vice chair.

Burns' climb to the top of the corporate ladder is essentially a story about mentorship— those who mentored her and the hundreds of Xerox employees she mentors to ensure the company's longevity.

Patrice Motsepe

Born: January 28, 1962
Country: The Republic of South Africa

"People don't know that there were very successful black businessmen in the years of apartheid." [202]

Patrice Motsepe's rise to economic dominance in South Africa has attracted a fair share of critics. Nonetheless, this self-made billionaire wears controversy and criticism as a badge of honor, as he carves out a large space for himself among Africa's economic elite.

Born into a middle-class family in Soweto, Motsepe earned a BA degree from the University of Swaziland and a law degree from the University of the Witwatersrand. He practiced law for a stint, becoming the first black partner at Bowman Gilfillan, a noted white law firm in South Africa. At Bowman Gilfillan, Motsepe specialized in business and mining law. Shortly after Nelson Mandela became president of South Africa in 1994, "black empowerment" became buzzwords. The essence of the new ideology was that most business ventures needed black participation at the ownership level. Motsepe saw an opportunity, and he seized the moment.

Motsepe sharpened his black-power theme by forming a mining-services company. He hired employees at low wages, but with decent profit-sharing arrangements. Motsepe began purchasing gold mines in 1997, and he was able to negotiate favorable loans that enabled him to consolidate his place in the mining industry rather quickly.[203]

In 2002, Motsepe captured South Africa's Best Entrepreneur Award; he was selected thirty-ninth among Great South Africans in 2004. In 2008, on the *Forbes Magazine's* "World Billionaire" list, Motsepe ranked 503. He is the nonexecutive chairman of Harmony Gold— the twelfth largest gold-mining company worldwide. *Forbes Magazine* pegs his net worth at $2.9 billion.

Motsepe joined the Giving Pledge in 2013, which obligates him to give half of his assets to charity.

SECTION D

"PLEASURE"

CHAPTER VIII

Arts & Entertainment

INTRODUCTION
Arts & Entertainment

When Abraham Maslow enumerated the basic needs of mankind, he omitted the need for leisure and pleasure. No human endeavors satisfy these needs more than those found in arts and entertainment. Where would the world be without music, dancing, movies, television shows, comedy, Broadway shows, vaudeville, festivals, carnivals, and concerts? Without arts and entertainment, mankind would sorely miss a force for human upliftment, economic empowerment, and social change.

Music and dancing—two leading forms of art and entertainment—are in and of themselves multifaceted, presenting some gratification for every possible taste. In music, there's pop, country, rhythm and blues, jazz, gospel, classical, and rap—an almost endless spectrum of genres. (From time immemorial, no one questions the power of the songs, "Soon Ah Will Be Done," "We Shall Overcome," or "Kumbaya, My Lord.") Similarly, in dance, the mix and the mode include disco, salsa, ballroom, ballet, meringue, and tap dancing, among others.

This chapter required judges to review the annals of recorded history and construct a selection of ten individuals who used arts and entertainment to positively impact the world. This was a daunting, exhausting, yet illuminating task. In the end, final selections took into consideration such things as commercial success, world reach, socio-developmental impact, post-career durability, and enduring legacy. Also taken into account was geographical proportionality to ensure, as far as possible, that selections represented the motherland as well as the diaspora.

On this basis, it is postulated that in the arena of arts and entertainment, the ten black persons who did most to change the world for the better are as follows:

Marian Anderson

Born: February 27, 1897
Died: April 8, 1993
Country: United States of America

"As long as you keep a person down, some part of you has to be down there to hold him down, so it means you cannot soar as you otherwise might." [204]

One hundred years from now, when historians compile a listing of global musical titans, the name Marian Anderson will resonate as a towering luminary who rose above racism, hatred and bigotry to become one of music's greatest gifts to mankind.

Born in Philadelphia, Pennsylvania to struggling parents, Anderson began singing publicly at age six. Her father was so impressed by her talent he bought her a piano when she was eight years old. Four years later, Anderson's father died and shortly thereafter, her mother was stricken with a debilitating illness. This did not dim Anderson's focus nor deter her pursuit of a musical career.

In fact, even as a child, she was so gifted, her deep, rich contralto voice so compelling, she had become the star performer in her church choir. By the time she became a teenager, she was a child protégé – under the tutelage of a professional voice coach, paid for by funds raised by members of her church choir.

Anderson was not wired to swim with the prevailing tides. While gospel music was her first love, she leaned heavily towards operatic and classical music. This did not endear her to many black audiences. White audiences sought to confine her to more stereotypical genres–blues or jazz. Anderson saw herself in a different light–singing songs created by the great masters- Haydn, Schubert, Handel and others.

Her first big break came in 1925, when at the age of twenty-eight, she entered a New York Town Hall singing contest that featured some 300 contestants. She won. This earned her the opportunity to sing with the New York Philharmonic Orchestra – the first black to do so.

Despite these exploits, she could hardly make ends meet. For the most part, blacks were not drawn to her music and whites were not prepared to hear her. She relocated to England and studied there before moving back to the United States.

Still unable to earn a decent living from her performances within the United States, Anderson headed back to Europe and found tremendous success. She performed all over – Italy, Poland, Russia, Paris and beyond. At one point, she did a grueling 20-concert tour in Scandinavia. At the top of her career she had mastered more than 200 songs and could render performances in multiple languages.

Anderson was immortalized in 1939, when the Daughters of the American Revolution (D.A.R) relied on a stale provision enshrined in the by-laws of Constitution Hall in Washington D.C. to prevent her from performing there based on race. President Franklin Roosevelt's wife, Eleanor, was so outraged by DAR's decision that she cancelled her membership at Constitution Hall. Mrs. Roosevelt then used her influence to make it possible for Anderson to give a free open-air concert at the Lincoln Memorial, which drew some 75,000 attendees. When Anderson opened with "My Country 'tis of thee", stunned silence, universal respect and admiration swept across that expansive national landmark and throughout radio land.

It is widely believed that this event of quiet heroism sparked the modern civil rights movement and paved the way for Dr. Martin Luther King, Medgar Evers, Malcolm X and others. According to a New York Times article, Anderson "suffered the indignities imposed on her people without protest, and easily rose above them."

Her awards and honors include:
- 1930's – First African American to perform at the White House
- 1939 – NAACP Spingarn Medal
- 1955 – First African American singer to perform as a member of the Metropolitan Opera in New York.
- 1961 – Performed the national anthem at President John F. Kennedy's inauguration

- 1963 – Received the Presidential Medal of Freedom
- 1988 – received a Grammy Award for Lifetime Achievement

During her post-performance career, Anderson served as:
- Goodwill Ambassador for the US State Department
- Delegate to the United Nations Human Rights Commission

Marian Anderson's celebrated forty-year career (1925-1965) will forever shine as a symbol of triumph over adversity and determination over timidity.

Josephine Baker
(Freda Josephine McDonald)

Born: June 3, 1906
Died: April 12, 1975
Country: The United States of America & France

"Surely the day will come when color means nothing more than the skin tone, when religion is seen uniquely as a way to speak one's soul; when birth places have the weight of a throw of the dice and all men are born free, when understanding breeds love and brotherhood." [205]

Born Freda Josephine McDonald on June 3, 1906, in St. Louis, Missouri, Baker's journey to becoming the world-renowned exotic dancer, Josephine Baker, ultimately represents one of the most famous rags-to-riches stories of the twentieth century.

Raised in poverty during a period of deep segregation and instability for the black community in the United States, Baker grew up in a broken family and endured a laborious childhood. From a young age, she lived and worked in the homes of the white elite, completed household chores and at times, withstood harrowing abuse. She found solace from her unremitting situation in dance; she informally performed on the streets of St. Louis. As Baker grew older, racial tensions and discrimination against blacks simultaneously escalated. In 1917, the East St. Louis Race Riot broke out; black men, women, and children were violently attacked and murdered by whites. Eleven-year-old Baker was a witness to the riot, watching from the other side of the Mississippi river, as more than six-thousand terrified blacks were driven from their homes in search of safety.[206]

The 1917 Race Riot resonated deeply within Baker, instilling fear and insecurity regarding her own situation, and therefore, drawing her even closer to her passion for dance. Eventually, she made her way into the St. Louis Chorus vaudeville circuit, performing comedic dances for the program repertoire. She enjoyed success on the stage due to the appreciation of the crowd; her ambition was fueled. The exposure from her time with the St. Louis Chorus not only further developed her talent, but also opened the door to her future triumphs. She moved to New York City in 1921, during the boom of the Harlem Renaissance, and landed a spot in the seminal Broadway show, *Shuffle Along*.[207] Her career blossomed in New York. She became increasingly recognized in the industry for her comedy performances, which made her the highest paid chorus girl.[208] However, appreciation for Baker's talent and performances were limited in America, because of the racial climate at the time. This reality motivated her to seize the opportunity to sail to Paris, France, for the 1925 *La Revue Nègre*.

The performance Baker gave in *La Revue Nègre* shocked audiences and skyrocketed her to fame in France overnight. She was welcomed and embraced in France, because the attitude toward blacks was warm compared to the racist sentiments she endured in the United States. Baker went on to receive high praise for her dance performances. One of her most-recognized shows—*Danse Sauvage*—

became iconic, because she wore her legendary banana skirt. Following a decade of success in Europe and South America, Baker decided to return to the US. Her experiences, however, reminded her of why she had initially left. Despite her talents, she was not appreciated in the United States. She continued to face harsh criticism and discrimination. She eventually returned to France, where she was welcomed with great excitement. It was then that Baker made the decision to renounce her American citizenship.

It was not only Josephine Baker's talent as a performer that made her exceptional, but also her outlook on humanity. Having grown up under difficult circumstances, she possessed a personal understanding and deeply intelligent way of renouncing inhumanity. When World War II broke out, Baker took on a pivotal role, carrying out counter espionage for the French. She allowed the French to use her castle in Dordogne as a headquarters for the resistance. Her star status also provided cover for the French and access to gatherings with top officials from around the world. Even her sheet music was used to smuggle top-secret information across borders. The German invasion, however, forced Baker to leave France for the remainder of the war. She found refuge in North Africa, where reportedly, she fell ill. The newspapers eventually announced her death. This story, however, turned out to be a spoof and was perhaps created for Baker's protection.

In reality, Baker performed for the troops during the remainder of the war, when she again had a chance to make a difference. She made a demand: She would only dance for audiences when blacks were allowed at the front of the theater. Baker's demand was immediately met. Through her actions, Baker proved her love and loyalty to France and demonstrated her fearless activism for the betterment of humanity. She was awarded the Croix de la Reine, the honorary rank of sub-lieutenant in the French Air Force, the Médaille de la Résistance, and the Légion d'honneur. The accolades she received for her unwavering dedication to France elevated her to a position of great respect and sustained leadership. This station granted her the power to advocate for further peace in the world and eventually, turn her attention to America.

Following the war, Baker concentrated on her family. In 1950, she adopted twelve children from myriad countries—a mix of French, Korean, Japanese, Finnish, Belgian, and Venezuelan descents. While her "Rainbow Tribe" raised questions and invited criticism (even today), Baker loved them. In her later years, when she struggled financially, she worked hard to provide for them. Her mixed family reflected her vision of what the world should look like, demonstrating that no matter your culture or race, people can live in harmony and equality together.

Not long after Baker formed her "Rainbow Tribe," she was offered ten thousand dollars to perform at a nightclub in Miami (1951). Baker made it clear that she would reject the offer unless the club met her condition of admitting an integrated audience. The club agreed, and Baker's show ignited a successful tour, whereupon she entertained mixed audiences across the US.

All of her triumphs in the United States, however, crashed down upon her, following an incident at the Stork Club; Baker and her friends were refused dinner services. At the club that evening was writer, Walter Winchell. Baker had come to know Winchell over time, and he had written positively about her in his newspaper column. Yet, Winchell failed to defend Baker, and his inaction felt like betrayal to her. Out of anger, Baker denounced Winchell in her complaints to the press. Her verbal assaults turned Winchell against her completely. He retaliated in a column, accusing Baker of being a communist. Winchell's article proved to have serious consequences; Baker's contracts were cancelled and her visa was revoked. In many respects, her reputation was ruined. Baker returned to France.

Eventually, however, she returned to the United States. In 1963, she took part in the March on Washington, speaking alongside Martin Luther King Jr. During this time, the NAACP named her "Woman of the Year" and proclaimed May 20, Josephine Baker Day.

In April 1975, Josephine Baker was laid to rest. She suffered a cerebral hemorrhage and passed away in her sleep. Her funeral procession was her final show, as thousands of people in Paris commemorated her life by attending her service in acknowledgment of her unrelenting positive impact on the world. The French military honored her with a twenty-one- gun salute and buried her with French military honors.[209]

Celia Cruz
(Úrsula Hilaria Celia de la Caridad Cruz Alfonso)

Born: October 21, 1925
Died: July 16, 2003
Country: The Republic of Cuba & The United States of America

"Singing is my life. It has always been my life. It will always be my life." [210]

One only needs to exclaim her stage name, Azucar, to evoke appreciation for the Cuban-American treasure, Úrsula Hilaria Celia de la Caridad Cruz Alfonso (Celia Cruz). Born on October 21, 1925, in Havana, Cuba, Cruz was a lover of music from an early age. Her life, growing up in the Santos Suárez neighborhood of Havana, was marked by poverty. Yet, the area where she was raised had a profound influence on her musical inclinations. In Santos Suárez, Cruz was introduced to a diverse range of music. She sang Santeria songs, taught to her by her neighbor, who believed in the pantheistic Afro-Cuban religion. Subsequently, Cruz learned folk songs in Yoruba, a Niger-Congo language—one of the major languages spoken in Nigeria and West Africa. Enthusiastically, Cruz would go on to add even more music and dance styles to her repertoire. She embraced boleros and tangos, and was ultimately dubbed the "Queen of Salsa."

When Cruz was eleven years old, she was already singing to her younger siblings and extended family members. There are accounts of how she attracted small crowds and passersby with her beautiful voice; these displays were merely her first performances in a vibrant career.[211] When Cruz was a teenager, she presented music and dance shows around her community and continued experiencing popularity, drawing more crowds and winning many competitions. This further drove Cruz's desire to pursue music and dance as a career. However, Cruz's parents wanted to ensure that their daughter's future was secure and pushed her into selecting a more traditional route of becoming a teacher. Cruz, therefore, began taking literature courses at the National Teachers' College; nevertheless, she continued to hone her musical talents. Eventually, she made the decision to enroll in Havana's National Conservatory of Music, where her instructors quickly recognized her talent.

In 1947, Cruz's aunt and cousin persuaded her to enter a radio talent show with Radio Garcia Serra for the program "La Hora del Té (The Tea Hour).[212] Proclaimed the winner, this victory spurred her participation on other radio shows in Cuba, including the Radio Cadena Suaritos.

A few years later (July 1950), Cruz finally caught her big break. At the time, the renowned Puerto Rican singer, Myrta Silva—who built a successful singing career performing with Cuba's legendary band, La Sonora Mantancera—decided to leave the musical group. Having already garnered significant attention for her talents, Cruz was invited to meet with the members of La Sonora Mantancera by an agent. They offered Cruz the chance to replace Silva in the orchestra, and she accepted, launching her exciting professional career.

Joining La Sonora Mantancera changed Cruz's life dramatically. She toured Cuba and Mexico with the group, appeared in several movies, and recorded full-length albums. Cruz became widely recognized for her amazing talents and eccentric stage outfits. In 1957, Cruz appeared in New York for her first performance at the Palladium Ballroom as well as in other well-established venues across the city. That year, she was awarded her first US gold record.

The world was beautiful for Celia Cruz, but by 1959, the political climate in Cuba changed. The Cuban Revolution had come to an end with Fidel Castro assuming leadership of the country. Cruz did not want to live under the new Cuban regime, and by way of Mexico, she and the band left Cuba soon thereafter. Cruz made her way to New York City, became a US citizen, and in 1962, she married La Sonora Mantancera's trumpet player, Pedro Knight.

In the US, Cruz's professional music career progressed, and in 1966, she collaborated with Tito Puente, the Puerto Rican "King of Latin Music." The albums they produced at Tico Records, however, did not attract the strong following they expected. In 1973, Cruz played the part of Gracia Divina in the Latin opera, *Hommy*, which featured salsa tunes. This show became a hit and resulted in Cruz recording her first US salsa record.

Salsa had reached its maturity by this time. Originating in New York, salsa mixed Cuban, Puerto Rican, Dominican, Columbian, and Brazilian styles of music that were rooted in African traditions. The sudden success of the opera propelled Cruz to continue to sing salsa tunes, allowing her to make her mark in a male-dominated genre. She enjoyed fame and celebrity for almost 30 more years. Fondly known as the "Queen of Salsa," "Queen of Latin Music," and "La Guarachia de Cuba," Cruz emerged as the renowned female voice of salsa music. Never straying far from her Cuban roots, two of her best-selling albums contained songs in Lucimi, a dialect of Yoruba. Even hip-hop and rap found their ways into her songs. Indeed, while in her seventies, Cruz's music still enjoyed tremendous popularity. She is best known for her salsa, bolero, and cha-cha-cha songs.

Cruz's accomplishments and accolades include the following: three Grammys; four Latin Grammys; twenty-three gold records; seventy-two albums; eleven films; a star on the Hollywood Walk of Fame (1989); numerous honors; several lifetime achievement awards; and three honorary doctorates (Yale University 1989, Florida International University 1992, University of Miami 1999). She is the founder of the Celia Cruz Foundation, which provides resources for cancer research and scholarships to young Latino music students.

Per her wishes, two funerals were held, one in Miami (where more than 250,000 mourners passed through the Freedom Tower) and the second in New York at the Frank E. Campbell Funeral Chapel. The services for Cruz were the most-attended funerals that each city had hosted.

Sir Sidney Poitier

Born: February 20, 1927
Country: The United States of America & The Commonwealth of The Bahamas

"I never had an occasion to question color, therefore, I only saw myself as what I was...a human being." [213]

The appearance of Sidney Poitier on the screen in Hollywood changed perceptions in the 1950s and paved the way for black people in cinema and entertainment in the years that followed. Poitier's ability to land roles—that did not reflect the stereotypical parts blacks played on the big screen at that time—opened new opportunities for countless black actors.

Born prematurely on February 20, 1927, in Miami, Florida, to Bahamian farmers, Poitier's parents traveled to Miami regularly; they sold produce that they grew on their farm on Cat Island. The Bahamas was under British rule during Poitier's formative years. Given the remote rural location of Cat Island (an island in The Bahamas), Poitier was sheltered from the black-and-white controversy that enveloped the Bahamas' urban centers. At the age of eleven, however, his family moved to the capital, Nassau, where Poitier lived with his parents until he was fifteen. Shortly thereafter, Poitier was sent to live in Miami with his brother.[214] Poitier decided to relocate to New York City, where he worked as an unskilled laborer to support himself. Working as a dishwasher in Harlem, he learned about New York's American Negro Theater.[215] After arranging an audition, he realized that he needed to memorize a script. Because Poitier had no experience in acting or mastering scripts, he purchased the women's magazine *True Confessions* and memorized all that he could. Following the audition, Poitier received the unwelcomed news that he had not been granted the part. His resourcefulness, however, helped him negotiate a job as a janitor at the American Negro Theater in exchange for being allowed to take acting classes at the academy.[216]

Poitier was overjoyed with the opportunity to attend drama classes. He didn't mind doing the janitorial work in trade, because his ambition was to gain acting experience. Potier's time at the academy proved to be turbulent and short-lived, however. He was kicked out of the arts school, because he did not show much promise. His fellow classmates supported him and pleaded with the administration to allow Poitier to stay. After some discussion, he was allowed to remain, as an understudy to Harry Belafonte, who was already a well-known actor. Belafonte was expected to be the main character in the upcoming play, *Days of Our Youth*. As understudy, Poitier learned Belafonte's part as best he could, and on the night of a show, Belafonte could not make it. Poitier rose to the occasion and, despite being a novice, he impressed the crowd in his public debut.[217] One audience member, who had previously directed the play, was particularly enthused.

The director approached Poitier with a request for him to briefly audition for a Greek comedy play called *Lysistrata*. Though a small part, this 1946 Broadway show marked Poitier's debut as his first acting job. Nerves got the better of Poitier that night; he confused his lines so badly that his performance was comedic to the audience. Anyone watching the play that night, unfamiliar with *Lysistrata*, could not tell. Poitier ended up receiving many positive reviews, raising interest in him. Fortuitously, a potentially disastrous occasion became Poitier's saving grace and helped him land another part in the play, *Anna Lucasta*. From here his career took off, and soon, Poitier was acting with the play's touring company.

In 1950, Poitier made his Hollywood debut in the film, *No Way Out*. In the lead role, he was cast as a doctor, who was responsible for treating a prejudiced white man, played by Richard Widmark. This role established a precedent for Poitier in his career. He would only play roles he believed in, and he demanded respect. At one point, his agent, Mart Baum, recommended him for a role in *Phoenix City*. Although Poitier had a second child on the way and needed the money, he turned down the role and the $750 payment that came with it. The story did not align with his principles. Poitier sought to portray black characters with dignity. This decision did not diminish his career; instead, it attracted greater interest in him as an actor.

The success of his role in *No Way Out* propelled Poitier forward, and in 1955, he acted his breakout role in *Blackboard Jungle* as a troublesome, but talented, music student. In 1958, Poitier accepted the role as a prison escapee in *The Defiant Ones*. Up to that point, he had been the supporting character in many films; this opportunity proved to be life changing, because he became the first black male actor to receive an Academy Award nomination. As lead in the musical, *Porgy and Bess*, and subsequently, in the dramatic adaptation, *Raisin in the Sun* (1961), Poitier became a recognized star.[218] Also, for his role in *Lilies of the Field* (1963), he received the Academy Award for Best Actor, making him the first black actor to win this award.

Poitier continued to challenge racial stereotypes throughout his professional career, taking care to only accept roles that did not reflect poorly on blacks or encourage racism. In the movie, *In The Heat of the Night* (1967), Poitier was cast to play a homicide detective. The film, which was directed by a group of white men, called for a scene in which a white man slapped Poitier and walked away. Poitier initially refused to do the scene, stating that it would send the wrong message; such an action, particularly as executed against a black man, would be signified as acceptable. Instead, Poitier demanded in an agreement that he be allowed to respond to the assault by returning a slap. Due to Poitier's insistence, the scene was powerful and defiant. Other roles in which Poitier's unwavering beliefs stood out included *Guess Who's Coming to Dinner* (1967) and *To Sir, with Love* (1967), both of which addressed the controversial topic of interracial relationships.

In 2001, Poitier was recognized for his contributions to American cinema, and he accepted an Honorary Academy Award. From 2002 to 2007, he served as the Bahamas Ambassador to Japan and the Bahamas Ambassador of UNESCO. Her Majesty Queen Elizabeth II of England named Poitier a Knight Commander of the Order of the British Empire. He was also awarded the Presidential Medal of Freedom in 2009 by President Barrack Obama. In March 2014, Poitier received a standing ovation when he appeared on stage with Angelina Jolie to present the Academy Award for Best Director.

The roles that Poitier played will forever remain iconic, showcased in films that will interminably represent mankind's nobler virtues.

Miriam Makeba
(Zenzile Miriam Makeba)

Born: March 4, 1932
Died: November 9, 2008
Country: The Republic of South Africa

"Age is…wisdom, if one has lived one's life properly." 219

A powerful singer and outspoken civil rights activist, Miriam Makeba was a woman who charmed the world with her talented performances, charisma, strength, and resolute commitment to improving humanity. She was born Zenzile Miriam Makeba in Johannesburg, South Africa, on March 4, 1932, to a Swazi mother and a Xhosa father, who passed away early on in her childhood. Her name at birth, Zenzile, is a Zulu name, meaning "you're responsible for what you've become."220 Makeba's birth name reflected greatly in her persona; later, she used her position of fame to influence change across the globe, especially in her home of South Africa. Makeba dedicated herself to empowering disadvantaged people against discrimination. She advocated for fundamental human rights and continues to be revered as the legendary "Mama Africa" and the "Empress of African Song."

As a young girl, Miriam Makeba moved to her grandparents' home; they regularly took her to church, where Makeba began singing and developing her passion for music. In addition, Makeba sang with her school choir and often performed at other events.[221] Her formative years were interrupted, when South Africa's Nationalist Party established apartheid throughout the country in 1948. The all-white government promoted racial segregation and reinforced already existing policies of discrimination. Forced to live under apartheid, nonwhite South Africans became the subject of severe oppression and hate. The unforgiving circumstances of life under apartheid rule also changed the course for Makeba, who left school at the age of sixteen. She found work as a child caretaker and maid in the homes of South Africa's dominating white inhabitants,[222] but these jobs did not last long. At the age of seventeen, Makeba became pregnant and gave birth to her first child. Shortly thereafter, she was diagnosed with breast cancer. Makeba survived the battle with cancer with the help of her mother, who practiced holistic medicine. Makeba then made the decision to move back to Johannesburg in search of new opportunities, leaving her daughter with her mother.

In Johannesburg, Makeba performed at various venues around the city with her cousin's band, the Cuban Brothers,[223] providing a basis for her professional career and allowing her to gain more singing experience. Being part of the band gave her exposure in the community, and she was invited to join The Manhattan Brothers in 1954, a popular band at that time in South Africa. Her time with The Manhattan Brothers led to fame and turned her passion for singing into a career. Makeba and the band toured neighboring countries, winning great acclaim and expanding her singing career. Around this time, Makeba also performed with the all-female quartet, The Skylarks; she and the group recorded over one hundred songs with many of the melodies becoming big hits, including "Pata Pata" and "The Click Song."[224] Despite all of her celebrity, Makeba was not satisfied with her life in South Africa. She understood the great restrictions that apartheid automatically placed on her life and future career.

In 1957, Makeba was invited to perform with the African Jazz and Variety Review, a show that brought together some of Johannesburg's best musical artists.[225] With the Variety Show she toured Africa for a year and a half. Through this experience, Makeba began acting and performed in the King Kong musical for a mixed audience. The increased recognition and experience in acting ultimately led to Makeba meeting American filmmaker, Lionel Rogosin. Rogosin specialized in making political films; he cast Makeba in his documentary feature, *Come Back Africa*. She sang two songs in the film. The documentary was controversial, because it addressed the struggles of living under apartheid. Makeba's participation in the film would later prove to be problematic for her.

The screening of *Come Back Africa* took place at the Venice Film Festival in 1959, and Rogosin invited Makeba to attend. Her performance in the film was met with instant applause. Makeba enjoyed more international recognition through this experience, and she subsequently flew to London. In London, she was introduced to the "King of Calypso," Harry Belafonte; he took an instant liking to Makeba and her musical talent. Belafonte assisted her in obtaining an American visa so that she could move to New York City. While in America, Makeba's performances on *The Steve Allen Show* and her successful opening at the Village Vanguard accelerated her career, bringing her immediate fame.

In 1960, a twenty-eight-year-old Makeba learned about the increased unrest in South Africa that culminated in the Sharpeville Massacre. Makeba's mother sent her daughter, Bongi, to the United States; on the day of Bongi's arrival, Makeba discovered that her mother had passed away. Makeba attempted to return to South Africa to honor her mother properly at her funeral service. Makeba learned that her South African citizenship had been revoked, blocking her from returning home for her mother's funeral.[226]

This period marked a time of unimaginable difficulty for Makeba, beginning with a long thirty-year exile from her homeland. Her international experiences and exposure, coupled with the revocation of her South African passport, heightened her activism. Makeba proved to not only be a pioneer of African music, but also a key activist on social and civil rights issues across the globe. Her career in America had taken off and propelled her to stardom. She partnered with well-known and well-respected artists for both music and activism, including Marlon Brando, Bing Crosby, Nina Simone, Abbey Lincoln, Steven Allen, Paul Simon, Hugh Masekela (also her husband for a period of time), and Marilyn Monroe. She even performed for John F. Kennedy's birthday celebration. Makeba was a trailblazer for women globally and African women especially, becoming the first African woman to receive a Grammy that she won for her highly successful album, *An Evening with Belafonte/ Makeba*.

In 1963, Makeba spoke before the United Nations on the issue of apartheid, and she raised a clarion call to action:

"I ask you and all the leaders of the world, would you act differently? Would you keep silent and do nothing, if you were in our place? Would you not resist if you were not allowed rights in your own country, because the color of your skin is different to that of your rulers?"

Makeba's powerful words led to any punishments that the ruling authority of South Africa could imagine; it had already revoked her right to return, but now, the government also banned her music and records. Even in the US, Makeba was ostracized at one point, because of her fearlessness in speaking out against injustices. This led to her record deals and tours being cancelled. Many countries offered Makeba citizenships, and in 1968, she accepted the offer from New Guniea and continued to advocate for civil rights. While living in New Guinea, she came to know President Ahmed Sekou Toure, and he appointed her the country's ambassador to the United Nations. This international platform gave her the power to advocate for civil rights; during this time, she continued to perform at shows throughout Africa and Europe.[227]

By 1990, Nelson Mandela was released from prison, due to pressure from the international community. South Africa's government began to lose power. Apartheid ended in 1994. Nelson Mandela welcomed Miriam Makeba back to South Africa for the first time in over three decades. The official end of apartheid marked one of the most important periods in South African history. For Makeba, the abolition of apartheid was monumental, because she had dedicated much of her life to condemning the atrocities against her people. Makeba's captivating voice and profound outlook on the world were reflected in the many accolades she received for her performances and her advocacy. She held ten honorary citizenships and nine passports in her lifetime.

In 2005, Makeba "retired," but continued to tour by performing in each of the countries she had visited previously; it was her way of saying goodbye. In November 2008, she passed away in Italy after a heart attack that she suffered while performing in Naples. Makeba's insightful, captivating voice will resonate through the ages, giving everlasting life to a legacy that we should all emulate.

Bob Marley
(Robert Nesta "Bob" Marley)

Born: February 6, 1945
Died: May 11, 1981
Country: Jamaica

"The greatness of a man is not in how much wealth he acquires, but in his integrity and his ability to affect those around him positively." [228]

More than thirty years after his passing on May 11, 1981, the timeless music of this Jamaican artist is still appreciated. Many of his accolades came posthumously: an induction into the Rock and Roll Hall of Fame in 1994; *Time* magazine's "Album of the Century" in 1999 awarded to *Exodus* (recorded in 1977); "One Love" honored as the "Song of the Millennium" in 1999 by the British Broadcasting Corporation (BBC); Grammy Lifetime Achievement Award (2001); star on the Hollywood Walk of Fame from the Hollywood Historic Trust and the Hollywood Chamber of Commerce (2001); and finally, in 2006, the renaming of Church Street in Brooklyn, New York, to Bob Marley Boulevard.

Born to Norval and Cedella Marley on February 6, 1945, Marley grew up in the rural community of Nine Miles in the parish of St. Ann in Jamaica. This area was steeped in African tradition, and it helped shape his storytelling style of music. As a youth, he moved to Trench Town, Jamaica, where he lived in a low-income community. The move presented Marley with the opportunity to form a vocal group with his friends. Initially called The Wailing Wailers, the band consisted of his childhood friend, Neville Livingston (aka Bunny Wailer), and Peter (Macintosh) Tosh.

The band formed in 1963, in the wake of Jamaica's independence in August 1962. The genesis of the group was relatively symbolic, because the band was seeking its identity, while Jamaica was searching to find its own cultural equilibrium. Part of Jamaica's character was reflected in the popularity of its reggae music. Reggae melodies originated from the traditional ska style.[229] The Wailing Wailers soon signed with Coxsone Dodd at Studio One record label as The Wailers, and the band produced the single "Simmer Down."

The song emerged as a top hit in 1964, catapulting the group's popularity to new heights. As time progressed, however, Marley became disenchanted, because he was not able to pursue music the way *he* wanted. To add to his difficulty, the band struggled to receive fair pay for their work, barely earning enough money to get by. The Wailers disbanded in 1966. That same year, his Imperial Majesty Emperor Haile Selassie I, King of Ethiopia ("Lord and Savior" according to Rastafarian beliefs), visited Jamaica. Marley, ironically, never met the emperor, but he still became greatly influenced by Rastafarianism, a religion that looks to Selassie as the Messiah.

Marley emigrated to the United States to be near his mother in Newark, Delaware; he found employment at a hotel as a cleaner and as a factory worker at Chrysler. Shortly thereafter, He moved back to Jamaica, and upon doing so, The Wailers reunited. Marley officially converted to Rastafarianism, which influenced his long signature dreadlocks. The Wailers also devoted themselves to this religious sect. In 1969, the band signed on with Jamaican music producer, Lee "Scratch" Perry, who specialized in the music styles of reggae and dub. The group came to be recognized as a black rock group. Marley understood that, in order to become successful, The Wailers had to reach an audience outside of Jamaica. The band set off to the United States in 1973 for their first overseas tour. While the group did not gain much popularity in America at the time, they attracted an impressive following across Africa and Europe. Some of their top hits abroad included "No Woman No Cry" (1975); "Exodus" (1977); "Waiting in Vain" (1977); "Satisfy My Soul" (1978); "Jamming" (1977); "Punky Reggae Party" (1977) and "Is This Love" (1978).[230]

The recognition that Marley gained allowed him to share his life experiences with the world through his songs and performances. He had the ability to connect with people cross- culturally and across borders, because his messages resonated with diverse groups, giving them hope. Once he had a measure of success, Marley relocated to a wealthier neighborhood in Jamaica. By so doing, he made a statement. Previously, Rastafarians were not welcome in certain parts of Jamaica. Marley proved to be a mover and a shaker and someone who did not care about what other people thought of him. His independent attitude dominated his outlook and secured his position as a great influence on others, especially in Jamaica.

Marley advocated effectively for issues that he otherwise would not have been in a position to change. In 1976, Jamaica experienced an escalation in political unrest, as the country approached general elections. Deep community divisions existed between political parties in Kingston (Jamaica's capital). Daily violence erupted due to the tensions between the People's National Party (PNP), historically associated with communism, and the Jamaican Labor Party (JLP), that some associate with fascism. Marley advocated for peace during this turbulent period; he spoke against the divisions among the people—particularly young Jamaicans—due to the clashes between the political parties. During this time, Marley performed with Stevie Wonder, who donated his show earnings to the Salvation Army. Wonder's gesture impressed Marley, inspiring him to do a free show in association with the Cultural Section of the Prime Minister's office.[231] Thereafter, politicians saw Marley as someone to draw to their side, because Jamaicans valued reggae artists. Leaders knew that by winning Marley's respect, the people's respect would follow.

Marley's free concert—named "Smile Jamaica"—would prove to be polarizing, because of the political climate. During the rehearsal, Marley, his wife (Rita), and his band were targets of assassination attempts. Marley and others were shot, but everyone survived the attack. The assault led to concerns about the safety of all during "Smile Jamaica," but Marley refused to cancel the show. Concert attendance was massive, and Marley gave an amazing performance. In the end, however, political tensions in Jamaica forced him to escape to Nassau, Bahamas, and then London. During this time, Marley continued to write songs. He eventually produced *Exodus*; a hit album that garnered acclaim.

Not long thereafter, Marley was diagnosed with Melanoma, and his doctors recommended amputating a toe. He rejected the idea, and the cancer worsened. In 1978, despite his illness, Marley was invited to headline the concert "One Love One Peace" in Jamaica; he agreed, remarking that his life was only important if he made a difference for others. Fans welcomed him back home with great excitement, and he performed to a crowd of over thirty thousand.

Marley enjoyed a vibrant career until 1980, when he performed his last concert. Although strenuous for him, Marley prevailed and managed to play two encores.

Marley began receiving chemotherapy over the course of eight months in Germany. In October 1981, he was discharged from the hospital, because there was nothing else his doctors could do for him. The cancer had taken its toll. Marley passed away in Miami on May 11, 1981. His legacy lives on, and his timeless message of love, self-pride and acceptance is appreciated by generations, who enjoy and are inspired by his music.

Michael Joseph Jackson

Born: August 29, 1958
Died: June 25, 2009
Country: The United States of America

"Let us dream of tomorrow where we can truly love from the soul, and know love as the ultimate truth at the heart of all creation." [232]

"We are The World," "Beat It," "Smooth Criminal," "ABC," and "Man in the Mirror:" these are tunes known worldwide. These songs have both entertained and called us to action to improve the human condition.

Michael Joseph Jackson was born August 28, 1958, in Gary, Indiana, to Joseph and Katherine Jackson. He was the eighth of ten children. Jackson began his singing career early on with his brothers, as the energetic lead vocalist for the Jackson 5.[233] They gained popularity, performing shows in the chitlin circuit, a group of theaters and nightclubs that allowed the band to safely play during a period of racial segregation. In 1967, after a few years touring the US, the Jackson 5 released its first two singles to acclaim. When the Jackson 5 signed with Berry Gordy Jr.

from Motown record company, the band was an instant sensation.[234]

The Jackson 5 was highly acclaimed for its enthralling choreographed productions, and Michael Jackson was the star who truly shined. In 1971, Motown launched his solo career, and Jackson reached the top ten with his first single, "Got to Be There."[235] A series of four popular albums followed; they included the hit songs "Ben" and "Rockin' Robin." In 1975, all but two of the Jackson brothers decided to make the move to Epic Records, perhaps due to disagreements in creative control. The Jackson 5 reformed as the Jacksons. The band toured and produced an additional six albums. Meanwhile, in 1979, Jackson's fifth studio album *Off the Wall* catapulted his career.[236] He penned some of the songs on the album, including the Grammy-winnng "Don't Stop 'Til You Get Enough." Although enjoying wide acclaim, Jackson's ambition was not satisfied. In 1982, Michael Jackson finally fulfilled his dream with the release of *Thriller*, winning several Grammys, music awards, and the Award of Merit.[237]

Following the enormous success of *Thriller*, in 1984, Jackson completed his final engagements as a member of the Jacksons. The Victory Tour took place in Canada and the United States, showcasing the band and Jackson's popular singles. The Victory Tour experienced ticket-pricing problems. Following the concerts, Jackson announced in a press conference that he would donate his earnings (an estimated $3 to $4 million dollars) to charity. Jackson had reached fame and was loved the world over, not only for his musical talents as the "King of Pop," but also for his acts of charity around the world.

In 1985, Jackson co-wrote with Lionel Richie, "We Are the World" with the purpose of ending famine in Africa.[238] The single was produced in collaboration with forty-five of the biggest pop artists of the time. In 1993, Jackson founded the Heal the World Foundation, granting access to his Neverland Ranch to underprivileged children. His foundation also donated millions of dollars in support of disadvantaged children who face threats of war, famine, abuse, poverty, and disease.[239]

Michael Jackson was a great humanitarian, who always considered the plight of others. He is known to have supported thirty-nine different charities in addition to his own. The *Guinness Book of World Records* recognized him with its "Most Charities Supported by a Pop Star" award for his philanthropy. Jackson holds the distinction of being the sole dancer—from pop and rock music—inducted into the Dance Hall of Fame. Jackson was also inducted into the Rock and Roll Hall of Fame twice, and the Songwriter's Hall of Fame. Michael Jackson's stunning accomplishments include the following: twenty-six American Music Awards, thirteen number-one singles, top ten singles on the *"Billboard Hot 100"* in five different decades, thirteen Grammy Awards, and a Grammy Lifetime Achievement award, making him the most awarded recording artist in the history of popular music.

With estimated sales of over four hundred million units worldwide, few people have not been touched by his music. Michael Jackson was an entertainer, a humanitarian, an innovator, and a king in many more respects than simply the world of pop music.

Youssou N'Dour

Born: October 1, 1959
Country: The Republic of Senegal

"People need to see that, far from being an obstacle, the world's diversity of languages, religions, and traditions is a great treasure, affording us precious opportunities to recognize ourselves in others." [240]

Youssou N'Dour was born on October 1, 1959, on West Africa's peninsular coast in Dakar, Senegal. His mother's family came from a traditional West African griot cast. While he was not raised with this particular tradition, N'Dour learned about the traveling poets, musicians, and storytellers mostly from his grandparents. The oral history of West Africa would later prove to give lyrical influence to his songs.

N'Dour's father was not supportive of his son's gravitation toward music and hoped that he would select a more traditional and respected career path, becoming a doctor or lawyer. However, N'Dour's mind was made up. When he was twelve years old, he performed with Star Band; the popular Senegalese group was formed in 1960 to honor Senegal's independence. His initial exposure to singing on stage gave N'Dour fulfillment and emboldened him to continue pursuing music.

A spin-off from Star Band, called Étoile de Dakar ("Star of Dakar"), premiered in 1979. With N'Dour as the leader, the band evolved into Super Étoile de Dakar. By the early 80s, N'Dour established himself as a popular singer across Africa.

In order to build upon his acclaim, in 1983, N'Dour traveled to Paris. Performing in Paris was not as satisfying as N'Dour expected; he did not take to the city in the same way other African artists had. In Paris, N'Dour's audiences were largely African. He yearned to reach a wider audience and performed a concert in London, where the audience was mostly British. N'Dour recalled that people approached him after the show, excited about his music. At last, N'Dour found the acclaim and acceptance he had hoped for. British singer-songwriter Peter Gabriel attended his London concert and became a source of great support. Gabriel invited N'Dour and the Super Étoile de Dakar with him on his world tour.[241]

In 1985, N'Dour organized a tour that supported the release of South Africa's anti-apartheid revolutionary, Nelson Mandela, who was still imprisoned. Another fulfilling moment for N'Dour transpired when he co-headlined with Gabriel and other major artists (including Bruce Springsteen, Sting, and Tracy Chapman) on the Human Rights Now! tour for Amnesty international. Twenty concerts over a period of six weeks in fourteen countries, the tour commemorated the fortieth anniversary of the Universal Declaration of Human Rights.[242] As he witnessed the millions of people united in front of the stage, N'Dour realized the immense power and captivating influence that music has on politics and humanity.

N'Dour released his first album through Virgin Records in 1989, called *The Lion*. His album was not as popular as anticipated, and he was eventually dropped from Virgin Records. In 1991, N'Dour joined Spike Lee's 40 Acres and a Mule Musicworks label. In 1994, he released the trilingual best-selling song, "7 Seconds." On this tune, he collaborated with Neneh Cherry, a Swedish artist whose roots were from both Sweden and Sierra Leone. A continued association with Spike Lee led him to produce the album, *Eyes Open*, utilizing N'Dour's studio in Dakar. Released in June of 1992, N'Dour received a Grammy Award nomination in the Best World Music Album category.[243]

Youssou N'Dour became a symbol for Africa and a leading symbol for world music. Using his platform—as an inspiration in Africa and around the world—N'Dour has championed universal human rights. N'Dour campaigned for immunization efforts in Senegal. He also used his global connections to found Senegal Surround Sound, an initiative to caution and educate Africans about the dangers of malaria. In addition, N'Dour has held many prestigious positions, including his long-term role as a UNICEF Goodwill Ambassador (April 1991). N'Dour held this post for twenty years before stepping down to pursue his candidacy for president of Senegal.

In October 2000, N'Dour was nominated for the role of Goodwill Ambassador to the United Nations Food and Agriculture Organization. In 2007, he became a member of the World Future Council and subsequently, in 2008, he joined the La Fondation Chirac, a foundation formed by former French President Jacques Chirac. N'Dour also served as the president of the Honorary Committee of the

Cardio Pediatric Cuomo in Dakar in association with the French organization, La Chaine de l'Espoir.[244] In 2012, N'Dour was appointed Senegal's Tourism and Culture Minister and subsequently, the Minister for Tourism and Leisure.

Having developed a style of Senegalese music known as Mblax, *Folk Roots* magazine called N'Dour the "African Musician of the Century." In 2008, he wrote and performed the official song for the FIFA World Cup; in 2011, Yale University conferred on him an honorary doctoral degree in music; and in 2013, he shared a $150,000 Swedish prize for his music and efforts to promote cross-cultural understanding. Today, N'Dour has a fan base of millions around the world.

For a performer like Youssou N'Dour, music is considered the "first language" that everyone speaks, because its universality breaks barriers and brings people together.[245] Throughout his life, N'Dour has proven that music has the power to draw attention to critical issues of concern—locally, nationally, and internationally. One of Africa's most legendary sons, N'Dour strives to leave his imprint on the world by uniting people through music and activism.

Angélique Kidjo
(Angélique Kpasseloko Hinto Hounsinou Kandjo Manta Zogbin Kidjo)

Born: July 14, 1960
Country: The Republic of Benin

"It doesn't matter what challenge you face, the most important thing is, when you fall, how you rise and how high you want to go, where you want to go from that rise on." [246]

Growing up in the West African country of Benin, Angelique Kidjo was heavily influenced by the progressive views in her family. Her father educated her brothers on the value of respecting women, even though their society did not always teach this lesson. Kidjo, the seventh of eight children, grew up with the understanding that she should always be treated with great respect. Her grandmother taught her that she should always do the right thing, not doubt herself, or worry about criticism. Her mother, who belonged to a forward-thinking women's group that encouraged women to exercise their rights, urged Kidjo to be an independent, free thinker. Her enlightened upbringing inspired her to become a self-reliant and confidant woman.[247] In addition to Kidjo's raw and powerful talent, her liberal childhood largely contributed to her stardom and international success.

From the early age of six, Kidjo gained experience as a performer, when she sang traditional African music with her mother's theater group. In school she further honed her natural talent and passion for singing as part of her school band, Les Sphinx. Due to the negative stigma attached to being a musician in her society, Kidjo endured name-calling from her peers. This period was also challenging for her, because of the jealousy she experienced from some of her classmates. Her parents, however, valued and supported Kidjo's endeavors, standing in opposition to the traditional cultural views of their society.[248] Kidjo's parents advised her to never quit out of fear of being negatively judged and insulted. She drew inspiration from these lessons and understood that no one had the power to discourage her dreams.

Another source of inspiration in Kidjo's life was her idol, Miriam Makeba. The first single that Kidjo recorded was a rendition of Makeba's song, "Les Trois Z." Played on national radio in Benin, Kidjo's record brought about considerable recognition of her musical talent. She collaborated with her brother and Cameroonian producer, Ekambi Brilliant, to record her first album, *Pretty*, in 1981.[249] The popularity of her first album prompted a tour throughout West Africa.

During this time, however, Kidjo became increasingly dissatisfied with the communist regime in her home country, and this discontentment cast a shadow on her future life and career in Benin. The government had not only limited freedom of speech, but it had also banned popular music from bands such as the Beatles and the Jackson 5, allowing only communist propaganda to air. In 1983,

Kidjo left Benin for Paris in order to escape communism and the suppressive politics in her home country.[250]

While in Paris, Kidjo dabbled in opportunities outside of music, but always reverted to singing. Paris proved to be a challenge, but one that she embraced, leading her to meeting her husband, Jean Hebrail. Kidjo built up Western recognition after a couple of years, and in 1985, she sang with the band Pili Pili. In the late 1980s, Kidjo gained recognition in Paris. Chris Blackwell, founder of Island Records, signed her to its label in 1991. Kidjo remained with Island Records as long as Blackwell did, recording four separate albums during her time with the company. She later signed a deal with Columbia Records. In 2007, she released her eighth studio album, Djin Djin, receiving a Grammy Award for Best Contemporary World Music Album in 2008.

Kidjo accepted many nominations and more than forty awards throughout the course of her career, including a second Grammy Award in 2015 for her world music album *Eve*. She was also awarded honorary doctorates from Yale University, Berklee College of Music, and Middlebury College. Kidjo was invited to perform at the Nobel Peace Prize concert in Oslo in 2002, honoring former US President Jimmy Carter. She also sang at the Nobel Peace Prize ceremony in 2011, honoring Ellen Johnson Sirleaf, Leymah Gbowee, and Tawakul Karman.

The distinguished musical talents of Kidjo elevated her to fame through which she represents those in need. In addition, Kidjo gives voice to people who may otherwise not be heard.[251] She was named goodwill ambassador to UNICEF in 2002, allowing her to collaborate on numerous humanitarian aid projects in Benin, as well as other countries throughout Africa. In Benin, Kidjo has been a dynamic presence, fighting against domestic abuse, child marriage, and female genital mutilation—a troika of evils. She collaborated in 2012 with the Italian Mission to the United Nations and performed a concert at the UN General Assembly Hall called "Raise your Voice to End Female Genital Mutilation."

Kidjo speaks eight languages fluently and uses these vocal skills to speak for defenseless people—especially women—across the world. Her position of stardom on the world stage motivates her to push on important humanitarian agendas. Her music inspires, and her tireless actions address challenging issues, giving hope and strength to humanity around the globe for a better future.

Misty Copeland

Born: September 10, 1982
Country: The United States of America

"The best piece of advice that I remember probably on a daily basis is to accept everything about me that is different. That is what makes me special." [252]

At the age of thirteen, Misty Copeland's ballet training began, which was later than the typical age for ballerinas. Nonetheless, she quickly excelled, dancing on point after only three months. From this impressive beginning, Copeland went on to impress audiences, rising to stardom as one of the best dancers of all time.[253]

She was born on September 10, 1982, in Kansas City, Missouri; she moved with her mother and siblings at a young age to San Pedro, California.[254] Much of Copeland's childhood was spent living at a quaint motel named Sunset Inn. Copeland would pretend that the Sunset Inn balcony was her studio, utilizing the railing for her daily exercises.[255] Copeland's interest in dance was unexpected. One of her teachers took notice of her raw talent and natural dancing ability and advised Copeland to look into classes at the Boys and Girls Club in San Pedro.

Copeland took her teacher's advice. At the club, she met Cindy Bradley. Her skills were honed by Bradley, who took Copeland into her home. Bradley provided her with an environment conducive to learning where Copeland could focus on her studies and dance.

Eventually, a legal custody battle ensued between Bradley and Copeland's mother, whereby Copeland attempted emancipation from her mother through the courts. However, she was unsuccessful. Copeland returned to her mother's home and attended San Pedro High School while training at Lauridsen Ballet Centre.[256] In 1999, she was awarded a scholarship to attend a summer ballet program through the American Ballet Theater (ABT).

Kevin McKenzie, who served as the theater director of the American Ballet Theatre (ABT), immediately noticed Copeland's talent, and her career began to take flight. Despite the naysayers and racial challenges, she persisted. Not only has Copeland demonstrated a raw talent and passion for ballet and the arts, but she also has proven to be a trailblazer, a pioneer, and an activist. Copeland is unafraid to use her gifts and her voice to accomplish the unexpected. She has danced in hundreds of ballet performances throughout the US and abroad. In 2015, Copeland made history as the first African American to become a principal dancer in the seventy-five-year run of the ABT.

CHAPTER IX
Communications & Media

INTRODUCTION
Communications & Media

Nowadays, with the advent of social media, distant communication has become seconds away. Before books and newspapers, there were slates; prior to e-mail, there was the facsimile; long before airplanes, there were steamboats; and telegrams predated telephones. Moreover, radios paved the way for televisions; beepers gave way to cellular telephones; and the computer has long made typewriters all but obsolete. Facebook competes with Twitter, and e-commerce, e-medicine, e-business, and e-classrooms are commonplace.

All of these advances bring people, who are great distances apart, closer. Thus, the world is smaller. In our rapidly changing environment, the universal urge is to know and to know *now*. At the same time, the media is pressured not just to inform, but also to educate, entertain, be "fair and balanced," "swear to the dogmas of no master," be accountable, be responsible, and help create a more enlightened citizenry.

Not everyone uses advancements in communications and media for positive purposes. These misapplications range from mail bombs to contemptible tabloids, from terrorist networks to gang bangers. But these craven employments are in the minority. In the mainstream, communications and media are beneficial tools for good, knitting people together.

Who are the leaders in Africa and the diaspora (past and present) that developed and expanded communications and media to challenge the status quo, debunk ancient myths, and shatter stereotypes? Who through the written and spoken word best-advanced information, activation, and reformation to promote justice, inclusion and equality?

It is postulated that in the arena of communications and media, the ten black persons who did the most to change the world for the better are as follows:

Alexander Sergeyevich Pushkin

Born: June 6, 1799
Died: February 10, 1837
Country: The Russian Federation

"It is better to have dreamed a thousand dreams that never were than never to have dreamed at all." [257]

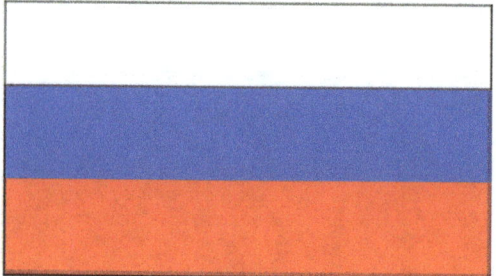

He was a poet, playwright, and novelist of the 1800s. Now, he is revered as the founder of modern Russian literature. Alexander Sergeyevich Pushkin was born in Moscow on June 6, 1799, to Sergei Lvovich Pushkin and Nadezhda Ossipovna Gannibal. Pushkin's great grandfather, Abraham Gannibal—an Afro-Russian nobleman from Cameroon—was raised by Peter the Great.

Pushkin engaged in writing poetry from an early age. At fourteen, he wrote his first poem (1813) as a student at Tsarskoe Selo Lyceum. Pushkin's writing talent flourished through his teenage years. He was particularly influenced by French poetry and literature as well as Russian Neoclassicism.[258]

Following his graduation in 1817, Pushkin joined the Russian Ministry of Foreign Affairs in 1818 and continued to practice his literary and poetry writing. In 1820, he gained widespread fame and recognition for his fairy- tale poem, "Ruslan and Ludmila." Although the poem drew attention to his abilities, it also created controversy, because the poem's style was unconventional in its verse methods. Pushkin's writing merged his views on Russian society with his works, particularly in his "Ode to Liberty"—a poem considered too critical of the Russian government. Consequently, Pushkin's writings were determined to represent thoughts that were too radical, resulting in his exile from St. Petersburg and Moscow.

Pushkin moved to several locations (Crimea, Caucasus in the south, and Chisinau) after being forced out of St. Petersburg. During this time, the Greek Revolution influenced his writing, and he diligently recorded the events of the war. In 1823, Pushkin moved to Odessa, where he wrote *Yevgeny Onegin* (also known as *Eugene Onegin*), a novel written in verse that eerily foreshadowed Pushkin's death. Over the course of seven years, Pushkin wrote *Yevgeny Onegin*, creating an entirely new style of prose.[259] Pushkin's literature continued to agitate government officials, and Odessa's governor insisted that the Tsar ban Pushkin from Odessa.

In 1825, Pushkin wrote *Boris Godunov*, which evolved into one of his most recognized plays. However, *Boris Godunov* was not performed until several years later, as it was government censored. Finally, in 1826, when Tsar Nicholas I came to power, Pushkin appealed to him for a pardon. Tsar Nicholas I granted the reprieve, and Pushkin returned to Moscow and St. Petersburg.[260]

Following his acceptance back into Russian society, Pushkin produced important literary works—some reflecting his time in exile. These writings included the narrative poem, *Prisoner of the Caucasus*.[261] He also wrote the novel, *The Captain's Daughter* in 1836; this work became notable, because it romanticized the Pugachev's Rebellion—one of Russia's largest peasant uprisings. Prior to this work in 1829, Pushkin met Natalya Goncharova, and they married in 1831.

Pushkin was highly regarded, despite the challenges and suppression he continued to face. In 1833, he was elected to the Russian Academy. By this time, his marriage to Natalya was marred by rumors of infidelity. Pushkin suspected that she was unfaithful to him, because many men pursued Natalya due to her beauty. George D'Anthès-Heeckeren in particular openly courted Natalya while she was married to Pushkin. Pushkin challenged D'Athnes to a duel with guns as the weapons of choice. He managed to wound D'Athnes, but Pushkin was not as fast as his opponent. Consequently, Pushkin was critically wounded by gunshot.[262] He survived for two days. On February 10, 1837, Pushkin passed away.

The final novel that Pushkin left behind, unfinished, was *The Moor of Peter the Great*. He wrote the story in honor of his grandfather and in celebration of his African heritage.[263] Devotees mourned his loss at his modest funeral. Pushkin's poetry and literature profoundly impacted art in his country and around the world. He is revered as an unofficial poet laureate of Russia. With nobility, Pushkin expressed his conscience, regardless of the consequences.

Leopold Sedar Senghor

Born: October 9, 1906
Died: December 20, 2001
Country: The Republic of Senegal

"I have always taken care to put an idea or emotion behind my words. I have made it a habit to be suspicious of the mere music of words." [264]

Leopold Sedar Senghor became the first president of Senegal, following the country's proclamation of independence. He was not only a revered politician, but also an acclaimed writer and poet, who contributed to the creation of the intellectual movement called negritude. In addition, Senghor was the first African to be elected into the prestigious Académie Française.

Born the fifth of six children on October 9, 1906, into a well-off Serer Catholic family, Leopold Senghor grew up in the coastal city of Joal–Fadiouth in Senegal (then French West Africa). Senghor began boarding school in 1914 at the age of eight in the small village of N'Gasobil. Almost a decade later, in 1923, he enrolled in the College Liberman in Dakar, where he excelled academically and passed the baccalaureate examination in 1927. For his achievements, he was granted a scholarship by the French government; this award allowed Senghor to travel to France in 1928, continuing his education at the Lycée Louis-le-Grand. In 1931, he studied French literature at the University of Paris (the Sorbonne). There, he met Francophone poet, Aimé Césaire.[265]

Through his friendship with Césaire, he formed other connections, mainly with African Americans and Caribbean citizens. Senghor also developed an interest in the Harlem Renaissance and New Negro Movement. In 1934, he was elected to the post of chairman of the student union. Senghor was inspired by the writings and teachings of blacks and, along with Césaire, founded the journal, *L'Étudiant Noir*. The concept of negritude was first explored by Senghor in his writings in 1936 and spurred from his observations of racist sentiments toward blacks in France and other Western cultures. Negritude, however, also garnered great criticism from white and black people.

With the outbreak of the Second World War, Senghor joined the French infantry ranks; he was taken prisoner by Germans for over a year (1940). While captive, he continued to write, and later, he published his poems and articles (1943). Upon his release, he joined the French Resistance for a time. Eventually, Senghor returned to his teaching career.[266]

Near the end of the war, Senghor met Lamine Gueye, a Senegalese politician, who convinced him to run for the Assemblée Nationale Française elections. After his win, he received great support from the Senegalese people; however, over the years, he became increasingly dissatisfied with party politics. Consequently, he created his own party, the Bloc Democratique Senegalais; this organization joined an independent group of the Assemblée Nationale Française. Throughout these years, Senghor's writings and poems were immersed with his political activities and beliefs.

West African countries demanded independence, and eventually, the French Parliament passed the Loi-Cadre (Reform Act) in 1959.[267] This new law provided greater autonomy to French African territories. Senghor ultimately led the independence movement for Senegal by appealing directly to French President Charles de Gaulle later that year. He became the first freely elected president of newly independent Senegal in 1960. Two years into his presidency, there was an attempted coup d'état; the overthrow was quickly suppressed with the support of the Senegalese people. In 1963, Senghor was reelected president and survived in 1967 an assassination attempt, successfully serving until he voluntarily left office in 1980.

Senghor's many accomplishments demonstrated his ability to build bridges among cultures via effective communication, regarding religion, culture, or politics. He was able to meet the needs of the Senegalese people, who were predominantly Muslim, despite the fact that he was raised a Serer Catholic. His political wit and ability to express his ideas clearly— through speech and written works—proved that Senghor was capable of reaching both the African and Western audiences. While he deeply supported his own Senegalese people, he also had a genuine appreciation for France and the French language. Senghor implemented modern educational systems throughout Senegal and maintained French as one of the central languages.

Over the course of his long and eventful life, Leopold Senghor was decorated with many honors. He was the recipient of thirty-seven honorary doctoral degrees. Senghor was presented the Grand-Croix of the Légion d'honneur and the Grand Croix of l'Ordre National du Mérite. In 1971, he was awarded the Commemorative Medal for the 2,500th Anniversary of the founding of the Persian Empire, and in 1978, Senghor was granted the Prix mondial Cino Del Duca. In 1994, he was the recipient of the African Studies Association's Lifetime Achievement Award, honoring his efforts to make the world a better place. Leopold Senghor passed away on December 20, 2001.

John Harold Johnson

Born: January 19, 1918
Died: August 8, 2005
Country: The United States of America

"It's better to get smart than to get mad. I try not to get so insulted that I will not take advantage of an opportunity to persuade people to change their minds." 268

John H. Johnson was born on January 19, 1918, and raised in Arkansas City, Arkansas. A tragic sawmill accident claimed his father's life, so he was raised by his mother and stepfather. His childhood was challenging, due largely to the segregation that the black community faced at that time. Growing up in a rural area under segregation meant that African American high schools did not exist for him. Johnson repeated the eighth grade in order to stay in school an extra year. This time period was also marked by considerable financial hardships for the family due in part to the Great Depression.

At the age of fifteen, Johnson accompanied his mother to Chicago, Illinois, for the 1933 Chicago World's Fair. The northern city event opened their eyes to the possibilities the region had to offer, and his family moved permanently to Chicago that same year.[269] The opportunities in Chicago ultimately contributed to Johnson's future successes.

In Chicago, Johnson's parents endeavored to find steady jobs. Eventually, they found employment, and Johnson did as well. He worked at the National Youth Administration (NYA), a division that operated under the Works Progress Administration (WPA), where Johnson's stepfather was employed. Before long, Johnson resumed his studies by attending DuSable High. His classmates included future celebrities—jazz musician, Nat King Cole and comedian, Redd Foxx.

Johnson excelled in school. He was voted student-council president. In addition, he was editor of the school's newspaper. When he graduated in 1963, he was offered admission to the University of Chicago with a full-tuition scholarship. Initially, he decided he would not be able to attend, because the scholarship did not cover additional room-and-board costs.

As fate would have it, because of his academic achievements during high school, he was invited to speak at an Urban League dinner. His speech impressed the president of Supreme Life Insurance Company, Harry Pace. As a result, Pace offered Johnson a job in order to help him pay his additional university expenses. This position gave Johnson the funds he needed to attend both the University of Chicago and Northwestern University.

Through the inspiration he gained from his studies in journalism, his position as Pace's assistant, and with *Reader's Digest*, Johnson endeavored to create his own magazine. In order to accomplish his goal, he needed to complete a couple of steps. The first action was to calculate the demand for a magazine that targeted black audiences. His position at Supreme Life Insurance Company allowed him to poll people's interest by sending letters offering prepaid subscriptions. Next, Johnson needed to secure money for the postage stamps to mail the letters of inquiry. His mother put her furniture up as collateral for the $500 postage costs.

The polling paid off, and in 1942, Johnson produced his own magazine for black readership called the *Negro Digest* and founded his business, the Johnson Publishing Company. Unfortunately, Johnson found that securing vendors for *Negro Digest* was difficult. Many vendors initially refused to sell his magazine on their newsstands, because it was geared to black customers. Johnson was persistent and rallied friends to influence vendors, and thereby, he achieved his goal by catching the attention of distributor, Joseph Levy. Johnson collaborated with Levy in the development of marketing plans for his magazine. Their strategies improved distribution and secured vendors in major cities.[270]

Negro Digest was popular, selling an estimated three thousand copies in its first press run. Readership soon expanded to fifty thousand copies monthly. The content of the magazine highlighted African American interests, literature, and news regarding social challenges. *Negro Digest* also attracted the attention of United States First Lady Eleanor Roosevelt, who contributed to the "If I Were a Negro" column of the magazine. Her article doubled sales overnight.[271]

The success of his first magazine inspired Johnson to remain in the industry, and in 1945, he created the monthly periodical, *Ebony*. This publication also focused on African American interests. The first press run for *Ebony* magazine sold out its twenty five thousand copies.[272] The magazine's circulation soon exploded to approximately 1.7 million monthly; the tremendous sales accelerated Johnson's career to new heights.

His first magazine, *Negro Digest*, was renamed *Black World*, and its evolution focused more on black political, social, and economic concerns. However, *Black World* was discontinued in 1976, allowing another publication Johnson created, Jet magazine, to flourish due to less competition. *Jet* magazine (founded by Johnson in 1951) was referred to as a mini Bible for blacks during the civil rights movement. *Jet* was last sold, in printed form, in June 2014.

Ebony magazine remains John H. Johnson's primary legacy. He was the first African American to be recognized on the *Forbes Magazine* "400" list, ranking amongst America's wealthiest.

From small and impoverished means, Johnson worked tirelessly to build his publishing empire, and ultimately, he branched into other areas of business. He became the president and CEO of Supreme Life Insurance Company, and he further diversified his interests by delving into the cosmetics industry and serving on the board of directors of other corporations.

During his lifetime, Johnson was the recipient of many awards, including the 1966 NAACP Spingarn Medal for his positive contributions to improving race relations. In 1951, the United States Chamber of Commerce honored him with the Young Man of the Year award, designating him as the first African American to receive the honor. President Bill Clinton presented Johnson with the Presidential Medal of Freedom. Johnson passed away on August 8, 2005.

Chinua Achebe
(Albert Chinualumogu Achebe)

Born: November 16, 1930
Died: March 21, 2013
Country: The Federal Republic of Nigeria

"One of the truest tests of integrity is its blunt refusal to be compromised." [273]

Things Fall Apart was published in over fifty languages and remains the best-known and best-remembered literary work by Nigerian author, Chinua Achebe. His 1958 novel about the life of the ambitious protagonist, Okonkwo—who was forced into exile following a series of unfortunate events—became a modern classic. The central themes highlight the clash of cultures between colonialism and traditional societies in Nigeria, as well as touching upon gender, masculinity, fear, and legacy.

Born Albert Chinualumogu Achebe on November 16, 1930, in Ogidi, Nigeria, Achebe grew up with the traditions of the oratory Igbo culture.[274] This environment taught him the significance and captivating power of storytelling. He was strong academically, demonstrating his intelligence at a young age. This helped him to excel and in his early teens, he moved to a new school in Nekede, Nigeria. There, Achebe was exposed to the traditional art practices of the Igbo tribe called Mbari; they left a lasting impression on him. At the age of fourteen, he was accepted into the prestigious Government College in the southern Nigerian city of Umuahia. While at Government College, Achebe explored every book the library had to offer, particularly classic novels. From his reading, he learned about the plight of Africans during colonization, but strangely, he identified with the colonialists, rather than his fellow Africans.

Aspiring to continue his education, Achebe took the entrance exam to attend the newly opened University of Ibadan in 1948. While at university, he studied medicine through a bursary he received as a result of his high test scores. However, the literary world beckoned him. After he read Joyce Cary's novel, *Mister Johnson*, he was struck with a deep realization, regarding the negative portrayals of black people and the kinds of justification and acceptance much of the world granted to colonialist subjugation and racism.[275] Achebe switched his major from medicine to English studies. He began to write and publish his first articles and stories in the university newspaper. Achebe completed his studies in 1953, and several years later, he published *Things Fall Apart*.

Eventually, Achebe left Nigeria and headed to the United States; there, he wrote about Nigeria's past, including colonialism and its degradation of the value of African literature and its other negative impacts on the world. In 1977, Achebe examined and criticized Joseph Conrad's book, *Heart of Darkness* in his lecture, "An Image of Africa: Racism in Conrad's 'Heart of Darkness'" to prove how ingrained and degrading this kind of writing about colonial Africa was. Achebe was a pioneer for African literature and an unrelenting voice that could not, for any reason, be quieted. More importantly, people listened to what Achebe had to say. He gained significant recognition for his work and advocacy that his compelling story could not be ignored.

Achebe was awarded the Nigerian National Merit Award in 1979, and he taught at universities across the US and in Africa. After his retirement from teaching in 1982, Achebe entered politics; he became the deputy national vice president of the People's Redemption Party, but failed in his bid to obtain power.

In 1987, he was nominated for the Booker McConnell Prize for *Anthills of the Savannah*; however, he did not win. Subsequently, in 2007, he won the Man Booker International Prize for fiction.[276] Achebe was also the recipient of a Rockefeller Scholarship and a UNESCO Fellowship for Creative Artists.

In 1990, Achebe was in a serious car accident that left him paralyzed and permanently dependent on a wheelchair. He accepted a post to teach at Bard College that he held for more than a decade. Later, Achebe joined Brown University's faculty for Africana Studies and was appointed the David and Marianna Fisher University professor.[277]

In 2010, Achebe was awarded the Dorothy and Lillian Gish Prize. His last book, *There Was a Country: A Personal History of Biafra*, was released in 2012; it addressed the Nigerian Civil War. Achebe passed away March 21, 2013.[278]

Derek Alton Walcott

Born: January 23, 1930
Died: March 17, 2017
Country: Saint Lucia

"Break a vase, and the love that reassembles the fragments is stronger than that love which took its symmetry for granted when it was whole." [279]

Derek Alton Walcott was born January 23, 1930, on the island of Saint Lucia in the capital city of Castries. He developed his natural talent for writing throughout his life and was the recipient of the Nobel Prize in Literature in 1992. Raised with his twin brother, Roderick, and sister, Pamela, Walcott acquired his love of poetry at an early age. He was greatly influenced by his mother—a teacher who recited poetry—and his father—a painter and poet. Walcott's father tragically passed away from mastoiditis before he and his brother were born. Fortunately, the paintings and poetry his father left behind served to inspire him.[280]

Walcott possessed an artistic inclination, perhaps partly inspired by his mother and partly spurred from his genetics. Greatly inspired by the French artist,

Cézanne, Walcott demonstrated a talent for painting at an early age. He studied with Harold "Harry" Simmons—a good friend of Walcott's late father. At the age of fourteen, Walcott gravitated towards writing as well.[281] The local St. Lucia newspaper, *The Voice*, published his first poem, "1944."[282] At the age of eighteen, Walcott had his first poetry collection (*25 Poems*) printed with his mother's financial support. The next year (1949), his second collection of poems, *Epitaph for the Young: XII Cantos*, was published. Walcott's works garnered acclaim from many, including Barbadian writer and poet Frank Collymore.

The talent that Walcott demonstrated earned him a Colonial Development and Welfare Scholarship; the prize allowed him to attend the University College of the West Indies in Kingston, Jamaica, where he studied poetry and literature. In 1951, he published his next volume of work, called *Poems*.[283]

Following graduation from university, Walcott relocated to the United States with the funding from a Rockefeller Foundation Fellowship; thereby, he became a student of theater. When he completed his stint in the US, he moved to Trinidad (1953), where he continued writing poetry, stories, and plays. Walcott and his brother, Roderick, founded the Trinidad Theatre Workshop in 1959. A few years later (1962), he published one of his most recognized works, *In a Green Night: Poems 1948–1960*, that highlighted his Caribbean heritage. Through this collection of poems, Walcott expressed his deep-rooted attachment to his Caribbean and African roots as well as his European ancestry. The poems also raised concerns about colonialism and its aftermath.[284]

In addition to his many stories and poems, Walcott worked as director of the Trinidad Theatre Workshop. Several years later, he accepted a post as an English professor at Boston University.[285] In 1970, he produced his popular play, *Dream on Monkey Mountain* that was broadcast on NBC. Produced off-Broadway by the Negro Ensemble Company, *Dream on Monkey Mountain* was honored with an Obie Award for Best Foreign Play (1971).[286]

As a teacher at Boston University, Walcott established the Boston Playwrights' Theatre (1981), where he taught courses in literature and writing for two decades. The same year (1981), he was awarded the prestigious MacArthur Foundation Fellowship, because his writing powerfully touched upon the relationships that man has with God and society.

Walcott's numerous plays, stories, and essays became increasingly popular and recognized. In 1988, he had the great honor of receiving the Queen's Medal for Poetry. One of his most notable written works was called *Omeros*, published in 1990. The epic poem depicts the story of two fishermen from the Caribbean, who make the long journey home to West Africa. Walcott received the W. H. Smith Literary Award in 1990 for *Omeros*. Two years later (1992), he was awarded the Nobel Prize for Literature. Walcott received many other honors for his breakthrough work, including the Anisfield-Wolf Book Award for Lifetime Achievement (2004); T. S. Eliot Prize (2011); and Knight Commander of the Order of Saint Lucia (2016). In addition, Walcott was a professor of literature, an honorary member of the American Academy and Institute of Arts and Letters, and a professor of poetry at Essex University in the UK, where he received an honorary doctorate (2008).

Wole Soyinka
(Akinwande Oluwole Babatunde Soyinka)

Born: July 13, 1934

Country: The Federal Republic of Nigeria

"Books and all forms of writing are terror to those who wish to suppress the truth." [287]

Akinwande Oluwole Babatunde Soyinka was born in west Nigeria in a city called Abeokuta on July 13, 1934. Inquisitive and observant, he often asked his parents questions about religion, traditions, and beliefs. Soyinka was raised with the influences of both Anglicanism and the traditional teachings of Yoruba. His mother was a highly religious market owner. His father was an Anglican Minister and head of Soyinka's school.[288]

Soyinka's observant nature characterized him as one who could draw conclusions and challenge people. From a perceptive young man, he flowered into a playwright, poet, novelist, Nobel Prize winner, and political activist. Soyinka published numerous works that continue to raise important questions that provoke his followers to think and observe.

In 1952, Soyinka studied at the University College in Ibadan, where he assisted in organizing a group of political activists (Pyrates Confraternity); this group spoke out against injustices in Nigeria. In 1954, when Soyinka was approximately twenty years old, he moved to England to pursue his BA in English at the University of Leeds. Already focused on writing during this time, he served as editor of the university's magazine, *The Eagle*.

Following graduation, Soyinka remained at the University of Leeds to earn his master's degree. He became involved with London's Royal Court Theatre. During this time, his earlier plays, such as *The Swamp Dwellers* (1958) and *The Lion and the Jewel* (1959), gained attention.[289] In 1960, Soyinka returned to Nigeria to pursue African and theatre studies after accepting the Rockefeller bursary award. That year, Soyinka founded a theatre group, The 1960 Masks, and wrote *A Dance of the Forest*. This work was honored as the official play for Nigerian Independence Day, because it raised political arguments and highlighted criticisms of Nigeria's political leaders.

In 1962, Soyinka taught English at the Obafemi Awolowo University in Ile-Ife, where he was outspoken about the Nigerian government. He released his first film, *Culture in Transition*, in 1963, and in 1964, he published *The Interpreters*, a novel that gained international recognition. Soyinka also created the Orisun Theatre Company, where he trained actors.[290] In 1964, Soyinka was arrested for acting against the central government. As a consequence, he was forced to spend two months in prison.[291] After his release, Soyinka championed the cause for peace in Nigeria. He was rearrested, based on accusations that he conspired with Biafra rebels. While in prison he published a letter that detailed the illegality of his arrest; he wound up in solitary confinement for twenty-two months. Soyinka managed to publish *Idanre and Other Poems* while imprisoned. He continued to write extensively until his release in 1969, following the defeat of the Biafran.

Following his imprisonment, Soyinka sought refuge in the South of France. Eventually, he returned to Nigeria and the University of Ibadan, as director of the Department of Theater Arts. Here, he was responsible for overseeing play and film productions. However, tensions from the civil war persisted; he was forced to move back to Europe, where he accepted teaching posts at Oxford and Cambridge Universities. In 1975, Oxford University Press published one of Soyinka's best-known plays, *Death and the King's Horseman*. That same year, he moved to Ghana, where he worked for *Transition* magazine as its editor. Soyinka strived to be a political agitator, writing columns in his magazine that criticized politics in Africa.[292]

Soyinka was honored with the Nobel Prize for Literature in 1986, making him the first African author to win the prestigious award. Soyinka dedicated the honor to Nelson Mandela in his acceptance speech, "This Past Must Address Its Present". His address at the ceremony helped to draw particular attention to the turmoil that South Africa was withstanding under apartheid.[293]

Following his Nobel Prize honor, Soyinka produced more written works, including the 1988 collection, *Mandela's Earth and Other Poems*. In 1994, Soyinka was appointed UNESCO Goodwill Ambassador. He eventually moved to the US, following the ascension of a new political dictator in Nigeria, General Sani Abacha. Throughout the US, Soyinka taught at top universities, including Yale, Emory, and Harvard. Soyinka remains a compelling voice, not only in popular literature and plays, but also via his incorruptible stand against injustices and abuses of power around the world.

Catherine L. Hughes
(Catherine Elizabeth Woods)

Born: April 22, 1947

Country: The United States of America

"It is not enough for you to do your very best. You must do what is required of the situation." [294]

Catherine Elizabeth Woods was born on April 22, 1947, in Omaha, Nebraska. She has become one of the leading African American radio and television personalities. Hughes was raised in the north-side housing projects in Omaha. Her father was the first African American to earn an accounting degree from the University of Creighton, and her mother was a nurse. Hughes' parents bought her a radio when she was nine years old, precipitating her love for radio and communications. She became pregnant at the age of 16 with her son, Alfred Liggins. Becoming a mother motivated Hughes to succeed even more.[295]

Like her father, Hughes attended the University of Creighton as well as the University of Nebraska. In 1969, while attending university, she landed her first job in radio at Omaha's black radio station, KOWH. Increasingly noticed, she enjoyed popularity at KOWH. In fact, Dean Tony Brown of Howard University's School of Communications visited the station in 1971, and Hughes made a good impression on him. Consequently, Brown offered her a full- time position with Howard University as a professor and the post of assistant to the dean in the Department of Communications. These appointments bolstered her career in communications. Hughes moved to Washington DC to take on her new roles.

In 1973, Hughes also began to work for WHUR-FM radio station, eventually becoming its general sales manager in 1975.[296] Her efforts and natural expertise in the industry greatly increased the radio station's ratings, placing the station at number three and producing a significant return on its investment in her. Subsequently, the station's revenue increased from $300,000 dollars per year to over $3 million dollars a year.[297] Hughes also became the first female head of a station in Washington DC during her tenure with WHUR-FM.

In 1979, Hughes purchased her first radio production set, and by 1980, she was motivated to purchase and run her own radio station. After reaching out to over thirty banks, she was finally granted a loan; she bought the failing Washington DC station WOL-AM. This proved to be a challenging investment for Hughes; the debt was more of a burden than she initially anticipated, leading to a period of great struggles in her life. She lost her home and car. In addition, she was forced to live at the WOL-AM office with her son, using the public bathrooms. Despite the setbacks, Hughes pushed forward, and eventually, Radio One came into fruition.

On her radio station, Hughes created the *Cathy Hughes Show*. Her talk show proved to be a success, ultimately staying on air for fourteen years. By 1986, Radio One finally turned a profit, and Hughes applied the returns to a purchase of another radio station. Hughes then bought WMMJ-FM, marking another victory for her. (The number of stations Hughes controlled eventually grew to sixty-five.) In 1994, she struck one of the largest deals ever made among minority-owned stations by acquiring WKYS-FM; over the next five years, Hughes continued to acquire more radio stations, building a positive reputation for business.[298]

When others tried to persuade her to play more music, rather than talk shows, Hughes was unwavering in her programming vision. Despite challenges, she remained steadfast in providing the public with a platform to discuss issues critical to African Americans.

In 1997, Hughes stepped down from her CEO position at Radio One, becoming chairperson and secretary of the company. Her son took her place as CEO, and he turned Radio One into a public corporation; it earned $172 million dollars during its initial public offering. While Hughes was no longer Radio One's CEO, the station remained in the family, and the downsizing of her responsibilities allowed for her to launch TV One in 2004. TV One, a cable-television station, was launched on Martin Luther King Jr. Day with the African American community as its target audience.

Hughes' life demonstrates that when one has powerful ideas and the perseverance to implement them despite obstacles, great successes can follow. Today, both Radio One and TV One operate profitably with Radio One becoming a multibillion-dollar company and the largest African American-owned station in the United States with a public outreach of over fourteen-million listeners. Hughes' personal fortune amounts to approximately $300 million dollars. Becoming the first African American woman to lead a major public media company will be her legacy.

Oprah Gail Winfrey

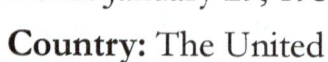

Born: January 29, 1954
Country: The United States of America

"Be thankful for what you have; you'll end up having more. If you concentrate on what you don't have, you will never, ever have enough." [299]

Over the years, she has topped many lists for her outstanding achievements, including "One of the Most Influential People" (*Forbes Magazine* 2013) and the "*Time 100: The Most Important People of the Century.*" "Orpah" Gail Winfrey was born in Kosciusko, Mississippi, on January 29, 1954. Her name, "Orpah," came from the Book of Ruth in the Bible, but people continuously mispronounced her name as Oprah—it eventually stuck. Winfrey's childhood beginnings were unstable. Her mother was a teenager when she gave birth to Winfrey, and the pregnancy had been unexpected. During her early years, Winfrey was left under the protection of her grandmother, who took good care of her. She attended church with her grandmother and as a result of living with her, learned to read at an early age.

After six years, Winfrey's mother returned, and mother and daughter relocated to Milwaukee, Wisconsin. Her mother, some would say, was a negligent parent, and Winfrey suffered the consequences of this inadequacy. When she was nine years old, she was brutally raped and subsequently molested until she was fourteen. Winfrey wanted to escape her horrific circumstances, so she ran away from home. When she was fourteen, she gave birth; tragically, the child passed away prematurely. Winfrey suffered alone and felt betrayed by her own family, because they would not believe the abuse she had been forced to endure.

She managed to attend school and quickly proved to be one of the brightest students in her class. She was eventually enrolled at a well-off school; her bus rides were difficult, because other students would tease her for being poor. Her high marks and excellent oratory skills led her to win a full-tuition scholarship at Tennessee State University.[300] After graduation, Winfrey began her career in communications as a news anchor for WLAC-TV, where she enjoyed the prestige of being the first black female news anchor.[301]

In 1976, Winfrey moved to Baltimore to anchor the news at WJZ-TV. From this point, her career blossomed; more opportunities emerged, not only in news, but also in other areas of television. After several years as news anchor and a television personality on Baltimore talk shows, Winfrey relocated to Chicago (1983). The morning talk show for WLS-TV initially reported low ratings, but with Winfrey's presence, the numbers surged.[302] Her charm and intelligence caught the attention of Roger Ebert, who helped Winfrey eventually sign a deal with King World Productions. By 1986, *The Oprah Winfrey Show* was born.

The Oprah Winfrey Show introduced audiences to a new type of talk show—one that ultimately revolutionized communications on television. Winfrey made guests—from all walks of life—feel comfortable, offering her couch, her attention, and a warm setting. Her sincerity and wisdom combined with an intimate environment led to her guests exploring and divulging their darkest secrets or most difficult periods in their lives. What would normally be a private matter was shared with the world; rather than being intrusive, the interviews proved to be therapeutic for all. Winfrey's outgoing, empathetic personality touched the hearts of millions of viewers. She became a sensation, and her show quickly soared to the highest spot in television ratings.[303]

By the end of the first year, *The Oprah Winfrey Show* played on over one hundred channels, enthralled millions of viewers, and grossed $125 million. Later, Winfrey gained ownership of her show, giving her the freedom and means to create her own production company, Harpo, ("Oprah" backwards).

Winfrey's success as a cultural phenomena opened opportunities for her to expand her career.[304] She acted in her first film, *The Color Purple*, directed by Steven Spielberg (1985); the narrative—based on the novel by Alice Walker—addressed issues of sexual abuse and racism. While she did not win the trophy, Winfrey was nominated for a Golden Globe Award for Best Supporting Actress.[305]

In 2000, Winfrey launched her popular periodical, *The Oprah Magazine*, geared toward women; it reached a total circulation of over two-million people. Throughout her career she has received numerous accolades, including Emmys,

NAACP Image Awards, People's Choice Awards, and Academy Awards. President Barack Obama honored Winfrey with the Presidential Medal of Freedom in 2013.

In 2011, she established the Oprah Winfrey Network, replacing the Discovery Health Channel. As an African American woman in the entertainment business, who grew up in abusive and impoverished circumstances, Winfrey transcended her humble beginnings to become a symbol of self-propelled success. Indeed, her sensational story is crowned by a net worth of over $3 billion.

"Oprahfication" and "The Oprah Effect" aptly describe the influences Winfrey wields over her fans and the public. Her endorsements of politicians, books, ideas, and celebrities have a magnetic pull. People trust her opinion, recommendations, and outlook. Many times her endorsements have resulted in very substantial booms for the receivers. Oprah has also been revered for being incredibly generous and philanthropic. Her financial donations and humanitarian aid have set her apart as a benevolent African American woman. Many of her most significant donations were given in support of educational causes.

In 2002, Winfrey founded Oprah's Angel Network, an organization that collects donations to sustain early education. She also established the Oprah Angel Network Katrina; this group raised substantial funds to benefit the victims of Hurricane Katrina in 2005. In 2007, Winfrey donated huge sums of money to establish the Oprah Winfrey Leadership Academy for Girls in a small town outside of Johannesburg, South Africa. The school is part of her initiative to educate girls who come from impoverished backgrounds (much like she did), and demonstrate academic and leadership promise.

Winfrey inspires, uplifts, and positively influences people of all backgrounds. Her ability to connect with any person—understand them and advocate for them—has proven to be one of her strongest and most admirable qualities. She is a universal symbol of hope, radiating her power and progressive outlook to the world.

Mo Abudu
(Mosunmola Abudu)

Born: September 11, 1964
Country: The United Kingdom & The Federal Republic of Nigeria

"Your ability to make things happen is what makes you different." [306]

Often referred to as the Oprah Winfrey of Africa, Monsunmola Abudu, better known as Mo Abudu, was named in *Forbes Magazine* as "Africa's Most Successful Woman." Abudu was born in London, England, on September 11, 1964. She moved to Lagos, Nigeria, with her family at the age of seven. Abudu was raised on her grandparent's cocoa farm, which was located in South West Nigeria in Ondo State. Abudu attended school in Nigeria until the age of eleven, when her father passed away. Soon after the loss of her father, Abudu lived with a guardian in the UK. She attended school as one of three black girls among the white students.

Abudu's childhood behavior reflected her great strength and courage. From her time as a schoolgirl in Tunbridge Wells, she was required to stand up for herself constantly. Abudu has stated in many interviews that she would often be asked "ridiculous and ignorant questions" by her peers about her African roots and life growing up in Nigeria.[307] Abudu believes that those uninformed inquiries partially inspired her to someday rewrite the story of Africa. Her goal was to debunk the ideas that many in the Western world legitimately believed about her home county, and in the process, change the negative and unfounded perspectives that many people harbored.[308]

Abudu attended West Kent and MidKent Colleges. She obtained her master's degree from the University of Westminster, London, in Human Resource Management (HRM). She landed her first job as a recruitment consultant (1987). Next, she joined the Starform Group (1990 to 1992), where she managed the Corporate Credit Management Exhibition. Abudu was also employed by Esso Exploration and Production Nigeria Ltd. (ExxonMobil), where she headed the Human Resources and Administration department. In this position, she honed her business skills, particularly concentrating on corporate organization and operations.[309]

While Abudu excelled in her career in the oil and gas industry, she held a greater ambition. Since her days in Tunbridge Wells, she desired to tell Africa's story, relaying its narrative as the host of a talk show, much like *The Oprah Winfrey Show* in America. She also aspired to create a show catered to African audiences. Abudu became serious about fulfilling these dreams in 2006.

Her main challenge, initially, was her lack of experience working in television. Reportedly, she tried reaching out to Oprah Winfrey for advice via e-mails without success. Abudu persisted in fulfilling her dreams through other means eventually pitching her idea to DStv Satellite, suggesting to the producers that Africans should have their own shows, similar to Oprah's or Ellen DeGeneres'. The producers agreed and created a series with her. Since the inception of her television show, *Moments with Mo*, Abudu has interviewed major figures from around the world.[310]

While she had made progress toward her ambition, *Moments with Mo* was a regional broadcast. Abudu realized that she had not completely fulfilled her initial objective to host a large-scale talk show. She insisted on hosting a show on a grander scale, and in July 2013, EbonyLife Television was launched. This network expanded across the continent as Africa's first-ever global entertainment source. The shows, produced in English, cover a range of topics that extend from domestic abuse to fashion.

The success of EbonyLife TV programming has placed Abudu in a position from which she can dedicate her life's work to changing the skewed perceptions and negative connotations associated with Africa. Abudu has the forum that she always wanted, and she has provided Africans with their own platform, whereupon their voices are heard.

Abudu's efforts to address the misunderstandings associated with Africa have carried her on a successful journey. She is recognized globally for improving her country's image. She continues to dispel misrepresentations and address racist stereotypes on a daily basis through her network of shows. She has faced obstacles, not only as a black person, but also as a woman in show business. She combats double standards and forms of discrimination more than ever by continuing to fight.[311]

Over the course of her career, Abudu has been the recipient of numerous awards, highlighting her achievements as well as her service to humanity. She is considered by *Forbes Magazine* to be one of the "Most Powerful Women in Global TV." She was also awarded an honorary doctorate by Nigeria's Babcock University, and in 2009, she founded the nonprofit organization, Inspire Africa Foundation.

Rebecca Enonchong

Born: 1967

Country: The Republic of Cameroon

"African tech companies must be held to the same standards as companies anywhere else in the world. But we must also be given the same respect. As long as we are treated as valuable partners, we can succeed." [312]

Born in Cameroon in 1967, Rebecca Enonchong has become one of Africa's most popular technology entrepreneurs. Her father, Dr. Henry Ndifor Abi Enonchong, founded the Federal Cameroon Bar Association and worked as a popular barrister. When Enonchong was a teenager, she moved with her family to the United States. At the age of fifteen, she worked a part-time job, delivering newspaper subscriptions to area residents.

Enonchong stated that her time working with the newspaper subscription company taught her to persevere, even when she encounters obstacles. At the age of seventeen, Enonchong was promoted to manager of the company; her new position taught her business and management responsibilities as well as race relations. According to Enonchong, her biggest breaks came from white men, who appreciated her business talents and understood the plight of women (particularly black women) in business.[313]

Enonchong obtained her bachelor's and master's degrees in economics from the Catholic University of America in Washington DC. Upon completion of her studies, she began her professional career at the Inter-American Development Bank (IDB) in 1996. She worked at the IDB as a consultant for two years before joining Oracle as a consultant in 1998. In 1999, she founded her company, AppsTech, a global entity that provides enterprise technology products, applications, and services with a particular focus on Oracle software.

In 2000, Enonchong was promoted to chairman of the Africa Technology Forum, an initiative working to encourage and educate women in Africa on the use of technology; she held this post for five years. Enonchong, at the time of this writing, served as: chairman of ActivSpaces; board member for Salesforce.com Foundation; member of Advisory Board of VC4Africa; co-founder, treasurer, and vice president of Africa Business Angels Network; co-founder of I/O Spaces; and CEO of TechApps.[314]

As the founder and leader of TechApps, Enonchong continuously addresses the challenges that women in tech must overcome. She initially founded TechApps in the United States, but quickly realized the significant positive impact it could have on women in Africa.[315]

In 2005, Enonchong and her team folded the Africa Technology Forum, because the costs could no longer be sustained. As a result, the African Center for Technology, Innovation, and Ventures became Active Spaces with the support of other business partnerships. Active Spaces supports young technology entrepreneurs in Africa by providing them with offices and mentorships in order to help them realize their ideas and business ambitions.[316] The organization also provides legal and tax advice, areas often overlooked by tech entrepreneurs.

Enonchong invested in the Cameroon Angels Network, leading to the creation of the Africa Business Angels Network. Additionally, she established Africa IT Women, supporting women in their tech entrepreneurial endeavors as well as with job placements. Africa IT Women provides free training for women, but men must pay; their fees fund the technical training at the organization. Finally, Enonchong's most recent organization, I/O Spaces, is a tech hub and co-working space that assists entrepreneurs and supports Africans in the United States and Africa.[317]

Enonchong paved the way for others by changing the way that business is done across Africa. She provides education and access to information, even for those citizens who do not have internet access. Enonchong also supports the parents of young entrepreneurs through her initiative, Gifted, by purchasing materials and school supplies for their children; she arranges a generous payment plan for those struggling with finances.

Enonchong has received many awards for her inspiring work in support of young entrepreneurs (female entrepreneurs in particular) in Africa and the United States. In 2014, she was named on *Forbes Magazine* list of "10 Female Tech Founders to Watch in Africa." *IT News Africa* identified Enonchong on its "10 Africans Making Waves in Technology" list. *Black Enterprise* recognized her as a "Women of Power." She was presented with *Enterprise Africa's* African Entrepreneur Award (2001) and the World Economic Forum's Global Leader for Tomorrow honor (2002). She has also made significant contributions globally to the empowerment of women in entrepreneurship and technology.

CHAPTER X

Sports

INTRODUCTION
Sports

The Olympic Games are comprised of some forty sports; many do not enjoy universal appeal. Some of the less popular events include archery, canoe sprint, fencing, rowing, synchronized swimming, trampoline, water polo, and badminton. While the ten sports chosen for this chapter—baseball, basketball, boxing, cricket, football, golf, gymnastics, soccer, tennis, and track and field—are by no means exhaustive, they enjoy near universal appeal.

It will become readily apparent that profile selections were not based purely on individual achievements in a chosen sport. (As examples, the following athletes would have been noted if this were the only criterion met: Wilt Chamberlain or Michael Jordan for basketball, Tiger Woods for golf, Serena Williams for tennis, Usian Bolt for track and field, and Mohammed Ali for boxing.) In addition to individual success, an athlete must have played a pivotal, pioneering role in utilizing the sport to effect change.

This chapter seeks to profile the trailblazers, not only because they excelled in a sport, but also because each utilized a particular sport as a vehicle to effect fundamental change or provide a sustained measure of pleasure to enthusiasts on a global scale.

Therefore, on the basis of the foregoing, it is felt that the following black persons did more than all others to change the world through sports:

Robert "Bob" Douglas

Born: November 4, 1882
Died: July 16, 1979
Country: The Federation of Saint Kitts and Nevis

Long before Wilt Chamberlain, Bill Russell, Magic Johnson, Michael Jordon, Julius Erving, Kobe Bryant, and Stephen Curry, there was Robert "Bob" Douglas, a native of St. Kitts and Nevis, who migrated to the United States and came to be known as "The Father of Black Professional Basketball." This designation was in large part due to Douglas' formation of the first wholly professional all-black basketball team in the US or elsewhere. From 1922 to 1949, Douglas not only owned, but also coached the New York Renaissance, a professional basketball team that pre-dated the National Basketball Association (NBA, founded 1946).

It is common knowledge that during the 1920s through the 1960s, intense, overt discrimination was prevalent throughout most of the United States.[318] Douglas and his team, the "Rens," did not allow discrimination to deter them from spreading the gospel of basketball. At that time, no regular basketball league existed. Consequently, Douglas and the Rens would drive—hundreds of miles if necessary—looking for black or white teams to challenge. Very often, the team suffered the indignities of sleeping in the bus and eating stale, cold food, because they were denied admission to hotels and restaurants.

Under Douglas' guidance, the Rens became an unstoppable force. The team enjoyed almost complete dominance, winning some 2,500 games; in the 1932 to 1933 campaign, the Rens won an incredible eighty-eight straight games. No team (with the possible exception of the Harlem Globetrotters) has surpassed this landmark achievement.

Douglas' Rens were victorious at the World Professional Championship in 1939, and in 1948, the team was runner-up to the Minneapolis Lakers of the National Basketball League (NBL), forerunner to today's NBA. As a significant contributor to the sport, Douglas was the first African American to be enshrined in the National Basketball Association Hall of Fame (1972).

Jesse Owens
(James Cleveland "Jesse" Owens)

Born: December 12, 1913
Died: March 31, 1980
Country: The United States of America

"The only bond worth anything between human beings is their humanness." [319]

While Usain Bolt and Carl Lewis are the champions of gold medals in track-and-field of all time, irrespective of race, James Cleveland "Jesse" Owens will forever be king. What Joe Louis did for boxing, Jesse Owens did for track and field—positively changing perceptions among blacks and whites about the athletic prowess of black athletes.

One of ten children, Owens was born to sharecropper parents, Henry and Emma Owens. He left his birthplace of Oakville, Alabama, with his family at an early age; they settled in Cleveland, Ohio—looking for a better life. The family did not realize that racism was as rampant in the north as it was in the south. Only perhaps in the north, it was more disguised. His parents found only menial work in Ohio; therefore, in primary and high school, Owens worked to make family ends meet.

After graduation, Owens was admitted to the University of Ohio; despite his outstanding high school, track-and-field career, the college did not offer him a scholarship. Owens labored to support himself while at the university. In addition, he endured unvarnished discrimination by fellow athletes and fans. The racism was especially horrifying when he travelled out of town to compete.

Owens came to national prominence in 1935 at a Big Ten Track and Field competition in Michigan, when he set three world records and tied for a fourth. These accomplishments all but assured Owens a spot on the 1936 United States Olympic team, set to compete in Germany. This was Adolph Hitler's Germany, and Hitler saw the Olympics as a grand stage to prove the superiority of the white race.

Owens shocked Hitler by winning four gold medals in the 100-meter, 200-meter, triple-jump, and 400-meter relays. Hitler refused to shake Owens' hand—a courtesy he had extended to white gold medalists. Yet, new ground had been broken. Owens became the first American (black or white) to win four gold medals in a single Olympic meet. It took forty-eight years for this feat to be duplicated, when Carl Lewis duplicated Owens' heroics in the same events (1984).

In his book, *The Jesse Owens Story*, he recounts with obvious lamentation that upon his return to the United States from Berlin, the authorities still made him ride in the back of the bus. And Owens received no invitation to visit the White House, as was customary.[320] Indeed, when he and his wife arrived at the hall in New York—where he was being honored with a ticker-tape parade and reception after the Olympics—the doorman allowed Owens' track coach admission through the front door, but made the Owens enter via the back door.[321]

During his post-Olympic days, Owens merely scraped by; he was effectively shut out from earning a living via professional sports. So, as time went on and things grew tougher, Owens accepted a gig to race against horses as entertainment. Eventually, he found employment as a radio disc jockey, a public speaker, and founder of a public-relations firm. By his fifties, Owens enjoyed a measure of financial stability.[322]

For all Owens' enormous talents, black athletes continued to face segregation in football, basketball, and baseball. Professional boxing imposed a quota on its number of black boxers for fear that too many black fighters would keep the white fans away. Owens had opened the door to acceptance and appreciation of black athletes. Yet, it would be some time before professional sports were desegregated.

President Gerald Ford awarded Owens the Medal of Freedom in 1976. Ten years following Owens' death in 1980, President George H. W. Bush presented the Congressional Gold Medal to the Owens family. In tribute to Owens' personal achievements and contributions to world peace and outstanding, a street in Berlin—leading to a stadium—was renamed Jesse Owens Parkway.[323] In 1983, Owens was inducted into the US Olympic Hall of Fame as a charter member.

Joe Louis
(Joseph Louis Barrows)

Born: May 13, 1914
Died: April 12, 1981
Country: The United States of America

"Every man's got to figure to get beat sometime." [324]

Ask the average world citizen if he's familiar with Joseph Louis Barrows, and chances are there would be a negative response. Ask that same citizen if the name Joe Louis rings a bell, and the probability is high that the respondent's eyes would sparkle with an affirmative reply. Thirty-five years after his death, no one has surpassed Louis' record (twelve years) as the longest reigning heavyweight champion of the world.

Born in the quaint town of Lafayette, Alabama—smack in the middle of cotton fields—Louis' great grandparents were slaves, and his parents picked cotton for a living. He barely knew his father, considering that when he was a toddler, his father was admitted to a hospital with mental illness.

Louis didn't get very far in school, because he worked odd jobs to help his mother after the family relocated to Detroit, Michigan. He shifted from job to job and even attempted trade school, thinking he could become a cabinetmaker. A classmate suggested that he try his hand at boxing. Louis agreed. His first bouts were not encouraging, especially considering that he hit the canvas three times in his inaugural fight. Louis was not discouraged. At the amateur level he competed in fifty-four fights, knocking out forty-three (or 80 percent) of his opponents. Louis had found his niche; he had identified his talent and decided to pursue professional boxing in 1935.[325]

He was an instant success, earning a small fortune his first year. The next year, however, Louis (now known as the "Brown Bomber") encountered a rough and tumble German gladiator, Marx Schmeling, an Adolf Hitler acolyte. Schmeling knocked Louis out in the twelfth round. The defeat stunned and crushed Louis, not only from an athletic standpoint, but also as a black American taking on Nazi symbol. Next, Louis took on heavyweight champion, Jim Braddock (1973), and he was ready. He vanquished Braddock in the eighth round. For the next twelve years, Louis sustained zero losses. In addition, during Louis' career he defended his title twenty-five times; three of these matches went the distance.[326]

Louis was as generous in his charity, as he was in his knockouts. On more than one occasion, he donated the purse from a fight to military relief funds. The extent of Louis' contributions explains in part his post-career tax problems and impoverished state.[327]

While a boxing icon of the first order, Louis was instrumental in breaking down walls of discrimination against blacks on golf courses across the United

States. In his day, the Professional Golfers Association (PGA) did not allow black players, but Louis used his fame to access golf courses under a sponsor's exemption provision.

By the time he retired in 1949, as the undefeated heavyweight champion of the world, Louis had fought seventy matches (amateur and professional) with sixty-six wins—fifty-two of the victories by knockouts. Admirably, Louis rescued the sport from the clutches of powerful gambling interests due to his incorruptibility. Unfortunately, he earned and mostly frittered away $5 million. Louis ended up working as a casino host in Las Vegas.

The Joe Louis Arena—named in his honor—is home to the Detroit Red Wings, a professional hockey team. In 2005, the International Boxing Research Organization listed Louis as the top heavyweight boxer—bar none. Similarly, *Ring Magazine* ranked Louis as number one on its listing of "The 100 Greatest Punchers of All Time."

Jack "Jackie" Robinson

Born: January 31, 1919
Died: October 24, 1972
Country: The United States of America

"I'm not concerned with you liking or disliking me. All I ask is that you respect me as a human being." 328

He had an illustrious ten-year career as a professional baseball player. Not only was he the first black to play Major League Baseball (MLB), he also ended a sixty-year legacy of blacks—irrespective of their talents—being relegated to far less-funded and less-visible Negro Leagues. But breaking the color barrier is only the beginning of his story.

On April 15, 1947, Jack "Jackie" Robinson donned his Brooklyn Dodgers uniform for the first time, and by October 10, 1956, when he wore the uniform for the last time, Robinson had etched himself into history, based on his stellar performances. In just ten years with the Brooklyn Dodgers, he appeared in six All-Star games, played in six World Series, and won the 1955 World Series. In

1947, Robinson was named Major League Baseball's "Rookie of the Year." In 1949, the MLB named him "Most Valuable Player."[329]

In 1969, Robinson was inducted into Baseball Hall of Fame, and thirty-five years later, Major League Baseball retired his uniform ("42"); in the history of baseball, Robinson was the first professional athlete to be so honored.[330] Since 2004, MLB has added a new twist to the distinction by instituting an annual "Jackie Robinson Day," requiring every player on every team to wear #42. Robinson's career statistics make him worthy of these honors: 311 career batting averages, 1,518 hits, 139 home runs, 734 runs batted in, and 197 stolen bases.

A product of Cairo, Georgia, he was one of five children born to Jerry and Mallie Robinson, both sharecroppers. He graduated from Pasadena Junior College in 1939 and enrolled in UCLA. Shortly thereafter, Robinson became the school's first athlete to win varsity letters in four sports: baseball, basketball, football, and track.

Needless to say, Robinson's road to stardom was fraught with difficulty. When the Dodgers went to Florida for spring training, he was not allowed to stay in the same hotel with the rest of the team. At times, the team would show up to practice, and the gates would be locked to protest his presence. Some of his teammates opted to sit out rather than play with him. The St. Louis Cardinals threatened to strike if Robinson played. Through it all, there is no evidence that Robinson ever became bitter or retaliated—except by his phenomenal performance on the field. After he had been in the league several years, more blacks were allowed to play, and today, MLB is 8.5 percent black, compared to 19 percent black at its peak. No doubt that this decline would sadden Robinson.

After his illustrious baseball career, Robinson became vice president and spokesperson for Chock Full o'Nuts coffee in New York and chairman of Freedom National Bank, where he initiated loans for minorities. After suffering the debilitating effects of diabetes, he passed away on October 24, 1972. Over two thousand fans attended Robinson's funeral service in Manhattan, and thousands more lined the streets of the city during his funeral procession to pay homage to a beloved hero.[331]

Charlie Sifford
(Charles Luther Sifford)

Born: June 2, 1922
Died: February 3, 2015
Country: The United States of America

"Just let me play." [332]

What Jesse Owens was to track and field, Jackie Robinson was to baseball, and Joe Louis was to boxing, Charles Sifford was to golf.

Considering the exploits of a young Tiger Woods on the golf course, it is difficult to imagine young Sifford—blessed with exceptional golfing skills—confined to compete in the National Negro Open tournaments. During the first many years of Sifford's professional career— beginning in 1948—the Professional Golf Association (PGA) did not allow blacks to participate—no matter how talented.[333]

Born June 22, 1922, in Charlotte, North Carolina, Sifford challenged the PGA multiple times, even in the face of death threats.[334] He was allowed on the courses in North Carolina as a caddie—earning less than a dollar a day—but that's as far as the PGA would allow him to advance. At one point, the PGA stopped him from even practicing on the North Carolina courses. That injustice prompted Sifford to move to Philadelphia.

He domineered non–PGA tournaments, winning five straight titles with the all-black United Golfers Association.[335] Finally, in 1961, Sifford shattered the glass ceiling, becoming the first black allowed to compete in the PGA. By then, he was thirty-nine years old. Sifford had a distinguished professional career in the PGA, winning several major tournaments: Great Hartford Open, 1967; Los Angeles Open, 1969; and Senior PGA Championship, 1975.[336] He is the first black to be inducted into the World Golf Hall of Fame (2004), and in 2014, President Barack Obama bestowed on him the coveted Presidential Medal of Freedom.[337]

Jim Brown

Born: February 17, 1936
Country: The United States of America

"The parents are the key." [338]

According to *Sporting News* magazine, Jim Brown is the greatest professional football player ever; the statistics tend to support this conclusion. In nine seasons with the Cleveland Browns of the National Football League (NFL), Brown was without peers. Not only did he lead the league in rushing for an unprecedented eight seasons, he also twice established new NFL rushing records. In addition, Brown participated in nine Pro Bowls.

The product of Saint Simons, Georgia, and star athlete at Syracuse University became the toast of the NFL for nearly nine years. Brown, at the age of thirty, hung up his cleats to seek the bright lights of Hollywood. He enjoyed years of a successful acting career. In 1988, he discovered his true calling, when he founded the Amer-I-Can foundation. The organization initially focused on at-risk youth in Cleveland and Los Angeles; now, it has blossomed into a national youth-empowerment program with enviable acclaim.

Under the banner, "Building a Better America, One Person at a Time," Amer-I-Can has nine focus points: motivation conditioning; goal setting; problem solving and decision making; emotional control; family relationships; financial stability; effective communication; job searching and retention; and drug and alcohol abuse awareness.[339]

NFL.com ranks Brown as the number two player of all time. He made the NFL's 50th and 75th Anniversary All Time Teams, and Brown is a college and professional football Hall of Famer.

Gary Sobers
(The Right Excellent Sir Garfield St. Auburn Sobers)

Born: July 28, 1936
Country: Barbados

The Right Excellent Sir Garfield St. Auburn Sobers is uniformly regarded as the greatest all-time cricket player, and in tribute to his stellar achievements on the pitch, he is a living legend and national hero of Barbados.

In 1975, Sobers was knighted by Queen Elizabeth during her official visit to Barbados. In 1998, the government of Barbados included him among ten national heroes awarded the prefix, "The Right Excellent." (This title is considered an equivalent to the British title, "The Right Honorable.") These awards were in recognition of Sobers' record-breaking

ninety-three Test matches for the West Indies team, whereupon he scored an amazing 8,032 runs. And for the leadership he displayed in 1970, when he captained the "Rest of the World XI" World Series Cricket (WSC) tournament; these matches were held in England without South African players—a response to the then crippling apartheid system that pervaded South Africa.[340] Sobers used the sport of cricket to break down deeply entrenched forms of racial discrimination and was successful in uniting cultures and making the case that like music, sports is a universal language.

Sobers played competitively for twenty years and served as captain of the West Indies Cricket team for a record seven years. He was selected as Cricketer of the Year seven times. In 2000, he was named Cricketer of the Century. The highly-prized Sir Garfield Sobers Trophy is awarded annually to honor the player judged to be at the top of his game by the International Cricket Council.

Cricket is a major competitive sport throughout Europe, India, Africa, and countries in the Commonwealth. For decades, cricket has brought diverse peoples and cultures together. Sir Garfield Sobers stands as one of the most appreciated cricket players for his exceptional athletic skills and his broadening of the sport across racial divides.

Pelé
(Edson Arantes do Nascimento)

Born: October 23, 1940
Country: The Federative Republic of Brazil

"Soccer is 'The Beautiful Game.'" [341]

His performance during the 1962 World Cup—a supreme international tournament held every four years—was so spectacular that many wealthy European teams tried to lure him. However, the government of Brazil had already declared Pelé, an "official national treasure," making his transfer out of Brazil most unlikely.

Today, decades after retirement, Pelé is still almost universally regarded as the greatest soccer player of all time. He was voted World Player of the Century by the International Federation of Football History and Statistics in 1999. Also that year, Pelé was elected Athlete of the Century by the International Olympic Committee. *Time* magazine listed him among its "100 Most Influential People of the 20th Century." In 2013, the Federation of International Football Association awarded Pelé the *Ballon d'Or Prix d'Honneur* in recognition of his career and achievements as a global icon of soccer.

Not only is Pelé the highest goal scorer in the world (541 league goals), he also scored close to 1,300 goals in 1,300 games for which he is listed in the Guinness World Records.

Pelé was born into poverty in Tres Coracoes, Brazil, but was raised in Sao Paulo, where his father taught him soccer. Unable to afford a ball, Pelé created one by covering a rock with newspapers and securing them with a string. At the age of fourteen, he led his team to seven state youth championships, and by age sixteen, Pelé was playing professionally for Santos.

Over the years, Pelé attracted such acclaim around the world that in 1968, the two sides involved in the Nigerian Civil War agreed to a forty-eight-hour ceasefire in order to watch Pelé play a friendly game in Lagos.[342] No wonder J. B. Pinheiro, former Brazilian Ambassador to the United Nations, once intoned, "Pelé played football for twenty-two years, and in that time, he did more to promote world friendship and fraternity than any other ambassador anywhere."

In 1962, following the loss by Beneficia to Pelé's team, Santos, Beneficia's goalkeeper, Costa Pereira said, "I arrived hoping to stop a great man. I went away convinced I had been outdone by someone who was not born on the same planet as the rest of us."

Pelé's athleticism was astounding. In Brazil, he accomplished 803 goals in 863 matches. Internationally, Pelé completed 479 goals in 503 matches.

He participated in fourteen World Cup tournaments and three World Cup championships. Pelé hung up his boots in 1999. Since retirement, he has been a UN Ambassador for Ecology and the Environment, Brazil's Extraordinary Minister of Sports, and a UNESCO Goodwill Ambassador.

Arthur Ashe
(Arthur Robert Ashe, Jr.)

Born: July 10, 1943
Died: February 6, 1993
Country: The United States of America

"One important key to success is self-confidence. An important key to self-confidence is preparation." [343]

Arthur Robert Ashe was more than a top-rated tennis player, winner of three Grand Slam titles, and the first black man to win three major singles championships (Wimbledon, Austrialian Open, and US Open); he was the game's conscience. With quiet dignity, but immutable resolve, Ashe fought for social justice and racial equality on and off the court.

Born in Richmond, Virginia—part of the segregated south at that time—Ashe faced discrimination from many quarters. Yet, by sheer determination, he was a standout at the amateur level, and thereby, Ashe won a scholarship to attend UCLA.

He played on the US Davis Cup team for close to a decade, winning the crown three times. In 1970, however, Ashe became the subject of international controversy, when he openly criticized South Africa's apartheid system. His remarks led South Africa to deny a visa for Ashe; he was unable to enter the country and compete in the South African Open. Although Ashe could not play in South Africa that year, he won the men's singles at Wimbledon (London) in 1975. Eventually, due to his celebrity, Ashe was allowed in South Africa. He was the first black to play in the country's World Championship singles.[344]

In 1983, Ashe, along with Harry Belafonte, chaired the Artists and Athletes Against Apartheid, a movement to raise awareness of the injustices of apartheid in South Africa.[345]

Ashe underwent heart surgery in 1979. Two years later, he announced that he had been diagnosed with human immunodeficiency virus (HIV); believed to have been contracted through a tainted blood transfusion that occurred during his heart operation. Shortly thereafter, Ashe became an international spokesman for HIV and AIDS awareness. He also devoted time to the sport of tennis, serving as United States Davis Cup captain until 1985. That same year, Ashe was inducted into the International Tennis Hall of Fame.

Ashe passed away on February 6, 1993 from AIDS-related pneumonia.[346] In 1993, he was posthumously awarded the Presidential Medal of Freedom by President Bill Clinton.[347] The US Open Tennis Championship is played annually at the Arthur Ashe Stadium—named in his honor—in New York.

Dominique Dawes

Born: November 20, 1976
Country: The United States of America

"I think in any industry, it is competitive. There are a certain number of slots out there and opportunities out there. So you need to make sure that you're always on the top of your toes, trying to get better." 348

At the age of six, Dominique Dawes began gymnastics lessons, culminating in her becoming the first black person to win an individual Olympic medal in women's gymnastics. Indeed, she is the first black person of any nationality or gender to win an Olympic gold medal in gymnastics.

A native of Silver Spring, Maryland, Dawes (at age nine) inscribed the word "determination" on a mirror, using crayon to embolden her for the arduous journey ahead. In every sense, at every turn, Dawes' determination paid off.

Dawes is one of only three female American gymnasts to compete in three Olympic medal- winning teams. Not bad, considering that when she showed up for her first tumbling class, the instructor canceled the class. From this inauspicious start, Dawes has made history. She has enjoyed the following accomplishments and honors: Essence Award (1997); induction into the USA gymnastics Hall of Fame (1998); AAUW Women of Distinction Award (2004); induction into the USA Olympics Hall of Fame (2008); and induction into the International Gymnastics Hall of Fame (2009).[349]

Dawes graduated from the University of Maryland, College Park in 2002. The same year, she became the first spokeswoman for the Girl Scouts of the USA's "Uniquely Me" self- esteem program. She served as president of the Women's Sports Federation and the foundation's youngest president (2004 and 2006). She is co-chair of President Obama's President's Council on Fitness, Sports, and Nutrition.[350]

Dawes' achievement in the field of gymnastics is legendary and positive proof that when fueled by undaunted determination, the sky is no limit.

Profile Index

Human & Civil Rights

Queen Ann Nzinga (Ana de Sousa Nzinga Mbande) 5

Olaudah Equiano (Gustavus Vassa) 8

Samuel Sharpe 11

Frederick Douglass (Frederick Augustus Washington Bailey) 13

Harriet Tubman (Araminta Ross) 18

Marcus Garvey (Marcus Mosiah Garvey, Jr.) 21

George Padmore (Malcolm Ivan Meredith Nurse) 24

Nelson Mandela (Nelson Rolihlahla Mandela) 27

Dr. Martin Luther King Jr. (Michael King Jr.) 31

Kwame Nkrumah (The Right Honourable) 35

Politics & Governance

Askia the Great (Askia Mohammad I) 40

Toussaint L'Ouverture 42

Anwar Sadat (Muhammad Anwar el-Sadat) 45

Kamala Harris (49th Vice President of The United States) 48

Sir Lynden Pindling 51

Colin Luther Powell 54

Kofi Annan 56

Ellen Johnson Sirleaf 58

Ngozi Okonjo–Iweala 61

Barack Obama (Barack Hussein Obama II) 63

Religion

Saint Augustine (Augustine of Hippo) 68
Saint Benedict the Moor, O. F. M. 70
Richard Allen (Bishop) 72
Haile Selassie 75
Elijah Muhammad 77
E. E. Cleveland (Pastor) 80
Francis Arinze (Cardinal) 83
Andraé Crouch (Andraé Edward Crouch) 85
T. D. Jakes (Thomas Dexter Jakes Sr.) 87
Chris Oyakhilome (Pastor) 89

Education

Daniel Payne (Bishop) 94
Alexander Crummell (Minister) 96
Patrick Francis Healy 98
Fanny Jackson Coppin 100
Booker T. Washington 103
W. E. B. DuBois (William Edward Burghardt DuBois) 105
Mary McLeod Bethune (Mary Jane McLeod) 108
Benjamin Elijah Mays 111
Dr. David Olaniyi Oyedepo (Bishop) 114
Melinda F. Emerson 116

Inventions

Thomas L. Jennings 120
Lewis Howard Latimer 122

George Washington Carver 124
Garrett Morgan (Garrett Augustus Morgan Sr.) 127
Frederick McKinley Jones 130
Marie Van Brittan Brown 132
George Edward Alcorn Jr. 134
Patricia Era Bath 136
Shirley Ann Jackson 139
Mark Dean 141

Science & Technology
Daniel Hale Williams 145
Percy Lavon Julian 148
Charles Richard Drew 152
Meredith Charles "Flash" Gourdine 155
Wangari Maathai 158
Charles Frank Bolden 162
Wanda M. Austin 164
Philip Emeagwali 167
Neil deGrasse Tyson 170
Juliana Rotich 173

Business & Entrepreneurship
Madam C. J. Walker 180
Reginald F. Lewis 183
Mohammed Hussein Al Amoudi 185
Folorunsho Alakija 187
Kenneth Chenault 189

Kenneth Frazier 192
Arnold W. Donald 194
Aliko Dangote 197
Ursula Burns. 199
Patrice Motsepe 201

Arts & Entertainment

Marian Anderson 207
Josephine Baker (Freda Josephine McDonald). 211
Celia Cruz (Úrsula Hilaria Celia de la Caridad Cruz Alfonso) 216
Sir Sidney Poitier 220
Miriam Makeba (Zenzile Miriam Makeba) 225
Bob Marley (Robert Nesta "Bob" Marley) 231
Michael Joseph Jackson 236
Youssou N'Dour 239
Angélique Kidjo (Angélique Kpasseloko Hinto Hounsinou Kandjo Manta Zogbin Kidjo). 243
Misty Copeland 247

Communications & Media

Alexander Sergeyevich Pushkin. 252
Leopold Sedar Senghor 255
John Harold Johnson. 259
Chinua Achebe (Albert Chinualumogu Achebe) 264
Derek Alton Walcott 267
Wole Soyinka (Akinwande Oluwole Babatunde Soyinka) 270
Catherine L. Hughes (Catherine Elizabeth Woods) 273

Oprah Gail Winfrey 276

Mo Abudu (Mosunmola Abudu). 281

Rebecca Enonchong 285

Sports

Robert "Bob" Douglas 291

Jesse Owens (James Cleveland "Jesse" Owens) 293

 Joe Louis (Joseph Louis Barrows) 296

Jack "Jackie" Robinson 299

Charlie Sifford (Charles Luther Sifford) 302

Jim Brown. 304

Gary Sobers (The Right Excellent Sir Garfield St. Auburn Sobers) 306

Pelé (Edson Arantes do Nascimento) 308

Arthur Ashe (Arthur Robert Ashe, Jr.) 311

Dominique Dawes 313

Citations

1. "Leadership." - *Queen Nzinga's And Legacy*. N.p., n.d. Web. 2016. <http://queennzingaleadershipandlegacy.weebly.com/leadership.html>.
2. Snethen, Jessica. "Queen Nzinga (1583-1663)." *Queen Nzinga (1583-1663) | The Black Past: Remembered and Reclaimed*. The Black Past: Remembered and Reclaimed, 2015. Web. <http://www.blackpast.org/gah/queen-nzinga-1583-1663>.
3. Dr. Y. "Queen Nzingha: Great Queen of Angola." *African Heritage*. African Heritage, 18 Mar. 2013. Web. <https://afrole-gends.com/2013/03/18/queen-nzingha-great-queen-of-angola/>.
4. Dr. Y. "Queen Nzingha: Great Queen of Angola." *African Heritage*. African Heritage, 18 Mar. 2013. Web. <https://afrole-gends.com/2013/03/18/queen-nzingha-great-queen-of-angola/>.
5. Bortolot, Alexander Ives. "Ana Nzinga: Queen of Ndongo." *The Met's Heilbrunn Timeline of Art History*. The Metropolitan Museum of Art, Oct. 2003. Web. 12 June 2016. <http://www.metmuseum.org/toah/hd/pwmn_2/hd_pwmn_2.htm>.
6. Engel, KeriLynn. "Ana Nzinga Mbande, Fearless African Queen." *Amazing Women In History*. AWH, 12 Jan. 2012. Web. 12 June 2016.
7. "Olaudah Equiano - Chapter I." *Olaudah Equiano - Chapter I*. N.p., n.d. Web. 2016. <https://history.hanover.edu/texts/equiano/equiano_ch1_a.html>.
8. "Olaudah Equiano." *PBS*. PBS, n.d. Web. 2016. <http://www.pbs.org/wgbh/aia/part1/1p276.html>.
9. "Olaudah Equiano." *PBS*. PBS, n.d. Web. 2016. <http://www.pbs.org/wgbh/aia/part1/1p276.html>.
10. Williamson, Jenn. "Summary of The Interesting Narrative of the Life of Olaudah Equiano, or Gustavus Vassa, the African. Written by Himself. Vol. I." *Summary of The Interesting Narrative of the Life of Olaudah Equiano, or Gustavus Vassa, the African. Written by Himself. Vol. I*. The University of North Carolina at Chapel Hill, 2004. Web. <http://docsouth.unc.edu/neh/equiano1/summary.html>.
11. Carey, Brycchan. "Olaudah Equiano: An Illustrated Biography." *Olaudah Equiano: An Illustrated Biography*. N.p., 2000. Web. 12 June 2016. <http://www.brycchancarey.com/equiano/biog.htm>.

12. Williamson, Jenn. "Summary of The Interesting Narrative of the Life of Olaudah Equiano, or Gustavus Vassa, the African. Written by Himself. Vol. I." *Summary of The Interesting Narrative of the Life of Olaudah Equiano, or Gustavus Vassa, the African. Written by Himself. Vol. I.* The University of North Carolina at Chapel Hill, 2004. Web.
<http://docsouth.unc.edu/neh/equiano1/summary.html>.

13. Williamson, Jenn. "Summary of The Interesting Narrative of the Life of Olaudah Equiano, or Gustavus Vassa, the African. Written by Himself. Vol. I." *Summary of The Interesting Narrative of the Life of Olaudah Equiano, or Gustavus Vassa, the African. Written by Himself. Vol. I.* Documenting the American South, 2004. Web. 12 June 2016.
<http://docsouth.unc.edu/neh/equiano1/summary.html>.

14. Williamson, Jenn. "Summary of The Interesting Narrative of the Life of Olaudah Equiano, or Gustavus Vassa, the African. Written by Himself. Vol. I." *Summary of The Interesting Narrative of the Life of Olaudah Equiano, or Gustavus Vassa, the African. Written by Himself. Vol. I.* The University of North Carolina at Chapel Hill, 2004. Web.
<http://docsouth.unc.edu/neh/equiano1/summary.html>.

15. "1832: Samuel Sharpe, "I Would Rather Die upon Yonder Gallows than Live in Slavery"" *ExecutedToday.com.* N.p., 23 May 2009. Web. 2016.
<http://www.executedtoday.com/2009/05/23/1832-samuel-sharpe-i-would-rather-die-upon-yonder- gallows-than-live-in-slavery/>.

16. Sam Sharpe Project." *Sam Sharpe Project.* N.p., 2012. Web. 12 June 2016.
<http://www.samsharpeproject.org/sam- sharpe>.

17. "Sam Sharpe Project." *Sam Sharpe Project.* N.p., 2012. Web. 12 June 2016.
<http://www.samsharpeproject.org/sam- sharpe>.

18. "Samuel Sharpe - Jamaican National Hero." *Jamaica Information Service.* N.p., 2016. Web. <http://jis.gov.jm/heroes/samuel-sharpe/>.

19. "Samuel Sharpe - Jamaican National Hero." *Jamaica Information Service.* N.p., n.d. Web. 12 June 2016. <http://jis.gov.jm/heroes/samuel-sharpe/>.

20. Wooten, Andre. "Sharpe, Samuel (ca. 1780-1832)." *The Black Past: Remembered and Reclaimed.* The Black Past: Remem- bered and Reclaimed, 2015. Web.
<http://www.blackpast.org/gah/sharpe-samuel-ca-1780-1832>.

21. "Frederick Douglass Quote." *BrainyQuote*. Xplore, n.d. Web. 2016. <http://www.brainyquote.com/quotes/quotes/f/freder-ickd107739.html>.

22. "Biography – Early Life." Frederick Douglass Heritage. N.p., n.d. Web. 31 May 2016.

23. "Frederick Douglass." *Wikipedia*. Wikimedia Foundation, 2016. Web. <https://en.wikipedia.org/wiki/Frederick_Dou-glass>./.latest_citation_text

24. "Frederick Douglass." *Wikipedia*. Wikimedia Foundation, 2016. Web. <https://en.wikipedia.org/wiki/Frederick_Dou-glass>./.latest_citation_text

25. "Frederick Douglass." *Wikipedia*. Wikimedia Foundation, 2016. Web. <https://en.wikipedia.org/wiki/Frederick_Dou-glass>./.latest_citation_text

26. "Frederick Douglass." *Wikipedia*. Wikimedia Foundation, 2016. Web. <https://en.wikipedia.org/wiki/Frederick_Dou-glass>./.latest_citation_text

27. "Frederick Douglass." *PBS*. PBS, n.d. Web. <http://www.pbs.org/wgbh/aia/part4/4p1539.html>.

28. "Frederick Douglass." *PBS*. PBS, n.d. Web. <http://www.pbs.org/wgbh/aia/part4/4p1539.html>.

29. "Douglass Establishes Abolitionist Paper - The North Star." *World History Project*. N.p., n.d. Web. 31 May 2016.

30. Chaffin, Tom. "Frederick Douglass's Irish Odyssey." *The Irish Times*. Th Irish Times, 02 Feb. 2015. Web. <http://www.irishtimes.com/culture/books/frederick-douglass-s-irish-odyssey-1.2084550>.

31. "Biographies: Frederick Douglas." *PBS*. PBS, n.d. Web. 12 June 2016.

32. "Harriet Tubman Quote." *BrainyQuote*. Xplore, n.d. Web. 2016. <http://www.brainyquote.com/quotes/quotes/h/harriet-tub310306.html>.

33. "Harriet Tubman." *PBS*. PBS, n.d. Web. 12 June 2016. <http://www.pbs.org/wgbh/aia/part4/4p1535.html>.

34. Rogers, Kevin. "Harriet Tubman Rescues Sister, Brother-in-law, and Children." *World History Project*. N.p., 2016. Web. <https://worldhistoryproject.org/1850/12/harriet-tubman-rescues-sister-brother-in-law-and-children>.

35. "John Brown's Raid on Harpers Ferry." *History.com*. A&E Television Networks, 2016. Web. <http://www.history.com/this-day-in-history/john-browns-raid-on-harpers-ferry>.

36. "Marcus Garvey Quote." *BrainyQuote*. Xplore, n.d. Web. 2016. <http://www.brainyquote.com/quotes/quotes/m/marcus-garv365148.html>

37. "American Experience Marcus Garvey." *PBS*. PBS, 1999. Web. 12 June 2016. <http://www.pbs.org/wgbh/amex/garvey/timeline/>.

38. History.com Staff. "Marcus Garvey." *History.com*. A&E Television Networks, 2009. Web. 12 June 2016. <http://www.his- tory.com/topics/black-history/marcus-garvey>.

39. "Introduction." *The Life and Struggles of Negro Toilers by George Padmore 1931*. N.p., n.d. Web. 2016. <https://www.marx- ists.org/archive/padmore/1931/negro-toilers/introduction.htm>.

40. Salter, Daren. "Padmore, George (1901-1959)." *The Black Past: Remembered and Reclaimed*. The Black Past: Remembered and Reclaimed, 2015. Web. <http://www.blackpast.org/aah/padmore-george-1901-1959>.

41. Salter, Daren. "Padmore, George (1901-1959)." *The Black Past: Remembered and Reclaimed*. The Black Past: Remembered and Reclaimed, 2015. Web. <http://www.blackpast.org/aah/padmore-george-1901-1959>.

42. "George Padmore." *Encyclopedia of World Biography*. Encyclopedia.com, 2016. Web. <http://www.encyclopedia.com/his- tory/historians-and-chronicles/historians-miscellaneous-biographies/george-padmore>.

43. Marable, Manning. "Remembering George Padmore." *Raceandhistory.com*. Race & History, 1998. Web. 12 June 2016. <http://www.raceandhistory.com/Historians/george_padmore.htm>.

44. Teelucksingh, Jerome. "George Padmore." *Encyclopedia.com*. HighBeam Research, 01 Jan. 2004. Web. 12 June 2016. <http://www.encyclopedia.com/topic/George_Padmore.aspx>.

45. "Nelson Mandela Quote." *BrainyQuote*. Xplore, n.d. Web. 2016. <http://www.brainyquote.com/quotes/quotes/n/nelson- mand178789.html>.

46. History.com Staff. "Nelson Mandela." *History.com*. A&E Television Networks, 2009. Web. 12 June 2016. <http://www.his- tory.com/topics/nelson-mandela>.

47. History.com Staff. "Nelson Mandela." *History.com*. A&E Television Networks, 2009. Web. 12 June 2016. <http://www.his- tory.com/topics/nelson-mandela>.

48. "Nelson Mandela Timeline 1940-1949." *Anonymous*. South African History Online, 2014. Web. 12 June 2016. <http://www.sahistory.org.za/topic/nelson-mandela-timeline-1940-1949>.

49. "Defiance Campaign 1952." *South African History Online*. South African History Online, 21 Mar. 2011. Web. <http://www.sahistory.org.za/topic/defiance-campaign-1952>.

50. "(1962) Nelson Mandela, "Address at the Conference of the Pan-African Freedom Movement of East and Central Africa"" *The Black Past: Remembered and Reclaimed*. The Black Past: Remembered and Reclaimed, 2015. Web. <http://www.blackpast.org/1962-nelson-mandela-address-conference-pan-african-freedom-movement-east-and-central- africa>.

51. History.com Staff. "Nelson Mandela." *History.com*. A&E Television Networks, 2009. Web. 12 June 2016. <http://www.his- tory.com/topics/nelson-mandela>.

52. "Martin Luther King, Jr. Quote." *BrainyQuote*. Xplore, n.d. Web. 2016. <http://www.brainyquote.com/quotes/quotes/m/martinluth101378.html>.

53. History.com Staff. "Martin Luther King Jr." *History.com*. A&E Television Networks, 2009. Web. 12 June 2016. <http://www.history.com/topics/black-history/martin-luther-king-jr>.

54. "King's House Is Bombed." *King's House Is Bombed*. Stanford University, n.d. Web. 12 June 2016. <http://kingencyclope- dia.stanford.edu/encyclopedia/chronologyentry/1956_01_30.1.html>.

55. History.com Staff. "Martin Luther King Jr." *History.com*. A&E Television Networks, 2009. Web. 12 June 2016. <http://www.history.com/topics/black-history/martin-luther-king-jr>.

56. "Askia the Great (62025 Hits)." *Askia the Great*. Black History, 25 Jan. 2008. Web. <http://blackhistory.com/content/62209/askia-the-great>.

57. Rouch, Jean Pierre. "Muhammad I Askia." *Encyclopedia Britannica Online*. Encyclopedia Britannica, 2016. Web.

58. "Toussaint LOuverture I Was Born a Slave, but Nature Gave Me the Soul of a Free Man." *Documents.mx*. N.p., n.d. Web. 2016. <http://documents.mx/documents/toussaint-louverture-i-was-born-a-slave-but-nature-gave-me-the-soul-of-a-free- man.html>.

59. Shen, Kona. "The Haitian Revolution 1792-1796." *History of Haiti*. Brown Department of Africana Studies, 27 Oct. 2015. Web.

60. Chandler, D. L. "Haitian Revolution Leader Toussaint L'Ouverture Was Born On This Day In 1743." *Black History*. News One, 20 May 2013. Web.

61. "Anwar Sadat Quote." *BrainyQuote*. Xplore, n.d. Web. 2016. <http://www.brainyquote.com/quotes/quotes/a/anwarsa- dat112116.html>.

62. Mahr, Krista. "Bread Is Life: Food and Protest in Egypt | TIME.com." *Science Space Bread Is Life Food and Protest in Egypt Comments*. TIME, 31 Jan. 2011. Web. 20 Mar. 2016.

63. "The People Have Spoken." *The Tribune*. N.p., n.d. Web. 2016. <http://www.tribune242.com/news/2012/may/14/the- people-have-spoken/>.

64. Colin Powell Quote." *BrainyQuote*. Xplore, n.d. Web. 2016. <http://www.brainyquote.com/quotes/quotes/c/colin- powel121363.html>.

65. "Biographies of the Secretaries of State: *Colin Luther Powell* (1937–)." Colin Luther Powell. U.S. Office of the Historian, n.d. Web. 2016.

66. "BBC NEWS | Americas | Full Text: Kofi Annan's Final Speech." *BBC News*. BBC, 11 Dec. 2006. Web. 2016. <http://news.bbc.co.uk/2/hi/6170089.stm>.

67. Annan, Kofi Atta. "How to Achieve Millennium Development Goals - *Kofi Annan Foundation*." Kofi Annan Foundation. The Korea Times, 21 Sept. 2010. Web. 12 June 2016. <http://www.kofiannanfoundation.org/in-the-news/how-to-achieve- millennium-development-goals/>.

68. "Ellen Johnson Sirleaf Quote." BrainyQuote. Xplore, n.d. Web. 2016. <http://www.brainyquote.com/quotes/quotes/e/el- lenjohns485530.html>.

68(b). "Ellen Johnson Sirleaf." World Bank Live. The World Bank, 2016. Web.

69. "Ngozi Okonjo-Iweala Quote." BrainyQuote. Xplore, n.d. Web. 2016. <http://www.brainyquote.com/quotes/quotes/n/ngoziokonj630493.html>.

70. "Lazard." *Wikipedia*. Wikimedia Foundation, 2 June 2016. Web.

71. "Finance Minister of the Year 2005: Ngozi Okonjo-Iweala, Nigeria @Euromoney." *Euromoney*. N.p., n.d. Web.

72. "Barack Obama Quote." *BrainyQuote*. Xplore, n.d. Web. 2016. <http://www.brainyquote.com/quotes/quotes/b/barack- obam409128.html>.

73. Silver, Nate. "Contemplating Obama's Place in History, Statistically." *FiveThirtyEight*. N.p., 23 Jan. 2013. Web. 19 June 2016.

74. Kim, Mallie Jane. "Survey Ranks Obama 15th Best President, Bush Among Worst." *US News*. U.S.News & World Report, 2 July 2010. Web.

75. "A Friar's Life.": *"Listen and Attend with the Ear of Your Heart"* N.p., n.d. Web. 2016. <http://afriarslife.blogspot.com/2013/07/listen-and-attend-with-ear-of-your.html>.

76. "St. Benedict the Moor (1526-1589)." *St. Benedict the Moor (1526-1589) | The Black Past: Remembered and Reclaimed.* Hu- manities Washington, 2007. Web. 2016.

77. Nash, Gary B. "Race and Revolution." *Google Books*. Rowman & Littlefield Publishers, Inc., 1990. Web. 2016.

78. "People & Ideas: Richard Allen." *PBS*. PBS, 11 Oct. 2010. Web. 19 June 2016.

79. Quote." *BrainyQuote*. Xplore, n.d. Web. 2016. <http://www.brainyquote.com/quotes/quotes/h/haileselas381375.html>.

80. Podesta, James, and Elizabeth Knowles. "Haile Selassie 1892–1975." *Encyclopedia.com*. HighBeam Research, 01 Jan. 1994. Web. 30 Aug. 2016. <http://www.encyclopedia.com/topic/Haile_Selassie.aspx>.

81. Podesta, James, and Elizabeth Knowles. "Haile Selassie 1892–1975." *Encyclopedia.com*. HighBeam Research, 01 Jan. 1994. Web. 20 June 2016.

82. "Elijah Muhammad Quote." *A-Z Quotes*. N.p., n.d. Web. 2016. <http://www.azquotes.com/quote/656244>.

83. Wankoff, Jordan, and John Bowker. "Muhammad, Elijah 1897–1975." *Encyclopedia.com*. HighBeam Research, 01 Jan. 1993. Web. 20 Mar. 2016.

84. "E.E. Cleveland Quote." *Flickr*. Yahoo!, n.d. Web. 2016.

85. Gates, Henry Louis, Emmanuel Akyeampong, and Steven J. Niven. "Dictionary of African Biography." *Google Books*. Ox- ford University Press, n.d. Web. 2016.

86. Dye, Mary, and James Manheim. "Crouch, Andraé." *Encyclopedia.com*. HighBeam Research, 01 Jan. 1993. Web. 2016.

87. "Ebony." *Google Books*. EBONY Magazine, Sept. 1982. Web. 2016.

88. Jones, Shannon. "TD Jakes Quotes on Life: 10 Memorable Statements From Evangelical Christian." Newsmax. *Newsmax*, 30 Apr. 2015. Web. 2016. <http://www.newsmax.com/FastFeatures/td-jakes-quotes-life-evangelical- christian/2015/04/30/id/641725/>.

89. "Chris Oyakhilome Quote." *A-Z Quotes*. A-Z Quotes, n.d. Web. 2016. <http://www.azquotes.com/quote/894407>.

90. "Quote by Daniel Payne." *Quotations101.com*. N.p., n.d. Web. 2016. <http://www.quotations101.com/quote/183179/Thats_my_top_goal_to_go_to_college>.

91. Fuller, Paul. "Black Methodists in America: A Success Story of a Model Minority Group." *Google Books*. America Star Books, 2012. Web. 20 June 2016.

92. "Alexander Crummell Quote." *A-Z Quotes*. N.p., n.d. Web. 2016. <http://www.azquotes.com/quote/1137185>.

93. "Alexander Crummell." *Bio.com*. A&E Networks Television, n.d. Web. 20 June 2016.

94. Ulke, Julius. "Patrick F. Healy, S.J. (1834-1910), President of Georgetown University from 1874 to 1882." Georgetown University, 2009. Web. 20 June 2016.

95. "Fanny Jackson Coppin Quote." *A-Z Quotes*. N.p., n.d. Web. 2016. <http://www.azquotes.com/quote/1184623>.

96. The Editors of Encyclopædia Britannica. "Fanny Jackson Coppin." *Encyclopedia Britannica Online*. Encyclopedia Britannica, 24 Oct. 2014. Web. 20 June 2016.

97. "Booker T. Washington Quote." *BrainyQuote*. Xplore, n.d. Web. 2016. <http://www.brainyquote.com/quotes/quotes/b/bookertwa132461.html>.

98. "W. E. B. Du Bois Quote." *BrainyQuote*. Xplore, n.d. Web. 2016. <http://www.brainyquote.com/quotes/quotes/w/web- dubo388223.html>.

99. Wormser, Richard. "Jim Crow Stories: W.E.B. DuBois." *PBS*. PBS, 2002. Web. 20 June 2016. 109. "Mary McLeod Bethune Quote." *BrainyQuote*. Xplore, n.d. Web. 2016. <http://www.brainyquote.com/quotes/quotes/m/marymcleod145817.html>.

100. Podesta, James, and Judith J. Culligan. "Bethune, Mary McLeod 1875–1955." *Encyclopedia.com*. HighBeam Research, 01 Jan. 1993. Web. 20 June 2016.

101. "American National Biography Online: Mays, Benjamin Elijah." *American National Biography Online: Mays, Benjamin Eli- jah*. N.p., n.d. Web. 2016. <http://www.anb.org/articles/15/15-01112.html>.

102. "Inspirational & Wisdom Quotes By Bishop David Oyedepo | Nollywood, Nigeria, News, Celebrity, Gists, Gossips, En- tertainment." *Nollywood Nigeria News Celebrity Gists Gossips Entertainment Atom*. N.p., n.d. Web. 2016. <http://naijagists.com/inspirational-wisdom-quotes-by-bishop-david-oyedepo/>.

103. "David Oyedepo." *Wikipedia*. Wikimedia Foundation, 3 June 2016. Web. 20 June 2016.

104. Emerson, Melinda F. "Become Your Own Boss in 12 Months." *Google Books*. Adams Media, 2015. Web. 2016.

105. Emerson, Melinda. "Melinda F. Emerson Foundation Launches Reinvention Weekend Event in Philadelphia » Succeed As Your Own Boss." *Succeed As Your Own Boss*. N.p., 03 Sept. 2013. Web. 20 June 2016.

106. "Jennings, Thomas L. (1791- 1856) | The Black Past: Remembered and Reclaimed." *Jennings, Thomas L. (1791- 1856) | The Black Past: Remembered and Reclaimed*. Blackpast.org, n.d. Web. 20 June 2016.

107. Chamberlain, Gaius. "Thomas Jennings." The Black Inventor Online Museum RSS2. N.p., 26 Nov. 2012. Web. 28 Aug. 2016. <http://blackinventor.com/thomas-jennings/>.

108. "Lewis Howard Latimer Quote." *A-Z Quotes*. N.p., n.d. Web. 2016. <http://www.azquotes.com/quote/665310>.

109. Chamberlain, Gaius. "Lewis Latimer." *The Black Inventor Online Museum RSS2*. The Black Inventor Online, 23 Mar. 2012. Web. 2016.

110. "George Washington Carver Quote." *BrainyQuote*. Xplore, n.d. Web. 2016. <http://www.brainyquote.com/quotes/quotes/g/georgewash103591.html>

111. "Iowa Roots, Global Impact: The Life and Legacy of George Washington Carver." *African American Museum* of Iowa. N.p., 2016. Web. 20 June 2016.

112. "Garrett Morgan Quote." *A-Z Quotes*. N.p., n.d. Web. 2016. <http://www.azquotes.com/quote/691105>.

113. Chamberlain, Gaius. "Garrett Morgan." *The Black Inventor Online Museum RSS2*. The Black Inventor Online, 23 Mar. 2012. Web. 2016.

114. "Frederick McKinley Jones.": *Refrigerator Inventions*. Famous Black Inventors, 2008. Web. 20 June 2016.

115. "Frederick McKinley Jones, Innovator of Many Devices." *Welcome To "Voices That Guide Us" Personal Narratives*. African American Registry, n.d. Web. 20 June 2016.

116. "Inventor Marie Van Brittan Brown Born." *Welcome To "Voices That Guide Us" Personal Narratives*. African American Registry, 2000. Web. 20 June 2016.

117. "Meet George Alcorn – Inventor Of The Imaging X-Ray Spectrometer." *How Africa*. N.p., 23 Feb. 2016. Web. 20 June 2016.

118. "Dr. Patricia E. Bath." *Dr. Patricia E. Bath*. N.p., n.d. Web. 2016. <http://www.blackhistorypages.net/pages/pbath.php>.

119. Stamatel, Janet. "Bath, Patricia E 1942–." *Encyclopedia.com*. HighBeam Research, 01 Jan. 2003. Web. 20 June 2016.

120. "Science Education: Time to Get Back to the Basics." *Big Think*. N.p., 27 May 2015. Web. 2016. <http://bigthink.com/words-of-wisdom/shirley-jackson-back-to-the-basics>.

121. "President's Profile - Rensselaer Polytechnic Institute (RPI)." *President's Profile*. Rensselaer Polytechnic Institute, 2012. Web. 2016.

122. "Dr. Shirley Ann Jackson." *Dr. Shirley Jackson: Telecommunications Inventions*. Famous Black Inventors, 2008. Web. 2016.

123. Hardawar, Devindra. "Mark Dean Designed the First IBM PC While Breaking Racial Barriers." *Engadget*. N.p., n.d. Web.2016. <https://www.engadget.com/2015/02/06/mark-dean-pc-pioneer/>.

124. "Dr. Mark Dean." The University of Tennessee Knoxville. N.p., n.d. Web. 2016. <http://www.eecs.utk.edu/people/fac- ulty/markdean>.

125. "Dean, Mark (1957-) | The Black Past: Remembered and Reclaimed." *The Black Past: Remembered and Reclaimed*. Black- past.org, n.d. Web. Mar. 2016.

126. "Dr. Mark Dean.": *Computer Inventions*. Famous Black Inventors, 2008. Web. 20 June 2016.

127. "Daniel Hale Williams and the First Successful Heart Surgery." *Columbia University Department of Surgery*. N.p., n.d.Web. 2016.

128. Bianco, David. "Williams, Daniel Hale 1856–1931." *Encyclopedia.com*. HighBeam Research, 01 Jan. 1992. Web. 21 June 2016.

129. "Daniel Hale Williams." *Bio.com*. A&E Networks Television, 2016. Web. 6 Apr. 2016.

130. "Daniel Hale Williams - Black Inventor Online Museum." *Daniel Hale Williams - Black Inventor Online Museum*. Black Inventor Online Museum, n.d. Web. 21 June 2016.

131. "Julian Speaks." *PBS*. PBS, n.d. Web. 2016.
    <http://www.pbs.org/wgbh/nova/julian/spea-nf.html>.

132. "Library Resource Kit Who Was Percy Julian?Expanded Version." *PBS*. PBS, 2007. Web. 12 May 2016.

133. Smith, Caroline. "Julian, Percy Lavon 1899–1975." Encyclopedia.com. HighBeam Research, 01 Jan. 1994. Web. 28 Aug. 2016.
    <http://www.encyclopedia.com/topic/Percy_Lavon_Julian.aspx>.

134. "The Life of Percy Lavon Julian '20." *DePauw University*. N.p., 19 Feb. 2009. Web. 21 June 2016.

135. "For Teachers." *Science Alive: Percy Julian*. Chemical Heritage Foundation, 2005. Web. 20 Mar. 2016.

136. Smith, Caroline. "Julian, Percy Lavon 1899–1975." *Encyclopedia.com*. HighBeam Research, 01 Jan. 1994. Web. 21 June 2016.

137. "Quote Addicts." *I Feel That the Recent Ruling of the Uni by Charles R. Drew*. N.p., n.d. Web. 2016.
    <http://quoteaddicts.com/825756>.

138. "Charles Richard Drew." *American Chemical Society*. American Chemical Society, 2016. Web. 4 Apr. 2016.

139. "Charles Drew." *Bio.com*. A&E Networks Television, 2016. Web. May 2016.

140. "Charles Drew Biography." Bio.com. A&E Networks Television, n.d. Web. 30 Aug. 2016.
    <http://www.biography.com/people/charles-drew-9279094#death-and-legacy>.

141. "Meredith Charles Gourdine." *Tescience2*. N.p., n.d. Web. 2016.
    <https://tescience2.wikispaces.com/+Meredith+Charles+Gourdine>.

142. "Meredith Charles Gourdine Biography." *Meredith Charles Gourdine Biography*. How Products Are Made, 2016. Web. Mar. 2016.

143. "Wangari Maathai Quote." *BrainyQuote*. Xplore, n.d. Web. 2016.
    <http://www.brainyquote.com/quotes/quotes/w/wan- garimaa416623.html>.

144. "Wangari Maathai - Biographical." *Nobel Prize*. The Nobel Foundation, 2004. Web. 2016.

145. "Wangari Maathai." *Nobel Womens Initiative*. Nobel Womens Initiative, 2004. Web. 21 June 2016.

146. "Biography." *The Green Belt Movement*. The Green Belt Movement, 2016. Web. 21 June 2016.

147. "A Quote by Charles F. Bolden." *Goodreads*. N.p., n.d. Web. 2016. <http://www.goodreads.com/quotes/1361576-always-do-your-best-in-whatever-you-do-set-goals>.

148. NASA. "Administrator Charlie Bolden." NASA. NASA, 18 Mar. 2016. Web. 30 Aug. 2016. <https://www.nasa.gov/about/highlights/bolden_bio.html>.

149. Dunbar, Brian. "NASA Rover Returns Voice, Telephoto Views From Mars." *NASA*. NASA, 27 Aug. 2012. Web. 20 June 2016.

150. "CHARLES F. BOLDEN, JR. (MAJOR GENERAL, USMC RET.) NASA ADMINISTRATOR." NASA. NASA, Sept. 2009. Web. 30 Aug. 2016. <http://www.jsc.nasa.gov/Bios/htmlbios/bolden-cf.html>.

151. "Dr. Wanda M. Austin." *The Aerospace Corporation*. N.p., n.d. Web. 2016. <http://www.aerospace.org/about-us/vision- and-values/corporate-officers/dr-wanda-austin-biography/>.

152. Hennigan, W.J. "How I Made It: Wanda M. Austin, President and CEO of Aerospace." *Los Angeles Times*. Los Angeles Times, 05 Jan. 2014. Web. 2 May 2016.

153. Osbourn, Christopher. "Dr. Wanda M. Austin." *NASA*. NASA, 20 May 2016. Web. 2016.

154. U.S. Department of Energy. "Wanda M. Austin." *Department of Energy*. Energy.gov, n.d. Web. 2016.

155. "Wanda Austin Selected to Serve on President's Council of Advisors on Science and Technology." *The Aerospace Corporation*. Aerospace, 26 Mar. 2015. Web. 2016.

156. "Philip Emeagwali Quote." *BrainyQuote*. Xplore, n.d. Web. 2016. <http://www.brainyquote.com/quotes/quotes/p/philipemea268348.html>.

157. "Autobiography of Dr. Philip Emeagwali." *Autobiography of Dr. Philip Emeagwali*. N.p., n.d. Web. 30 Aug. 2016. <http://bookbuilder.cast.org/view_print.php?book=25103>.

158. "Philip Emeagwali." *Wikipedia*. Wikimedia Foundation, n.d. Web. 2016. <https://en.wikipedia.org/wiki/Philip_Emeag- wali>./.latest_citation_text

159. Obioha, McLord. "Nigerian 'Calculus' Takes America by Storm." *Nigerian 'Calculus' Takes America by Storm*. The Niger- ian, June 1996. Web. <http://emeagwali.com/usa/nigerian/The_Nigerian_and_Africans_1996.html>.

160. "Autobiography of Dr. Philip Emeagwali." *Autobiography of Dr. Philip Emeagwali*. N.p., n.d. Web. 30 Aug. 2016. <http://bookbuilder.cast.org/view_print.php?book=25103>.

161. "Autobiography of Dr. Philip Emeagwali." *Autobiography of Dr. Philip Emeagwali*. N.p., n.d. Web. 30 Aug. 2016. <http://bookbuilder.cast.org/view_print.php?book=25103>.

162. "Dr. Philip Emeagwali." *Dr. Philip Emeagwali: Inventor of the World's Fastest Computer*. Famous Black Inventors, 2008. Web. 2016. <http://www.black-inventor.com/Dr-Philip-Emeagwali.asp>.

163. "Dr. Philip Emeagwali.": *Inventor of the World's Fastest Computer*. Famous Black Inventors, 2008. Web. 21 June 2016.

164. Hahz4k. "A Black Man Named Philip Emeagwali Created The Internet." *Atlnightspots*. N.p., n.d. Web. 2016. <http://www.atlnightspots.com/a-black-man-named-philip-emeagwali-created-the-internet/>.

165. Sanchez, Brenna. "Emeagwali, Philip 1954–." *Encyclopedia.com*. HighBeam Research, 01 Jan. 2002. Web. 5 Mar. 2016.

166. "Meet Dr. Philip Emeagwali From Nigeria, Inventor of the World's Fastest Computer." *African Leadership*. African Lead- ership Magazine, 29 Jan. 2015. Web. <http://africanleadership.co.uk/blog/?p=542>.

167. Gray, Madison. "Black History Month: Unsung Heroes." *Time*. Time Inc., 12 Jan. 2007. Web. 5 Apr. 2016.

168. "Neil DeGrasse Tyson on Stereotypes, Societal Expectations, and Women and Minorities in Science." *Dynamic Ecology*. N.p., 01 May 2014. Web. 2016.

169. "Neil DeGrasse Tyson." *Wikipedia*. Wikimedia Foundation, n.d. Web. 2016. <https://en.wikipedia.org/wiki/Neil_de- Grasse_Tyson>.

170. Andrew, Elise. "Beginner's Telescope Buying Guide." *IFLScience*. IFL Science, 27 May 2016. Web. 5 Apr. 2016.

171. "Curriculum Vitae." *Hayden Planetarium*. Hayden Planetarium, n.d. Web. 2016. <http://www.haydenplanetarium.org/tyson/curriculum-vitae#education>.

172. "Curriculum Vitae." *Hayden Planetarium*. Hayden Planetarium, n.d. Web. 2016. <http://www.haydenplanetarium.org/tyson/curriculum-vitae#education>.

173. "Commission on the Future of the U.S. Aerospace Industry." *Hayden Planetarium*. Hayden Planetarium, 2016. Web. 21 June 2016.

174. "Neil DeGrasse Tyson." *Wikipedia*. Wikimedia Foundation, 2016. Web. 21 June 2016.

175. "Juliana Rotich Quote." *BrainyQuote*. Xplore, n.d. Web. 2016. <http://www.brainyquote.com/quotes/quotes/j/julia- narot561826.html>.

176. Bellis, Mary. "Famous Quotes from Madam Walker." *About.com Inventors*. About.com, n.d. Web. 2016.

177. Bundles, A'lelia. "Madam C.J. Walker's Secrets to Success." *Bio.com*. A&E Networks Television, 2016. Web. Mar. 2016.

178. Evans, Tim. "Madam Walker Paved Way for Generations of Black, Female Entrepreneurs." *Indianapolis Star*. N.p., 02 Feb. 2015. Web. 30 Aug. 2016. <http://www.indystar.com/story/news/2015/02/01/madam-walker-paved-way-generations- black-female-entrepreneurs/22695831/>.

179. "Madam C.J. Walker." Bio.com. A&E Networks Television, 2016. Web. 30 Aug. 2016. <http://www.biography.com/peo- ple/madam-cj-walker-9522174#synopsis>.

180. History.com Staff. "Madame C. J. Walker." *History.com*. A&E Television Networks, 2009. Web. 5 Apr. 2016.

181. Leggs, Brent. "Preserving an Iconic Landmark in Business History: Madam C. J. Walker's Villa Lewaro | National Trust for Historic Preservation." Preserving an Iconic Landmark in Business History: Madam C. J. Walker's Villa Lewaro | National Trust for Historic Preservation. National Trust for Historic Preservation, 02 June 2014. Web. 30 Aug. 2016. <https://saving- places.org/stories/preserving-iconic-landmark-business-history-madam-cj-walker-villa-lewaro#.V3wry_krLIU>.

182. "Reginald F. Lewis." *Reginald F. Lewis Quotes (Author of Why Should White Guys Have All the Fun?)*. N.p., n.d. Web. 2016.

183. "Reginald F. Lewis." *Bio.com*. A&E Networks Television, 2016. Web. 5 Apr. 2016.

184. Confer, Molly B. "HLS Gets $3M Donation." *HLS Gets $3M Donation | News | The Harvard Crimson*. The Harvard Crim- son, 10 July 1992. Web. 21 June 2016.

185. Serafin, Tatiana. "Sheikh Mohammed Al Amoudi On Philanthropy." *Forbes*. Forbes Magazine, 5 June 2013. Web. 2016.

186. Ventures Africa. "The Ethiopian Billionaire: Sheikh Mohammed Al Amoudi." *Ventures Africa*. Ventures Africa, 20 July 2012. Web. 21 June 2016.

187. Taire, Morenike. "Secrets of My Success." *Vanguard News*. Vanguard News, 24 Mar. 2016. Web. 2016.

188. "The World's 100 Most Powerful Women." *Forbes*. Forbes Magazine, 21 June 2016. Web. 21 June 2016.

189. Dingle, Derek T. "Black History Month Quote of the Day: American Express' Kenneth Chenault." *Black Enterprise*. N.p., 4 Feb. 2013. Web. 2016.

190. "American Express Named One of the World's Most Admired Companies By Fortune Magazine." American Express. *American Express*, 2016. Web. 30 Aug. 2016. <http://about.americanexpress.com/news/pr/2014/amex-most-admired-compa- nies-fortune-magazine.aspx>.

191. "Kenneth Chenault." *Bio.com*. A&E Networks Television, 2016. Web. 21 June 2016.

192. Loftus, Peter. "Big Pharma's Delicate Dance on Drug Prices." *WSJ*. WSJ, 21 Feb. 2016. Web. 2016.

193. "Leadership." *Merck.com*. Merck, n.d. Web. 30 Aug. 2016. <http://www.merck.com/about/leadership/home.html>.

194. "Kenneth C. Frazier." *Frazier, Kenneth C. (1954-) | The Black Past: Remembered and Reclaimed*. Blackpast.org, n.d. Web. 21 June 2016.

195. Wood, Tim. "Carnival Officials: We Won't Sail to Cuba Until Cuban-Born Americans Can Join Us." *Travel Pulse*. Travel Pulse, 18 Apr. 2016. Web. 2016.

196. Sampson, Hannah. "One Year In, Carnival CEO Arnold Donald Is Working to Right the Ship." *Miamiherald*. N.p., 4 July 2014. Web. 21 June 2016.

197. Aribisala, Femi. "Femi Aribisala." *Aliko Dangote: The Quintessential Nigerian Entrepreneur*. N.p., 22 Jan. 2016. Web. 2016.

198. "Black Economics." *Black Economics*. N.p., n.d. Web. 30 Aug. 2016. <http://blackeconomics.co.uk/>.

199. Nsehe, Mfonobong. "Nigerian Billionaire Aliko Dangote Gets Highest National Honor." *Forbes*. Forbes Magazine, 28 Oct. 2011. Web. 21 June 2016.

200. "Ursula Burns Quote." *BrainyQuote*. Xplore, n.d. Web. 2016.

201. Shwayder, Maya. "Ursula Burns, First Female African-American CEO Of Fortune 500 Company Xerox." *International Business Times*. International Business Times, 14 June 2013. Web. 21 June 2016.

202. "Patrice Motsepe Quote." *BrainyQuote*. Xplore, n.d. Web. 2016.

203. Mars, Errol I. "Patrice Motsepe." : *Black Entrepreneurs, Black CEO, Black Executive, Black Billionaires, Entrepreneur Profile*. Blackentrepreneurprofile.com, n.d. Web. Mar. 2016.

204. Lewis, Jone Johnson. "Marian Anderson Quotes." *About Education*. N.p., 24 Mar. 2015. Web. 26 Aug. 2016. <http://womenshistory.about.com/od/quotes/a/marian_anderson.htm>.

205. "Josephine Baker Quote." *BrainyQuote*. Xplore, n.d. Web. 2016.

206. Wood, Ean. "The Josephine Baker Story." *Google Books*. Omnibus Press, 2010. Web. Jan. 2016.

207. JosephineBakerTube. "Joséphine Baker: The 1st Black Superstar." *YouTube*. YouTube, 13 Nov. 2011. Web. Jan. 2016.

208. "Josephine Baker." *Bio.com*. A&E Networks Television, 2016. Web. Jan. 2016.

209. "The Official Josephine Baker Website." *The Official Josephine Baker Website*. N.p., n.d. Web. 22 June 2016.

210. "Celia Cruz Quote." *BrainyQuote*. Xplore, n.d. Web. 2016. <http://www.brainyquote.com/quotes/quotes/c/celiacruz191644.html>.

211. Garcia-Johnson, Ronie-Richele, Debra Reilly, and Ramiro Burr. "Cruz, Celia." *Encyclopedia.com*. HighBeam Research, 01 Jan. 1994. Web. 5 Mar. 2016.

212. Garcia-Johnson, Ronie-Richele, Debra Reilly, and Ramiro Burr. "Cruz, Celia." *Encyclopedia.com*. HighBeam Research, 01 Jan. 1994. Web. 5 Mar. 2016.

213. "Sidney Poitier Quote." *BrainyQuote*. Xplore, n.d. Web. 2016. <http://www.brainyquote.com/quotes/quotes/s/sidney- poit272842.html>.

214. "Sidney Poitier." *Bio.com*. A&E Networks Television, n.d. Web. 2016.

215. "Sidney Poitier Biography." *Academy of Achievement*. Academy of Achievement, 12 Dec. 2014. Web. 2016.

216. "Sidney Poitier Interview." *Academy of Achievement*. Academy of Achievement, 12 Dec. 2014. Web. 2016.

217. "Harry Belafonte Fast Facts." *CNN*. Cable News Network, 1 Mar. 2016. Web. 30 Aug. 2016. <http://www.cnn.com/2013/07/07/us/harry-belafonte-fast-facts/index.html>.

218. Heldheim, Bob. "'A Raisin In The Sun'" *St. Augustine Florida's News*. St. Augustine Florida's News, 15 Feb. 2008. Web. 2016.

219. "The Quotations Page: Quote from Miriam Makeba." *The Quotations Page*. N.p., n.d. Web. 2016. <http://www.quota- tionspage.com/quote/33502.html>.

220. Mbeje, Audrey N. "African Studies Center-African Languages at Penn." *African Studies Center- African Languages at Penn*. University of Pennsylvania, n.d. Web. 2 Feb. 2016.

221. Kirkpatrick, Connor. "Miriam Makeba: Activist on Two Fronts by Connor Kirkpatrick." *South African History Online*. South African History Online, 20 June 2015. Web. 2 Feb. 2016.

222. Transformed122. "Miriam Makeba - Mama Afrika." *YouTube*. YouTube, 02 Mar. 2009. Web. 2 Feb. 2016.

223. Kirkpatrick, Connor. "Miriam Makeba." *South African History Online*. South African History Online, 9 Nov. 2015. Web. 2 Feb. 2016.

224. "Miriam Makeba." *Wikipedia*. Wikimedia Foundation, 15 June 2016. Web. 2 Feb. 2016.

225. "Mama Africa – The Life of Miriam Makeba." *Revive Music Mama Africa The Life of Miriam Makeba Comments*. Revive Music, 13 June 2011. Web. 23 June 2016.

226. Bigelow, Barbara; Pendergast Sara. "Miriam Makeba." *Encyclopedia.com*. HighBeam Research, 01 Jan. 2004. Web. 4 Feb. 2016.

227. "Miriam Makeba." *Wikipedia*. Wikimedia Foundation, 15 June 2016. Web. 2 Feb. 2016.

228. "Bob Marley Quote." *BrainyQuote*. Xplore, n.d. Web. 2016. <http://www.brainyquote.com/quotes/quotes/b/bobmar-ley578991.html>.

229. Cooper, Carolyn J. "Reggae." *Encyclopedia Britannica Online*. Encyclopedia Britannica, 15 May 2015. Web. 15 Apr. 2016.

230. "Legend (Bob Marley and the Wailers Album)." *Wikipedia*. Wikimedia Foundation, 22 June 2016. Web. 25 June 2016.

231. Denselow, Robin. "Bob Marley Presides over the Peace Concert." *The Guardian*. Guardian News and Media, 15 June 2011. Web. 04 July 2016.

232. "Michael Jackson Quote." *BrainyQuote*. Xplore, n.d. Web. 2016. <http://www.brainyquote.com/quotes/quotes/m/michaeljac389543.html>.

233. "Inductee Explorer | Rock & Roll Hall of Fame." *Rock & Roll Hall of Fame*. N.p., n.d. Web. 30 Aug. 2016. <https://rock- hall.com/inductees/the-jackson-five/bio/>.

234. "Michael Jackson 1958 - 2009." *Time*. Time Inc., 26 June 2009. Web. 5 Mar. 2016. 252 |

235. "Inductee Explorer | Rock & Roll Hall of Fame." *Rock & Roll Hall of Fame*. N.p., n.d. Web. 30 Aug. 2016. <https://rock- hall.com/inductees/the-jackson-five/bio/>.

236. Monde, Chiderah. "Michael Jackson 1979 Manifesto Reveals Singer's Career Goals." *NY Daily News*. NY Daily News, 20 May 2013. Web. 10 Feb. 2016.

237. Grow, Kory. "Michael Jackson's 'Thriller' Is First Album to Sell 30 Million Copies." *Rolling Stone*. N.p., 16 Dec. 2015. Web. 30 Aug. 2016. <http://www.rollingstone.com/music/news/michael-jacksons-thriller-is-first-album-to-sell-30-million- copies-20151216>.

238. Edwards, Gavin. "'We Are the World': A Minute-by-Minute Breakdown on Its 30th Anniversary." *Rolling Stone*. Rolling Stone, 06 Mar. 2015. Web. 5 Feb. 2016.

239. Varner, Jeff. "Michael Jackson's Donation HIStory." *BORGEN Magazine*. Borgen, 17 July 2015. Web. 30 Aug. 2016. <http://www.borgenmagazine.com/michael-jacksons-donation-history/>.

240. Colgrove, Rosemary. "Eye on the Sparrow." *Google Books*. Mill City Press, 2010. Web. 2016. Preface, xii

241. Smith, David. "Youssou N'Dour: The Singer Who Changed His Tune." *The Guardian*. Guardian News and Media, 07 Jan. 2012. Web. May 2016.

242. Zawisza, Marie. "How Music Is the Real Language of Political Diplomacy." *The Guardian*. Guardian News and Media, 31 Oct. 2015. Web. May 2016.

243. "Youssou N'Dour." African Music Encyclopedia: Janet Planet, 1998. Web. 30 Aug. 2016. <http://africanmusic.org/artists/youssou.html>.

244. "Concert Solidaire De Youssou N'Dour." *La Chaîne De L'Espoir*. La Chaîne De L'Espoir, 19 Feb. 2016. Web. May 2016.

245. Martin, Michel. "N'Dour's Popularity Continues to Rise." *NPR*. NPR, 26 Nov. 2007. Web. May 2016.

246. "Angelique Kidjo Quote." *A-Z Quotes*. N.p., n.d. Web. 2016. <http://www.azquotes.com/quote/1362020>.

247. K.Y.W. "About a Girl." *The Economist*. The Economist Newspaper, 24 Jan. 2014. Web. 10 Feb. 2016.

248. The Hour. "Angelique Kidjo on George Stroumboulopoulos Tonight: INTERVIEW." *YouTube*. YouTube, 03 Feb. 2014. Web. 5 Feb. 2016.

249. "Angélique Kidjo." *Wikipedia*. Wikimedia Foundation, 2016. Web. 3 Apr. 2016.

250. Pareles, Jon. "A Continent on Her Musical Map." *The New York Times*. The New York Times, 18 Jan. 2014. Web. 3 Apr. 2016.

251. Al Jazeera English. "One on One- Angelique Kidjo." *YouTube*. YouTube, 31 July 2007. Web. 4 Apr. 2016.

252. "Misty Copeland Quote." *A-Z Quotes*. A-Z Quotes, n.d. Web. 2016.

253. "The Official Website of Misty Copeland." Misty Copeland. N.p., n.d. Web. 30 Aug. 2016. <http://mistycopeland.com/about/>.

254. "The Official Website of Misty Copeland." Misty Copeland. N.p., n.d. Web. 30 Aug. 2016. <http://mistycopeland.com/about/>.

255. Brian, Scott. "60 Minutes Misty Copeland." *YouTube*. YouTube, 25 Aug. 2015. Web. 22 June 2016.

256. Blumberg, Naomi. "Misty Copeland." *Encyclopedia Britannica Online*. Encyclopedia Britannica, 26 May 2016. Web. 30 Aug. 2016. <https://www.britannica.com/biography/Misty-Copeland>.

257. "Translation." *Alexander Pushkin: It Is Better to Have Dreamed a Thousand Dreams That Never Were than Never to Have Dreamed at All.* N.p., n.d. Web. 2016. <http://www.quotes.net/quote/41031>.

258. *"Alexander Pushkin."* Poetry Foundation. Poetry Foundation, 2016. Web. Feb. 2016.

259. Blagoy, Dimitry Dimitriyevich. "Aleksandr Sergeyevich Pushkin." *Encyclopedia Britannica Online.* Encyclopedia Britan- nica, 2016. Web. 30 Aug. 2016. <https://www.britannica.com/biography/Aleksandr-Sergeyevich-Pushkin>.

260. Kennedy, Patrick. "Alexander Pushkin: Author Profile." *About Education.* About Education, n.d. Web. 05 July 2016.

261. Lyles, John. "Bloody Verses: Rereading Pushkin's «Prisoner of the Caucasus»." *The Pushkin Review.* N.p., 2014. Web. 30 Aug. 2016. <http://pushkiniana.org/index.php/vol-16-17-articles/267-bloody-verses-rereading-pushkin-s-prisoner-of-the- caucasus>.

262. Iyengar, Shanto. "Explorations in Political Psychology." *Google Books.* Duke University Press, 1993. Web. Feb. 2016.

263. "Alexander Pushkin, Black Russian Poet and Novelist." *Welcome To "Voices That Guide Us" Personal Narratives.* African American Registry, n.d. Web. Feb. 2016.

264. "Leopold Sedar Senghor Quote." *A-Z Quotes.* N.p., n.d. Web. 2016. <http://www.azquotes.com/quote/1267582>.

265. Adi, Hakim, and Marika Sherwood. "Pan-African History." *Google Books.* Routledge, 2003. Web. Mar. 2016.

266. Decker, Ed. "Senghor, Leopold Sedar 1906—." *Encyclopedia.com.* HighBeam Research, 01 Jan. 1996. Web. Mar. 2016.

267. Halsall, Paul. "Modern History Sourcebook: France: The "Loi-Cadre" of June 23, 1956." *Modern History Sourcebook: France: The "Loi-Cadre" of June 23, 1956.* N.p., July 1998. Web. 30 Aug. 2016. <http://sourcebooks.fordham.edu/mod/1956- loicadre.html>.

268. "John H. Johnson Quote." *BrainyQuote.* Xplore, n.d. Web. 2016. <http://www.brainyquote.com/quotes/quotes/j/john- hjohn189577.html>.

269. "John H. Johnson Biography." *Childhood, Life Achievements & Timeline.* Childhood, Life Achievements & Timeline, n.d. Web. May 2016.

270. Jones, Jae. "The Negro Digest the Black Version of the Reader's Digest." *Black Then.* Black Then, 31 Aug. 2015. Web. May 2016.

271. "The Negro Digest." *Wikipedia*. Wikimedia Foundation, n.d. Web. May 2016.

272. Lowe, Frederick, and Trice Edney. "Iconic Ebony, JET Magazines No Longer Owned by Johnson Publishing Co." *Richmond Free Press*. Richmond Free Press, 24 June 2016. Web. May 2016.

273. "Chinua Achebe Quote." *BrainyQuote*. Xplore, n.d. Web. 2016.
<http://www.brainyquote.com/quotes/quotes/c/chinu-aache381166.html>.

274. "About the Author." *Cornell University*. N.p., 2005. Web. 30 Aug. 2016.
<http://reading.cornell.edu/reading_project_05/about.html>.

275. Franklin, Ruth. "After Empire." *The New Yorker*. The New Yorker, 19 May 2008. Web. Mar. 2016.

276. "About the Author." *Cornell University*. N.p., 2005. Web. 30 Aug. 2016.
<http://reading.cornell.edu/reading_project_05/about.html>.

277. "Chinua Achebe." *Bio.com*. A&E Networks Television, n.d. Web. Mar. 2016.

278. "Achebe Wins Booker Prize for Fiction." *The New York Times*. The New York Times, 13 June 2007. Web. 30 Aug. 2016.
<http://www.nytimes.com/2007/06/13/arts/AP-Booker-International.html?_r=1>.

279. "Derek Walcott - Nobel Lecture.": *The Antilles: Fragments of Epic Memory*. N.p., n.d. Web. 2016.
<http://www.nobel-prize.org/nobel_prizes/literature/laureates/1992/walcott-lecture.html>.

280. Hirsch, Edward. "The Paris Review: Derek Walcott." *Paris Review*. Paris Review, 2016. Web.

281. Hirsch, Edward. "The Paris Review: Derek Walcott." *Paris Review*. Paris Review, 2016. Web.

282. "Derek Walcott." *Poets.org*. Academy of American Poets, n.d. Web. 2016.

283. "Derek Walcott." *Poetry Foundation*. Poetry Foundation, 2010. Web. 2016.

284. "Literary Articles." *Treatment of the Colonial History in Derek Walcott's Poetry*. Literary Articles, n.d. Web. 2016.

285. Derek Walcott - Derek Walcott Biography - Poem Hunter. "Derek Walcott - Derek Walcott Biography." *Poemhunter.com*. Poemhunter.com, n.d. Web. May 2016.

286. "Dream on Monkey Mountain and Other Plays." *Macmillan*. Macmillan, n.d. Web. 2016.

287. "Wole Soyinka Quote." *BrainyQuote*. Xplore, n.d. Web. 2016.
<http://www.brainyquote.com/quotes/quotes/w/wole-soyink385160.html>.

288. "Wole Soyinka." *Bio.com*. A&E Networks Television, n.d. Web. Mar. 2016.

289. "Wole Soyinka." *Wole Soyinka - Biographical*. Nobelprize.org, 1986. Web. Mar. 2016.

290. "Laureate - Wole Soyinka." *Laureate - Wole Soyinka*. Mediatheque, n.d. Web. Mar. 2016.

291. Marren, Susan, and Kevin McNeilly. "Wole Soyinka." *Encyclopedia.com*. HighBeam Research, 01 Jan. 1993. Web. Mar. 2016.

292. Mazrui, Alamin M., and Willy Mutunga. "Debating the African Condition: Race, Gender, and Culture Conflict." *Google Books*. Africa World Press, Inc., 2004. Web. Mar. 2016.

293. Soyinka, Wole. "Wole Soyinka - Nobel Lecture.": *This Past Must Address Its Present*. Svenska Akademien, 2011. Web. 05 July 2016.

294. "Cathy Hughes." *The History Makers*. The History Makers, n.d. Web. 2016. <http://www.thehistorymakers.com/biogra- phy/cathy-hughes-39>.

295. "Cathy Hughes." *The History Makers*. The History Makers, 2016. Web. May 2016.

296. "She Made It" *The Paley Center for Media*. The Paley Center for Media, n.d. Web. May 2016.

297. "Cathy Hughes." *The History Makers*. The History Makers, 2016. Web. May 2016.

298. "She Made It" *The Paley Center for Media*. The Paley Center for Media, n.d. Web. May 2016.

299. "Oprah Winfrey Quote." *BrainyQuote*. Xplore, n.d. Web. 2016. <http://www.brainyquote.com/quotes/quotes/o/oprah- winfr163087.html>.

300. "Oprah Winfrey." Notable Names Database. Soylent Communications, 2016. Web. 30 Aug. 2016. <http://www.nndb.com/people/466/000022400/>.

301. "Oprah Winfrey." *Notable Names Database*. Soylent Communications, 2016. Web. 30 Aug. 2016. <http://www.nndb.com/people/466/000022400/>.

302. "Oprah Winfrey." *Notable Names Database*. Soylent Communications, 2016. Web. 30 Aug. 2016. <http://www.nndb.com/people/466/000022400/>.

303. "Oprah Winfrey Biography." *Academy of Achievement*. Academy of Achievement, 31 Aug. 2015. Web. 2016.

304. Illouz, Eva. "Oprah Winfrey and the Glamour of Misery." *Google Books*. Columbia University Press, 2003. Web. 2016.

305. *IMDb*. IMDb.com, n.d. Web. 30 Aug. 2016. <http://www.imdb.com/title/tt0088939/?ref_=nm_flmg_act_24>.

306. "Mo Abudu Quote." *A-Z Quotes*. N.p., n.d. Web. 2016. <http://www.azquotes.com/quote/1137213>.

307. Nsehe, Mfonobong. "Africa's Most Successful Women: Mo Abudu." *Forbes*. Forbes Magazine, 1 Jan. 2015. Web. 3 Apr. 2016.

308. ""Africa's Africa": The Woman with Her Resolve to Rewrite Africa's Story." *IGazeti African Dream*. IGazeti African Dream, 10 Mar. 2015. Web. Apr. 2016.

309. Naija, Bella. "Mo Abudu Named Forbes Africa's Most Successful Woman | Talks Standing up for Herself & Her Media Journey." *BellaNaija*. BellaNaija, 8 Jan. 2015. Web. 2016.

310. Nsehe, Mfonobong. "Africa's Most Successful Women: Mo Abudu." *Forbes*. Forbes Magazine, 1 Jan. 2015. Web. 30 Aug. 2016. <http://www.forbes.com/sites/mfonobongnsehe/2015/01/01/africas-most-successful-women-mo- abudu/#1f75d97c6c8e>.

311. Smallman, Etan. "Meet Africa's Oprah: Why Mosunmola 'Mo' Abudu Wants to Change the World's View of Her Conti- nent." *The Independent*. Independent Digital News and Media, 15 Nov. 2015. Web. 2016.

312. "Rebecca Enonchong Quote." *A-Z Quotes*. N.p., n.d. Web. 2016. <http://www.azquotes.com/quote/815637>.

313. Douglas, Kate. "Meet the Boss: Rebecca Enonchong." *How We Made It In Africa*. How We Made It In Africa, 26 June 2013. Web. Apr. 2016.

314. "Rebecca E Enonchong - Rebranding Africa Forum." *Rebranding Africa Forum*. Rebranding Africa Forum, 22 Sept. 2015. Web. Apr. 2016.

315. Atagana, Mich. "African Women in Tech: Rebecca Enonchong." *Memeburn*. Memeburn, 03 Oct. 2014. Web. Apr. 2016.

316. ICWEGMBH. "Rebecca Enonchong, Founder and CEO of AppsTech, Cameroon." *YouTube*. YouTube, 10 June 2015. Web. Apr. 2016.

317. ICWEGMBH. "Rebecca Enonchong, Founder and CEO of AppsTech, Cameroon." *YouTube*. YouTube, 10 June 2015. Web. Apr. 2016.

318. "Bob Douglas, the Father of Black Basketball." *Welcome To "Voices That Guide Us" Personal Narratives*. African American Registry, n.d. Web. 2016.

319. "Jesse Owens Quote." *BrainyQuote*. Xplore, n.d. Web. 2016. <http://www.brainyquote.com/quotes/quotes/j/jesse- owens383871.html>.

320. "Jesse Owens." *Bio.com*. A&E Networks Television, n.d. Web. 2016.

321. Schwartz, Larry. "Owens Pierced a Myth." *ESPN*. ESPN Internet Ventures, n.d. Web. 30 Aug. 2016. <https://espn.go.com/sportscentury/features/00016393.html>.

322. Schwartz, Larry. "Owens Pierced a Myth." *ESPN*. ESPN Internet Ventures, n.d. Web. 30 Aug. 2016. <https://espn.go.com/sportscentury/features/00016393.html>.

323. Schwartz, Larry. "Owens Pierced a Myth." ESPN. ESPN Internet Ventures, n.d. Web. 30 Aug. 2016. <https://espn.go.com/sportscentury/features/00016393.html>.

324. "Joe Louis Quote." *BrainyQuote*. Xplore, n.d. Web. 2016.
   <http://www.brainyquote.com/quotes/quotes/j/joelouis378492.html>.

325. "Joe Louis." *Bio.com*. A&E Networks Television, n.d. Web. 2016.

326. "Joe Louis." *PBS*. PBS, 2004. Web. 30 Aug. 2016.
   <http://www.pbs.org/wgbh/amex/fight/peopleevents/p_louis.html>.

327. Schwartz, Larry. "'Brown Bomber' Was a Hero to All." *ESPN*. ESPN Internet Ventures, n.d. Web. 30 Aug. 2016. <https://espn.go.com/sportscentury/features/00016109.html>.

328. Drash, Wayne. "Jackie Robinson Breaks Barriers on Web." *CNN*. Cable News Network, 10 July 1997. Web. 30 Aug. 2016. <http://www.cnn.com/TECH/9707/10/site.seer.robinson/>.

329. "Jackie Robinson: A Biography." *Choice Reviews Online* 35.08 (1998): n. pag. *Jackierobinson.org*. The Jackie Robinson Foundation. Web. 30 Aug. 2016. <http://www.jackierobinson.org/wp-content/themes/jrfwebtwo/pdf/Jackie%20Robin- son%20bio.pdf>.

330. "Jackie Robinson." *Baseball Hall of Fame*. Baseball Hall of Fame, n.d. Web. June 2016.

331. Swaine, Rick. "Jackie Robinson." *Society for American Baseball Research*. N.p., 2006. Web. 30 Aug. 2016. <http://sabr.org/bioproj/person/bb9e2490>.

332. "Charlie Sifford Quotes." *BrainyQuote*. Xplore, n.d. Web. 2016.
   <http://www.brainyquote.com/quotes/authors/c/char- lie_sifford.html>.

333. "Charles Sifford Biography." *Bio.com*. A&E Networks Television, n.d. Web. 2016.

334. "Charlie Sifford." *Bio.com*. A&E Networks Television, 2016. Web. 30 Aug. 2016.
   <http://www.biography.com/people/charles-sifford-533282#early-life>.

335. "Golf Pioneer Charlie Sifford, 92, Dies." *ESPN*. ESPN Internet Ventures, 4 Feb. 2015. Web. 30 Aug. 2016.
   <http://espn.go.com/golf/story/_/id/12276698/charlie-sifford-golf-pioneer-dies-92>.

336. "Golf Pioneer Charlie Sifford, 92, Dies." *ESPN*. ESPN Internet Ventures, 4 Feb. 2015. Web. 30 Aug. 2016.
   <http://espn.go.com/golf/story/_/id/12276698/charlie-sifford-golf-pioneer-dies-92>.

337. "Golf Pioneer Charlie Sifford, 92, Dies." *ESPN*. ESPN Internet Ventures, 4 Feb. 2015. Web. 30 Aug. 2016.
   <http://espn.go.com/golf/story/_/id/12276698/charlie-sifford-golf-pioneer-dies-92>.

338. "Jim Brown Quotes." *QuoteHD*. N.p., n.d. Web. 2016.
   <http://www.quotehd.com/quotes/jim-brown-quote-the-parents- are-the-key>.

339. "Program Overview." *Program Overview*. AMER-I-CAN, n.d. Web. 1 July 2016.

340. "Garfield Sobers." *Wikipedia*. Wikimedia Foundation, 20 June 2016. Web. 2016.

341. "The Beautiful Game: Is Football Art?" *BBC*. N.p., n.d. Web. 2016. <http://www.bbc.com/culture/story/20140203-beau- tiful-game-is-football-art>.

342. The Editors of Encyclopædia Britannica. "Pele." *Encyclopedia Britannica Online*. Encyclopedia Britannica, n.d. Web. 2016.

343. "Arthur Ashe Quote." *BrainyQuote*. Xplore, n.d. Web. 2016. <http://www.brainyquote.com/quotes/quotes/a/arthurashe109755.html>.

344. "African American Athletes Arthur Ashe." *African American Athletes Arthur Ashe*. N.p., 2016. Web. 30 Aug. 2016. <http://www.myblackhistory.net/Arthur_Ashe.htm>.

345. "African American Athletes Arthur Ashe." *African American Athletes Arthur Ashe*. N.p., 2016. Web. 30 Aug. 2016. <http://www.myblackhistory.net/Arthur_Ashe.htm>.

346. "Arthur Ashe." *Bio.com*. A&E Networks Television, 2016. Web. 30 Aug. 2016. <http://www.biography.com/people/arthur-ashe-9190544>.

347. "Arthur Ashe." *Wikipedia*. Wikimedia Foundation, 2 July 2016. Web. 2016.

348. "Dominique Dawes Quote." *BrainyQuote*. Xplore, n.d. Web. 2016. <http://www.brainyquote.com/quotes/quotes/d/do-miniqued613878.html>.

349. "Dominique Dawes." *Wikipedia*. Wikimedia Foundation, 1 June 2016. Web. July 2016.

350. "President's Council on Fitness, Sports & Nutrition." *Fitness*. N.p., n.d. Web. 30 Aug. 2016. <http://www.fitness.gov/>.

From an article entitled "History's Black Hole" from the January 10, 2016 global edition of the New York Daily News, Arthur Browne opines, "Across every filed of endeavor, from the ministry to medicine and from education to entrepreneurship, book merchants balk at memoralizing black experience and accomplishments." Essentially, this book is a celebration of black accomplishments -over centuries and across continents- seeks to fill a portion of that "black hole."

Of the roughly 7 billion people who inhabit this planet, some 1.5 billion are classified as white and blacks account for 1.1 billion. The remaining over 4 billion are somewhere in the middle. Yet, throughout the years, a paucity of written materials have recorded the positive influences and myriad contributions that the great number of blacks citizens have made toward global peace, progress, prosperity and pleasure.

Dr. Elliston Rahming has a distinguished career in public service and academia. He served as an Ambassador at the United Nations and the Organizations of American States (OAS) in Washington, D.C. He holds a BA degree from Bethune-Cookman University as well as MSW and PhD degrees from Washington University, St. Louis, Missouri.

Contact: theintertechgroup@gmail.com

Distinction Publishing House, Dover, Denver.

www.ingramcontent.com/pod-product-compliance
Lightning Source LLC
Chambersburg PA
CBHW081406080526
44589CB00016B/2482